ASIAN AMERICAN MEDIA ACTIVISM

CRITICAL CULTURAL COMMUNICATION

General Editors: Jonathan Gray, Aswin Punathambekar, Nina Huntemann
Founding Editors: Sarah Banet-Weiser and Kent A. Ono

Asian American Media Activism

Fighting for Cultural Citizenship

Lori Kido Lopez

NEW YORK UNIVERSITY PRESS

New York

NEW YORK UNIVERSITY PRESS
New York
www.nyupress.org

© 2016 by New York University
All rights reserved

References to Internet websites (URLs) were accurate at the time of writing. Neither the author nor New York University Press is responsible for URLs that may have expired or changed since the manuscript was prepared.

ISBN: 978-1-4798-7819-2 (hardback)
ISBN: 978-1-4798-6683-0 (paperback)

For Library of Congress Cataloging-in-Publication data, please contact the Library of Congress.

Manufactured in the United States of America

10 9 8 7 6 5 4 3 2 1

Also available as an ebook

For Jason, my far better half

CONTENTS

ACKNOWLEDGMENTS

My research on Asian American media activism began at the University of Southern California, where I was lucky to work with many world-class scholars. I must first thank my advisor Sarah Banet-Weiser for seeing this project through from start to finish. She has been a fierce and loyal advocate, and I am so happy that our friendship has grown over the years. This project has also benefitted greatly from the guidance of Henry Jenkins, whose scholarship provides the foundation for all my cultural studies thinking, and whose generosity toward his students is without comparison. I am particularly grateful to have gotten in on the ground floor of Henry's research group at Annenberg, Civic Paths. It was during our weekly meetings that many of my ideas about Race-bending and fan-activism were developed and enriched, but also where I learned how rewarding it can be to do research as a team.

I have also received a tremendous amount of support at the University of Wisconsin-Madison. I feel like the luckiest girl in the world to have ended up with this dream job, a pleasure that mostly centers on having such wonderful colleagues—in particular, my Media and Cultural Studies colleagues Jonathan Gray, Jeremy Morris, Derek Johnson, Michele Hilmes, and Eric Hoyt. It is because of their smiling faces that I love coming in to Vilas Hall even in the dead of winter. I am very appreciative of their enthusiastic support for me and the work that I do, and I take great joy in getting to be an auntie to their adorable children.

There are many other members of my extended academic community who have helped me develop as a scholar. I am grateful to have been able to partner with and wrestle over ideas with Konrad Ng, who buoys my spirit with his endless positivity. Vincent Pham has also been a supporter of this project since the very beginning—I am very glad that when we discovered our work was on the same topic, we decided to become allies instead of arch nemeses. There are many other folks from Asian American studies who have given me a home outside my disciplinary home and strengthened my commitments to the larger political cause of ethnic studies. In particular, I am grateful for the mentorship and friendship of my colleague Timothy Yu, and for the Asian Americanist perspective that Viet Nguyen and Jane Iwamura provided on this project in its early days.

Life on the academic path would not be possible without the camaraderie of those who toil alongside you, so I want to express my love for Evan Brody, Allison Noyes Soeller, Beth Boser, Garrett Broad, and all the other members of our Annenberg fantasy football league who made it very difficult for me to leave Los Angeles. I also would be remiss if I did not acknowledge those who have guided me from the very beginning—Ming-Yuen Ma, who supervised my scholarship as an undergraduate and first taught me about Asian American media, and Radhika Parameswaran, who probably did not realize that when she took me on as a master's student that she was really signing up for a lifelong commitment. Warmest thanks to Alicia Nadkarni and Eric Zinner at NYU Press for helping this project become a book, to my anonymous reviewers for their many helpful suggestions, and to series editors Jonathan Gray, Aswin Punathambekar, and Nina Huntemann for strengthening my analysis.

Of course the true credit must be given to all the activists whose heroic work inspired this investigation, and who allowed me to share some of their stories: Alex Nogales, Alice Lee, Amy Uyematsu, Anderson Le, Anna Xie, Bill Imada, Buck Wong, Eddie Wong, Eric Kitayama, Evelyn Yoshimura, Dariane Nabor, Frank Kwan, Guy Aoki, Jeffrey Mio, Jon Yokogawa, Karen Narasaki, Kevin Vu, Lorraine Sammy, Marilyn Tokuda, Marissa Lee, Michael Le, Navin Narayanan, Nita Song, Phil Lee, Phil Yu, Sumi Haru, Sylvia Pham, and Telly Wong. I wish that I was not merely writing academic prose about their activism, but was able to continue in the trenches alongside them; I hope that they can take this book as a sign that I will always support the work from afar.

Finally, I would like to thank my family. My parents Sharlene and Doug DesRochers have always been my proudest fans since I was a little girl, and I am very appreciative of how seriously they continue to treat all my ridiculous aspirations. My mom's inquisitive mind and boundless generosity and my dad's unwavering strength and problem-solving resolve provide the backbone for my life. As a youngest child, I also owe so much to my siblings Keith DesRochers and Kelli Ledeen, who are two of the smartest, funniest people I know. Thanks to my wonderful in-laws Donna and Anthony Lopez, and my lifelong friends Caleb Oken-Berg and Katherine Adams. Above all, this book is dedicated to Jason Kido Lopez. Every aspect of my life has been shaped by Jason's wise counsel and philosophical probing, his humility and kindness, and his playful quirkiness. I cannot imagine a happier life than the one we share together.

Introduction

The Role of Asian American Media Activism

Starring Mindy Kaling as a hopelessly romantic gynecologist, *The Mindy Project* premiered in the fall of 2012 on FOX. It was the first network TV show to ever star an actor of South Asian descent. With Kaling serving as the lead actor, creator, writer, and (sometimes) director, the show stood alone in an industrial landscape dominated by white men both in front of and behind the camera. Given these facts, it might seem like *The Mindy Project* would have been considered a clear victory to those interested in improving Asian American representation in the media—it showcased the abundant talents of an Asian American woman and brought her story onto network television to be enjoyed by mass audiences. Yet if we look at the way the show was received by different audiences, we can begin to see how the work of Asian American media activism is not always so straightforward. During its second season, an activist organization called Media Action Network for Asian Americans (MANAA) publicly criticized the show for its cast of all-white male leads and romantic partners, and chastised Kaling for failing to "give back" to the community (AsianWeek 2014). At a panel at South by Southwest, Kaling responded to the flurry of critiques: "I look at shows on TV, and this is going to just seem defensive, but I'm just gonna say it—I'm a fucking Indian woman who has her own fucking network television show, OK?" (Bailey 2014). Kaling questioned why her show was being held to a different standard than other shows and emphasized that she worked in television, not politics.

These debates about how best to represent Asian Americans in the media similarly flared up around the ABC sitcom *Fresh Off the Boat*, a series created by celebrity chef Eddie Huang about his experiences as a child of Taiwanese immigrants in the 1990s. It was the first all-Asian American family sitcom since Margaret Cho's unsuccessful *All-*

The Mindy Project has been praised for having an Indian American female lead in Mindy Kaling, but also criticized for failing to diversify its cast of male suitors for Mindy.

American Girl twenty years prior, and was championed by many Asian American bloggers, journalists, and social media users. Asian American activists implored audiences to support the show, since they feared its failure might set back network television another twenty years before they would try another Asian American family show. Yet when news broke that the sitcom had been picked up for ABC's 2014–2015 prime-time lineup, a different community of Asian Americans responded with criticism on Twitter. They questioned the use of the phrase "fresh off the boat," which is a derogatory title used to mock recent immigrants that many Asian Americans feel can only be used by the "in-group." As Twitter user @KaitlynYin stated, "#FreshOffTheBoat normalizes the term. Whites will think it's acceptable to use w/o realizing historical origins" (Yin 2014). Creator Huang countered by arguing that the show's title was an attempt to reclaim the term FOB as one of pride, and connected his use of the term "fresh" to the hip-hop culture of the 1990s. Yet even before the show premiered, others were complaining about the fact that the actors playing immigrants had to use fake accents for the role and

Eddie Huang's *Fresh Off the Boat* is the first Asian American family sitcom since Margaret Cho's unsuccessful *All-American Girl* twenty years prior.

that the show's casting reinforced the ideology that all Asian American peoples and cultures could be indiscriminately lumped together.

These two incidents remind us that discussions concerning race and representation are inevitably heated and difficult, and that even when images of minority communities succeed in gaining visibility there can be disagreement about what political gains have really been achieved. But it is also important to note that these debates reflect more than a simple disagreement between two individuals. Rather, the disagreements described here are between organized collectives who are strategically working to impact change in the representation of Asian Americans in the media. This is perhaps more evident in the first example, where MANAA seeks to serve as a representative Asian American voice when asking FOX to make changes to the content of a show. But in the second example, we must also look at conversations on Twitter as more than just the voices of individuals each with their own opinions—in many cases, Asian Americans are actively using Twitter as a space for joining together, strategizing, and responding to media images as a collective. Activism that relies upon Twitter and other online tools does operate differently from more traditional face-to-face activism, and the culture of digital forms of activism is in a state of rapid development and flux. Nevertheless, it is important to take both these instances of media activism seriously and consider their motivations, strategies, and impact.

In exploring the work of those who see the media as a tool for impacting social change, we can better understand where these disagreements come from and what is at stake in the battle over the media. What kinds of representations of Asian Americans would be more or less problematic, and what counts as "Asian American" to begin with in a world where individuals embody multiple and shifting identities? How do we know what is gained in the fight to improve representation, and who benefits from this battle? Asian American media activists seeking to improve representations often take up positions that appear contradictory to the success of Asian American actors, shows, and storylines because they do not agree upon the answers to these questions. Yet if we simply rest upon the conclusion that representational politics are complicated, we foreclose the opportunity to use media activism to impact change. In this book I investigate not only how Asian American media activism takes place and evaluate what kinds of interventions might actually be effective, but I also use a media studies and cultural studies framework to argue that these disagreements about media representation reflect different understandings of what cultural citizenship looks like for Asian Americans. Battles over representations of Asian America reveal the way that activists seeking to improve the representation of Asian Americans in entertainment media are engaging in a fight for cultural citizenship, or a deeper sense of belonging and acceptance within a nation that has long rejected them. This argument advances our understanding of how cultural citizenship is connected to media representation, and in this investigation of the varied ways in which activists mobilize and deploy their strategies, what we discover are the different and potentially conflicting ways in which cultural citizenship is being claimed.

Sociologists and social movement theorists have explored a vast repertoire of activism and forms of protest, but media activism is a specific form of activism that demands the tools of media studies and cultural studies in order to best understand how it operates. As such, I do not purport to connect Asian American media activism to larger media reform movements or question how it functions as a social movement. Rather, when looking at the work of those fighting to improve the representation of Asian Americans in the media, I rely upon the core inquiries of media studies in order to make sense of what is occurring—asking how texts are imbued with ideology, how media industries are structured and controlled, and how audiences are actively participating in shaping meaning. More specifically, I look at how Asian American media consumers and producers deploy specific understandings of citizenship as a directive for shaping representation in mainstream entertainment media. *manifests of cultural citizenship ownerships in presentation.*

To argue that media activists are fighting for cultural citizenship implies that the latter can be actively claimed through activism, and through the specific examples of media activism that I explore here, we can more clearly see how activists and minority communities believe that empowerment will be achieved through cultural citizenship. Each community of activists relies on different understandings of what cultural citizenship will look like and how it will be achieved in structuring their media activism work. But despite their differences, I argue that they share one important similarity—Asian American media activists view cultural citizenship as a collective endeavor that cannot be accomplished at the level of the individual. This pushes back against assumptions that our neoliberal media landscape is inexorably moving citizenship toward the individual, and opens up a space for exploring the way that Asian Americans in particular are using media to create networks of cultural citizenship that seek to impact their broader community. This perspective on the way that Asian Americans are responding to media representations also serves to challenge a ubiquitous postracial media discourse that insists upon race as merely an individual quality. As Catherine Squire argues in her examination of the explosion of discourse about postracism in the media, a belief in the declining significance of race in today's society "[resonates] with neoliberal discourses because of their shared investment in individual-level analysis and concern with individual freedoms" (Squires 2014, 6). My focus on cultural citizenship and media activism reaffirms the necessity of collective racial designations such as "Asian American" even in our increasingly globalized landscape, where such an amalgam of national and racial identity may be questioned for its continued usage.

[handwritten annotations: "1) low rep quantity → w/in their roles"; "2) newly in storygraphy"]

Exclusion and Inclusion of Asian Americans in the Media

At its core, media activism for Asian Americans revolves around a very simple kind of injustice. Americans of Asian descent have historically been excluded from the media in multiple ways—the number of roles rarely reflects the actual percentage of Asian Americans in the United States, actors are forced to repeatedly embody tired and offensive stereotypes, and they are frequently relegated to the role of a sidekick or background character. Asian Americans are rarely shown with families, love interests, or well-developed back stories. Most egregious of all, they are almost never cast in starring roles. The problems inherent to Asian American media representation have been well documented within academic scholarship, beginning with Darrell Hamamoto's (1994) *Monitored Peril: Asian Americans and the Politics of TV Representation*, which presents an exhaustive survey of the racist depictions of Asian Americans from television's early days to the early 1990s. Robert Lee (1999) comes to similar conclusions in *Orientals: Asian Americans in Popular Culture*, in which he connects the history of the perception of Asian American immigration as a threat to the representation of Asian Americans in newspaper comics, songs, fictional stories, dramatic productions, and movies. Kent Ono and Vincent Pham's (2008) *Asian Americans and the Media* updates these works with an overview of the entire contemporary Asian American media landscape, including descriptions of the work of Asian American media producers and interventions by the community such as film festivals and media arts centers. Scholars have also delved into the nuances of how gender and sexuality are inflected within representations of Asian America, such as Gina Marchetti's (1994) examination of interracial relationships in *Romancing the Yellow Peril* and Celine Parreñas Shimizu's volumes on women in *The Hypersexuality of Race* (2007) and men in *Straitjacket Sexualities* (2012). While Marchetti focuses on textual analyses of the ways that power relations are upheld through depictions of interracial romances, Shimizu works to dislodge straightforward stereotype analysis by theorizing the way that Asian American viewers must negotiate their identities against even the most problematic media representations.

Through these works on representation it becomes clear that media invisibility and mistreatment impacts Asian American communities in profound ways. The limited number of representations serves to fix a particular image within the public imagination and restrict possibilities—both aesthetically within the world of imagery and within society, where racism has clearly material consequences. These images are also critical in the formation of national identities and cultural notions of citizenship, as the erasure of non-white bodies from the media can lead to assumptions of exclusion from our imagined nation as well. Indeed, one of the primary impacts of the way that Asian Americans have been represented is to shore up institutionalized racism—reproducing structures of dominance as if Asian Americans are categorically different, and in fact inferior, to other Americans.

These linkages between media imagery and the lived experiences of Asian Americans clearly demand changes in the way that they have been represented. Yet what drew me to this research was the impulse to answer the question, "Now what?" If we can so ably recognize the problems, it is incumbent upon those interested in representation to move beyond mere critique to consider sites for change, pathways toward demonstrating agency or empowerment within media structures, and courses of action that can realistically be taken up. This is no easy undertaking. We can see from the example of *The Mindy Project* and *Fresh Off the Boat* that there is much disagreement about what kind of changes we wish to see, let alone how to accomplish them. As media studies scholars have long demonstrated, mere visibility does not necessarily lead to empowerment, and the renewed propagation of injurious representations is certainly not a desirable outcome. LeiLani Nishime (2014) reminds us of this in her exploration of images of multiracial Asian American representations, which are increasingly plentiful. She argues that media analyses should not rest upon simple categorizations of stereotypical or oppositional, celebrated or condemned; rather, she reads the visibility and invisibility of multiracial bodies in the media for what they reflect about the continued significance of racial hierarchies and power-laden systems of value. These complexities remind us that images are always in flux, shifting beneath our feet. If we look at contemporary stories about Asian Americans in the media, we see that they continue to reflect the changing roles that Asians play in American society. This includes everything from the arrival of thousands of Asian immigrants in the years following the Immigration and Nationality Act of 1965, to shifts in popular culture toward embracing global forms of media, to the contemporary struggles to gain legal citizenship in a climate of increasing anti-immigrant hostility. In a famously risk-averse industry like network television, the fact that media executives took a gamble on these two programs featuring non-white stars reflects a media landscape irrevocably altered by demographic shifts in the United States and responding to changing perceptions of both Asian and American citizenship.

In recent years we have already begun to see many changes in the way Asian Americans have been portrayed. After *Fresh Off the Boat* debuted in February 2015, ABC greenlit a second Asian American family sitcom called *Dr. Ken*, starring comedian Ken Jeong, which premiered that fall. Mindy Kaling's *The Mindy Project* was canceled on FOX after three successful seasons and immediately picked up by Hulu, while ABC's *Quantico* debuted in the fall of 2015 with Indian actress Priyanka Chopra as the lead. Lucy Liu, Daniel Dae Kim, Grace Park, Ming Na, Aziz Ansari, Sandra Oh, Yun Jin Kim, and Danny Pudi have all been leads or prominent series regulars on network television programs ranging from sitcoms to medical dramas to musicals. In the world of film, Kal Penn and John Cho have shown that two Asian American men can anchor an extremely successful comedy franchise with *Harold and Kumar* and its sequels. There has also been an increase in the popularity and viability of movies that take place overseas and have entirely non-white casts, such as *Slumdog Millionaire* and *The Life of Pi*—both of which won Academy Awards. We can see that Asian Americans are slowly making inroads into mainstream representation with these specific roles. Each of these roles serves as a reminder that Asian American media activism chases after a moving target that cannot easily be reduced to a simple or universal set of demands.

Beyond the way that Asian Americans are represented within film and television, there are two other mediated realms that must be explored— advertising and online media. With regard to the former, we know that the images produced by advertisers swirl around us throughout our daily lives, invading our personal space more insistently than any other media. Researchers estimate that we each see over five thousand ads a day, including commercials on television and radio, billboards, sidebars and pop-up ads online, spam e-mails and physical junk mail, and countless other forms. As a *New York Times* headline proclaimed in 2007, "Anywhere the Eye Can See, It's Likely to See an Ad" (Story 2007). Ads are being placed on subway turnstiles, motion sickness bags, toll booths, bridges, and doctors' examination tables, immersing consumers in their imagery. Given this ubiquity, it makes sense to consider the realm of advertising when thinking about the impact of media imagery. As a visual medium that depicts society, advertising contains narratives about race and portrays racialized bodies just as television programs and movies do—albeit with a decisively commercial intent and a condensed time frame. The advertising agencies who produce these images are thus in a position of power that must be viewed alongside the media producers at film and television studios.

For the specific case of considering how minority communities are portrayed in advertising, we can turn to the work of multicultural advertising agencies. Although general market advertisers may include some token faces of color, the real work of representing and providing advertisements to communities of color belongs to advertising agencies who focus exclusively on minorities. Yet research on multicultural advertising has been scant. There have been some racially specific investigations, such as Jason Chambers's (2009) history of black consumer marketing, Arlene Davila's (2001) investigation of the Hispanic marketing industry, and Shalini Shankar's (2015) insightful work on the role played by Asian American advertising agencies in creating consumer markets. While these studies have laid the groundwork for understanding the political complexities of the minority marketplace—including the ways in which advertisements have historically contributed to social change—many academics are hesitant to connect the work of advertisers to activism. Given the anticapitalist focus of much work in critical race studies, advertising is often the target of criticism rather than a site for potential contributions to social justice. In this project I seek to view Asian American advertising as an important site where negotiations between consumers and image producers take place, and in which notions of cultural citizenship are produced and engaged.

Using the same logic that we must consider all mediated spaces where images of Asian Americans are regularly being created, viewed, and interpreted as potential sites for media activism, of course we must include the online realm as well. The number of hours Americans spend online increases every year, with adults in 2013 averaging well over three hours per day online (eMarketer 2013). Within the online arena there are countless spaces in which Asian American stories are shared. YouTube provides the most obvious example, given the resounding success of a number of Asian Americans in accumulating subscriber bases such as Kevin Wu, Freddie Wong, Ryan Higa, and Michelle Phan. Each of these individuals have literally millions of fans who regularly view their video blogs and scripted stories online. YouTube has also begun to offer a platform for more organized media production companies, such as Wong Fu Productions and YOMYOMF (You Offend Me You Offend My Family), both of which focus on producing Asian American-themed videos. Beyond YouTube, the internet and online social media can be seen to more generally enable Asian American media producers to disseminate their work using blogs, forums, Facebook, Twitter, or personal websites. The rise of digital media has provided many opportunities for media creators to bypass the gatekeepers of the traditional world of film and television and lowered barriers to access so that those with the proper technology can more easily participate in sharing their work. Alongside traditional media such as television and movies, I will also investigate the way that Asian American media activists are making sense of these digital interventions and opportunities.

Citizenship through Media

This conversation about the ability to participate in sharing one's ideas and stories, build resilient forms of community, and express one's emotions and needs is connected to our understanding of what it means to be a citizen. At its most basic level, citizenship can be seen as the set of laws and procedures that prohibit or grant an individual legal status to reside within the nation-state. Someone who is a member of the citizenry is assumed to possess a basic set of rights and protections such as the right to free speech and protection from unjust imprisonment. Legal citizenship has been connected to race in the United States since as far back as the birth of the country. Although founding documents such as the Declaration of Independence explicitly connected the concept of citizenship to notions of equality and freedom, in reality there were many restrictions and exclusions about who counted as a citizen. For blacks, women, and other minorities, the fight for the rights of American citizenship—including representation, the ability to vote, to possess land, and to live under the protection of the government—were long and arduous. Even the Fourteenth Amendment to the Constitution, which set forth a basic definition for citizenship that included birthright citizenship and therefore granted citizenship to African Americans, was not meant to apply to Native Americans or other nonwhite immigrants.

Yet these legal conflicts between citizenship and race do not embrace the full picture of how citizenship is lived out. Beyond legal rights and restrictions, we can also think of citizenship being granted through the fulfillment of certain cultural practices. For instance, citizens are those who participate in their civic duties and contribute to the upkeep of the national body by voting or volunteering their services, speaking up about important issues, or helping to police the community against wrongdoing. A citizen can also be culturally demarcated by their feelings of identification or belonging with the nation and its people. Given that citizenship encompasses such a broad range of concepts, it follows that the processes of granting and denying citizenship are similarly complicated. For each of these ways of viewing citizenship, there are particular identities and practices that can activate and close down membership and participation.

Although at its core the logic of citizenship assumes that those who possess citizenship ought to be treated equally, the reality is that many groups of people are systematically denied the privileges that citizenship is assumed to accord, and many groups constantly struggle for an equal share in what we might call "first-class citizenship." In his work on minority groups in Southeast Asia and Latinos in the United States, Renato Rosaldo (2003) points out that "when one enjoys the status of belonging to the national community, this belonging can easily be taken for granted and trivialized; but when such belonging is denied, its absence can prove devastating" (2). One arena in which these different degrees of citizenship can be seen at work is within cultural practices. In terms of culture, it is often assumed that the cultural practices of a citizen match those of the dominant culture. This means that people can be excluded from first-class citizenship for having non-normative cultural practices, such as ethnic traditions, sexual preferences, or religious practices. Indeed, many individuals whose cultural practices do not align with hegemonic norms—gays and lesbians, Muslims, or African Americans, for example—are made to feel as though they do not belong and that their lifestyle is somehow antithetical to the ideals of the nation. It is within our everyday lives that cultural citizenship is evidenced—by the way that one is treated and respected, whether one is allowed to speak up for oneself and his or her community, or whether one can participate in the public sphere. As Toby Miller claims, "citizenship has always been cultural" (2007, 51), as states have always demanded that citizens meet cultural requirements with regard to things like language, knowledge, allegiance, and behavior.

Yet the borders policing citizenship are a moving equilibrium, always shifting and allowing for redefinition. Just as the rules for who counts as a legal citizen have drastically changed in the last century, so too have definitions for who counts as a cultural citizen. William Flores and Rina Benmayor (1998) point to the efforts of Latinos in particular to redefine the shape of American culture. Latino immigrants who might not be legal citizens nonetheless strive to be "recognized as legitimate political subjects claiming rights for themselves and their children, and in that sense as citizens" (11). Such striving takes on many different forms in post–9/11 America for young immigrants of color, as Sunaina Maira (2009) finds in her exploration of the diverse ways in which cultural citizenship is produced in the lives of South Asian Muslim youth. For them, expressions of their relationship to the state can be flexible, multifaceted, and even reflective of dissent. Beyond simply a means for exclusion, then, cultural citizenship more importantly can be seen as offering a route toward restructuring and reordering society in such a way that minority groups can move in their own ways toward claiming these kinds of cultural rights. Thus cultural citizenship stands in opposition to normative assumptions about the necessity of assimilation. Those who stand on the margins remind us that we must widen our understanding of citizenship to include and embrace those whose cultural practices and identities do not match up with the mainstream, rather than assuming it is always best to conform and adopt the practices of the majority in order to be accepted. Through this recognition, we can begin to see how the kinds of cultural practices that are included within the category of "American" are always in motion, being slowly transformed through the process and performance of cultural citizenship.

Cultural citizenship is, then, intimately connected to media practices and images. In order for individuals to feel like their cultural practices are accepted and that people like them are included within the nation, they must see themselves and their specific communities represented within the media. When they are absent, sidelined, or mistreated, there is a real impact on the ability of communities to feel recognized and validated. Joke Hermes (2005) argues that popular culture and media consumption have "the power to make people bond and feel that they belong" (2), and in her audience ethnographies she traces the ways that people take up their role as cultural citizens through their interpretive practices. She argues that we do not have much agency over media production, so we must turn to interpretation as a viable source for creating citizenship. Similarly, Jillian Baez (2008) and Vicki Mayer (2003) have called for a turn to actual audiences as a site for identifying the production of cultural citizenship. Within their work we can see how studies of audiences show how individuals make sense of media in ways that resonate with their own cultural identities.

Yet these studies of how audiences make sense of media texts in relation to cultural citizenship also contribute to a widening division between citizenship at the level of the individual and citizenship for the collective. In *The Well-Tempered Self: Citizenship, Culture and the Post-Modern Self* (1993), Toby Miller argues that media and other popular culture serve as forms of discipline, tempering the individual into well-behaved citizens and consumers. In our increasingly neoliberal media culture, this focus on the individual begins to shape citizenship as something that everyone must attain for herself—whether through private enterprise, choices of what media to consume and how to interpret it, performances of participation, or other individual acts. Laurie Ouellette (2008) finds that reality television consistently emphasizes the neoliberal ideologies of self-reliance and taking care of oneself. Her exploration of television as a cultural technology reminds us of the profound impact of neoliberal ideologies on the shape of our society—including the move toward relying on businesses rather than government, privatizing social welfare, and connecting individual responsibility and self-empowerment to the attainment of citizenship. Within the realm of neoliberalism, the ideal citizen is one who is self-governing and independent.

This focus on the individual becomes particularly pronounced within discussions of new media, where the concept of Web 2.0 leads to the conclusion that everyone is a producer, capable of engineering his or her own destiny (Ratto and Boler 2014). What is lost in this focus on the individual is the potential to view cultural citizenship as a collective endeavor. John Hartley (2012) draws attention to this distinction in his discussion of Do-It-Yourself citizenship, or DIY citizenship. Although the idea of doing citizenship on your own harkens to this focus on the individual, he emphasizes the existence of a similarly framed "Do It With Others" citizenship. As he states, "DIY/DIWO citizenship is more individuated and privatized than previous types, because it is driven by voluntarist choices and affiliations, but at the same time it has an activist and communitarian ethic, where 'knowledge shared is knowledge gained'" (144). This framework points more clearly to what is at stake in the distinction between attaining citizenship for oneself and taking on a more community-minded activist goal of attaining citizenship for one's community.

In this book I argue that within the work of Asian American media activists we can see a fight for a specific kind of cultural citizenship—one that relies on a collective notion of cultural citizenship. All collectives are made up of individuals, but thinking about mediated cultural citizenship through the lens of activism helps to shake us free from this exclusive focus on the individual. I do not purport to contradict the notion that dominant media programming promotes the individual as responsible for his or her own citizenship; this has certainly been the case. Nor do I seek to criticize the works of scholars who have focused on the ways in which individuals have made sense of cultural citizenship, as this is a valuable contribution to our understanding of how media texts shape citizenship. Rather, I simply seek to shift our attention to a new arena that has yet to be fully explored—sites where mediated cultural citizenships are being deliberately engaged, formed, and re-created through the body of the collective. In doing so, I argue that there are ways to resist the harm to cultural citizenship that neoliberalism has wrought. Asian Americans provide a particularly important case for making this argument, as it is through those whose citizenship has been challenged at the level of the legal, political, and cultural that the need for collective action is required. Indeed, there are more ways to interact with media than simply to consume it. Media activism demonstrates a way that Asian Americans can and do interact with texts with the goal of changing them. For Asian Americans and other politically disenfranchised minorities, it isn't enough to simply take up individual forms of citizenship through cultural practices. Citizenship is a concept that must always connect back to collective forms of political action that contribute to social justice—whether that is by attaining legal citizenship, or simply working toward better living conditions for Asians in America. Through media activism, Asian Americans demonstrate their ability to perform cultural citizenship while working to achieve a broader movement toward cultural citizenship for others.

The Contradiction of Asian American Citizenship

This focus on Asian Americans is particularly important given that they have had a contradictory relationship with the concept of citizenship in both legal and cultural terms. On the one hand, Asian Americans have consistently been seen as "alien" throughout their history in the United States. As Mae Ngai (2004) argues, Asian Americans are uniquely marked by the category of the "alien citizen." Asians born in the United States hold birthright legal citizenship, and yet all Asians are nevertheless seen "as racially unassimilable and hence ineligible to naturalized citizenship" (170). In her examination of the treatment of Japanese Americans and Chinese Americans during World War II and the Cold War, she finds moments when alien citizenship is produced and sustained until 1965 when immigration restrictions are lifted. Lisa Lowe (1996) further examines the notion of Asian American citizenship in *Immigrant Acts*, arguing that "the American citizen has been defined over against the Asian immigrant, legally, economically, culturally" (4), and these anxieties of the U.S. nation-state come to be represented in images of Asians as "exotic, barbaric, and alien . . . a 'yellow peril' threatening to displace white European immigrants" (4). She examines the various exclusion acts and naturalization laws that have worked to regulate the national body of the United States within an Orientalist discourse that consistently marks Asian Americans as the enemy despite their role as a necessary labor force in maintaining the U.S. economy. Edward Said's (1979) concept of Orientalism, wherein "the East" is positioned as inherently inferior to "the West," emerges within such discourses and confirms the superiority of whiteness. Although many Asian Americans are native-born citizens or have become citizens through naturalization, Lowe argues that their conditions within the nation-state are so marked by these laws and policies that the idea of citizenship for Asian Americans remains a perpetual contradiction. Leti Volpp (2001) further explores the contradiction of Asian American citizenship by distinguishing between the different facets of citizenship—legal status, rights, political activity, and identity. Although each of these discourses possesses unique histories and relationships to one another, she finds that "race cuts against the promise of each of these citizenship discourses" (58). We can see that Asian Americans have not been conceptualized as American citizens for a number of reasons ranging from legal prohibitions to citizenship, the realities of white privilege, assumptions that Asian Americans are politically inactive, or the blatant assumption that immigrant communities are disloyal.

Yet the contradiction of Asian American citizenship is that Asian America as a cultural body is simultaneously rejected and embraced. Although Asian Americans have been considered unfit for legal citizenship, in many ways they are also seen as culturally desirable. One way of understanding this contradiction is in terms of Robert Lee's distinction between the "alien" and the "foreign" (Lee 1999, 3). While both terms point to someone distinctly "other," the foreign is perceived as benignly temporary while the much more threatening alien desires to stay and become a pollutant. Thus, although the foreign still serves to bar outsiders from cultural assimilation, foreignness can nevertheless be fetishized and even admired because it does not pose a threat.

We can see both sides of this contradiction embodied within media representations. On the one hand, Asian Americans have historically been portrayed as noncitizens—as unassimilable perpetual foreigners, and the foreboding threat known as the yellow peril. This kind of ideology can be seen materialized in fictional characters like Fu Manchu (Mayer 2014), the Chinese villain who appeared in countless British and American movies, radio programs, books, graphic novels, and television shows from 1912 to the 1960s. Fu Manchu embodied the mysterious, inscrutable, mystical power of the East, always plotting new ways to take over the world. As international relations between the United States and Asia shifted, different Asian populations served as the enemy—Chinese during the Gold Rush as they flooded the United States with cheap labor; Japanese during World War II, Koreans during the Korean War, and Vietnamese during the Vietnam War (Shim 1998). Threats of Asian Americans as the alien coincided with imagery of Asians in American media as grotesque beasts incapable of humanity.

But we can also see the way that Asian Americans have been conceived of as foreign—transitory outsiders who merely serve to amuse and entertain. This portrayal is visible in the stereotype of the model minority, or the racial group who has somehow managed to "make it" and serves as a supposed model for blacks and Latinos to aspire to (Wu 2014). The model Asian American is passive and nonconfrontational, possesses an aptitude for math and science, and is the picture of discipline and obedience. Frank Chin and Jeffery Paul Chan (1972) tie the yellow peril together with the model minority in two succinct images: "For Fu Manchu and the Yellow Peril, there is Charlie Chan and his Number One Son. The unacceptable model is unacceptable because he cannot be controlled by whites. The acceptable model is acceptable because he is tractable. There is racist hate and racist love" (Chin and Chan 1972). Asian Americans are poised at the intersection of this racist hate and racist love, both of which are made visible within media imagery.

Portrayals of Asians in mainstream U.S. media may make the notion of cultural citizenship in the United States seem tenuous at best, but Asian Americans can also be seen to create their own sense of cultural citizenship that relies on a more global sense of community. Many Asian Americans participate in the media cultures from Asia, particularly within countries where they have significant cultural ties. In examples such as Indian Americans keeping up with the latest Bollywood movies, Korean Americans participating in the Korean wave of interest in K-pop music, Vietnamese Americans partnering with film producers overseas to produce Vietnamese comedies, or Japanese Americans trading and translating anime and manga, many different communities of Asian Americans are laying claim to different cultural identities and feelings of belonging through the transnational flow of media between

Asia and the United States. The possession of competing cultural citizenships serves to undercut the assumed primacy of so-called American citizenship, as it offers routes to participation and acceptance other than those that are American-centric. If cultural citizenship includes participating in the normative cultural practices of a nation and therefore allowing for feelings of belonging and inclusion, then we must consider that many Asians moving through diasporic spaces can possess this kind of citizenship in places other than the United States. Media creation and media consumption offer particularly important moments for enacting this kind of citizenship. This helps us to see how the fight for legal citizenship within America needs to be viewed as only one desired result of the way that Asian Americans are interacting with media texts and representations—leaving open the possibility for other interpretations and desires for citizenship that exceed these limited perspectives.

The Roots of Asian American Media Activism

The fight for cultural citizenship through changing media representations has a long history within Asian America. In his exploration of the history of film censorship, Charles Lyons (1996) describes protests of Asian American portrayals as early as 1973. Those who were closest to the problem were among the first to take a stand—Asian American actors and industry professionals. First, a Chinese American actor complained about the use of the word "chink" in the film *Charlie Varrick* and got the line removed. A group of Asian American artists also protested the 1973 film *Lost Horizons* for its use of yellowface, which was the standard practice within the industry of white actors wearing make up to take on the role of Asian characters.[1] In subsequent protests, activist collectives also fought against the stereotyped performances of characters like Fu Manchu and Charlie Chan, demanding that Asian American roles be cast with Asian actors who spoke proper English and did not live in crime-infested Chinatowns. In 1985, the stereotype-ridden film *Year of the Dragon* inspired the first nationally organized protest by a number of different Asian American organizations. The numerous protests and rallies around the film's premiere culminated in a $100 million class action lawsuit against the film's producers at MGM/UA. They responded to the lawsuit with a disclaimer that ran before the film, stating:

This film does not intend to demean or to ignore the many positive features of Asian-Americans and specifically Chinese-American communities. Any similarity between the depiction in this film and any association,
organization, individual or Chinatown that exists in real life is accidental.
(Harmetz 1985)

The moderate success of the protests against *Year of the Dragon* and
the community organizing that took place laid the groundwork for the
founding of the Media Action Network for Asian Americans (MANAA)
in 1991, which remains the only watchdog group dedicated to responding to Asian American representations today.

Members initially joined together to protest news stories during the
fiftieth anniversary of the bombing of Pearl Harbor that revisited old
antagonisms between the Japanese and the United States. Almost immediately, they turned their advocacy away from just news in order to focus
on the world of entertainment media. As part of the Asian Pacific American Media Coalition (APAMC) and the larger umbrella organization
of the Multi-Ethnic Media Coalition (which also includes the National
Latino Media Council and American Indians in Film and Television),
MANAA also participates in the annual awarding of Diversity Report
Cards to the top four television networks. Since 1999, the coalition has
met to analyze statistics on how many Asian Americans are hired by
the major networks, and this information is then discussed during individual meetings with the networks, as well as publicized in press re-
leases. But as we can see in MANAA's mission of "advocating balanced,
sensitive and positive portrayals of Asian Americans," its work largely
consists of calling attention to the same antagonisms seen in previous
decades—offensive stereotypes employed to the exclusion of any other
kinds of roles for Asian Americans, the use of yellowface to allow white
actors to play Asian characters, and the exclusion of Asian Americans
from starring roles.

It is not a coincidence that Asian Americans began organizing to
protest racist media imagery in the early 1970s, as this was when a collective and politicized Asian American identity began to form. Prior to
1969, Asian immigrants tended to hold firmly to their distinct ethnic
identities and to "disidentify" with any Asian ethnic community being
politically or economically targeted. This was the case for Japanese dur-

ing the Chinese Exclusion and for Chinese during the Japanese American internment (Espiritu 1992). But this act of disidentification and its dampening impact on intraethnic coalitions stood in contrast to the fact that non-Asians still ascribed a collective identity to all Americans of Asian descent. Indeed, individuals of all Asian backgrounds were being treated in the same discriminatory ways—they had been allowed to immigrate because of the labor power that they could provide, but suffered from hostility and violence, as well as discriminatory anti-immigration laws.

As Asian immigrant families continued to settle in the United States throughout the twentieth century, ties to their home countries began to dissipate or transform. A sense of shared history and circumstance within the U.S. context began to come together under the title of "Asian American." This group identification was propelled by a burgeoning social movement that united many who aligned themselves with Third World organizations fighting against poverty, war, and racism. Despite the flaws inherent in the term "Asian American" and the vast community it could potentially blanket, activists mobilizing under its collective umbrella began to organize and mobilize. Asian immigrants had begun building alliances with labor organizers and other racialized communities, and their organizational infrastructure allowed them a space to develop their own consciousness and awareness of their common experiences. As Daryl Maeda (2009) states, "Asian American identity contested Asian nationalism, liberal assimilationism, and narrow ethnic and class-based radicalism by embracing multiethnic, interracial, and transnational solidarity" (39). In his examination of important moments such as the Third World Liberation Front strike at San Francisco State College, alliances of the Red Guard Party with the Black Panthers, and protests against the Vietnam War, Maeda finds that Asian American identity is intimately connected to both antiracism and anti-imperialism. Activists within the Asian American movement in the 1960s linked the struggles of working-class communities to Third World struggles, and in the process sought to mobilize Asian Americans across the country in their efforts to challenge a number of norms, including "systems of rank and privilege, structures of hierarchy and bureaucracy, forms of exploitation and inequality, and notions of selfishness and individualism" (Omatsu 2010, 304).

Although the forging of a collective Asian American identity in the 1970s was imbued with this kind of radical critique, the meaning of Asian American activism has shifted in recent decades. In some ways, the growth of the Asian American neoconservative class and the influx of Asian American professionals and business executives who have taken up the banner of Asian American identity have pushed the politics of the movement away from its radical counterhegemonic roots (Omatsu 2010). Instead of seeking to overthrow the structures of dominance that lead to oppression and inequalities, Asian American community groups who survived the economic turbulence of the 1980s and use the term now are often conspicuously lacking in the populations who first came together as activists—youth without college degrees, immigrant workers, gang members, the elderly, and the poor. This does not mean that all Asian American activists have shifted in this direction; there are many grassroots organizations and collectives of activists who continue to work from the margins (Das Gupta 2006). Yet it must be acknowledged that Asian American activism has never been and is certainly not today a monolithic or unified force, and discourses of the "model minority" who resists disruptions to the status quo can work to dampen politicization.

In pointing to the story of how this identity has shifted since its origination, I do not seek to deprive the term of meaning or political efficacy; on the contrary, I trace its lineage so that we can continue to more accurately chart its continued salience today. Given the transformation of the communities using the term "Asian American" and the wide diversity of communities who might fall under its indiscriminate umbrella, it is important to consider the political significance of continuing to use such a term. Gayatri Spivak's theories are helpful in understanding the significance of the strategic use of essentialism, where a master concept is strategically deployed for political action. Spivak acknowledges that there is a risk inherent in deploying essentialism in this way, as the strategy can serve to solidify an identity as if there were indeed a unifying essence to all those encompassed within it. But she hopes that "the strategic use of an essence as a mobilizing slogan or masterword like *woman* or *worker* or the name of a nation is, ideally, self-conscious for all mobilized" (Spivak 1993, 3). In bringing together different Asian communities, the term "Asian American" was constructed to strategically destabilize the existing racial order and empower individuals to speak out on behalf of their marginalized community.

In accordance with Spivak's hopes for only temporary alliances, Kent Ono (1995) has called for the "re-signing" of the term "Asian American" because of its failure as a collective assignation. As part of an effort to either re-sign or resignify the term, Ono asks us to think about what purpose the term still serves, and how it can be used in an era when the incommensurability of the diverse community to which it refers has not been addressed. As a broad category, the term "Asian American" has always served to exclude many of its members, and in looking at contemporary formations, has been dominated by only a minority of the community's most privileged participants. For instance, the larger East Asian ethnic groups of Chinese, Japanese, Filipino, Vietnamese, and Korean Americans are often recognized. Yet communities from South Asia such as those from India, Sri Lanka, Pakistan; the indigenous people of Hawaii and other Pacific Islands; ethnic groups such as the Hmong; and others have been neglected. As Ono argues, now more than ever the term needs to be reconsidered so that it can come to terms with changing social conditions without sacrificing dissent from within its ranks. It is my hope that media activism as I define it within this project can provide a site for such a re-signing, helping us to better understand the diversity of those encompassed by the term Asian American, as well as some of the practices—including participation in consumer culture, explicitly activist or political actions, and media production—that enable us to widen and redefine its boundaries.

Indeed, the fight for media representation that I examine here is not taken up as a radical act designed to rewrite the structures of American society. The activists in this book include organizers, policy makers, media producers and professionals, and everyday consumers—each of whom identify as Asian American, relying on the collective notion that their diverse and disparate voices are stronger when united than divided. As evidenced by the fact that many Asian American media activists have been active professional members of media industries—actors, filmmakers, and crew—it is clear that their model of activism falls under this more conservative, contemporary model. Rather than seeking to wholly remake the film industry or challenge the system of media structures that uphold racial hierarchies and inequalities, media activists are simply fighting for access to greater participation and a recognized voice in the process that already exists. In this way, media activists take on the collective political identity that developed out of the Asian American movement from the 1960s but do not share in its radical critiques.

Yet this is the labor of fighting for cultural citizenship—the recognition that there are political processes and identities that even privileged bodies are still seeking to claim, and that the fight to do so might look different from what our revolutionary forefathers imagined. Today's media activism is by no means free from criticism; indeed, throughout my investigation of Asian American media activism, I outline some of the limitations of what I consider to be a more conservative, assimilationist Asian American politics. Yet I also work to identify political potential in a mode of activism that relies on deep engagement with even the most devalued forms of popular culture—becoming an impassioned fan of a media franchise, creating advertisements, or partnering with McDonalds—as a vehicle for social change. It is important that this potential be acknowledged, as my examination of these different processes of activism serves to counter a romanticism for a kind of "authentic" or "real" activism that is limited in who it can stem from or what kinds of actions and alliances it can include. Moreover, in calling the disparate engagements depicted here "activism," I also expand the category of media activist to participants who might not normally be considered. In doing so, this book shows that the fight for cultural citizenship through media activism is one that can potentially benefit all the different communities within Asian America, including those who are most privileged and those who are most disenfranchised.

Expanding Definitions of Activism

Through this book I am interested in refining the definition of media activism so that the term can more accurately be deployed in conversations about who is participating in creating change in the media beyond those that affect Asian Americans. Academics and practitioners have long debated what should count as activism, given that activism-related activities span a broad range from those that are designed to bring about awareness or act as symbolic gestures, to governmental or legislative action, to activities that endeavor to actually bring about structural or institutional change. All activism begins with the identification of a social problem based on inequality, injustice, or harm to society. After identifying this core problem, activists engage in any number of activities designed to bring about social change. Such a project can be focused on just one facet of a social problem and may be limited in scope, but centers on a cause or set of causes with the goal of achieving societal change. Some examples of social causes that activists have organized around include AIDS, animal rights, environmental, gay and lesbian, feminist, and labor issues. The Asian American media activism described thus far includes tactics such as protesting problematic representations and organizing meetings with media producers to convey concerns.

I define activism as intentional participation in a political act designed to remedy a social injustice. Of course, the definition of what counts as political is not clear-cut, and within cultural studies there is a tendency to see nearly all social activity as being imbued with political meaning. But at the very least this definition helps to clarify that activism is intentional, meaning that activists must be aware of the intended consequences of their actions with regard to a cause. Unintentional consequences are of course inevitable and important to at least consider, but it is intention that marks one as an activist. If we are trying to understand who is involved in media activism, we can look for what I have defined as the necessary elements of activism—the identification of a social problem that exists within the media and the intentional action taken to remedy this mediated problem. Thus, my investigation of media activism depends upon the fact that media activists explicitly connect media representations to social realities; they are not simply seeking change because of a personal desire or preference. Their goal is to make meaningful, long-term change in the media landscape—whether that means changing the images that have been created, the structures that produce those images, or the way that images are understood by viewers.[2]

This book argues that while the stated goals of media activists might seem immediate—to recast a role, to demand an apology from producers, to hire an Asian American consultant or director, to produce more images of Asian Americans—what goes unstated is the connection between these achievements and the ultimate goal of cultural citizenship for Asian Americans. Activists who organize to improve the representation of Asian Americans in the media are critical of the second-class treatment of Asian Americans within American society, where Asian Americans are still routinely subject to discrimination and violence. This problem is attributed to two factors: first, the fact that images of Asian Americans fall into problematic and limiting categories in our visual imagination, reflecting a lack of respect and subordinate social status, and second, that Asian Americans are often distanced from the ability to control, direct, or even participate in telling their own stories. Thus, media activists seek to remedy the social problem of the oppression of Asian Americans by changing media representations. Although media activists can also be fans who share affective connections to the images that they seek to change, what I argue here is that activists are working first and foremost toward actualization as citizens, and fighting oppression through media is a necessary component of working toward this goal. Although the specific activist collectives and projects that I examine here cannot be understood outside an Asian American context and identity, the broader potential for using media activism to comment upon and redefine cultural citizenship is one that can be productively utilized in a variety of different communities. Although the specific cultural context for each community would impact what that citizenship looks like and means, my intention here is to identify who is participating in media activism so that we can better understand the broader cultural forces shaping media industries and our interactions with them as citizens.

In the chapters that follow, I look at Asian Americans in a variety of roles—as members of corporate advisory councils, cable channel owners, owners of advertising agencies, YouTube videographers, Twitter users, bloggers, and others. For each case, we can consider the theory of change being utilized and the kinds of actions being taken in the hope of leading to a better future for Asian Americans. Although not all the cases I examine fall under the category of activism as defined here, I am still interested in the individuals and organizations who are contributing to the same vision of social change through media representation that is so clearly defined by traditional activist groups. In doing so, I paint a more accurate picture of who it is that is actually contributing to the larger project of improving images of Asian Americans and what those improvements mean in terms of cultural citizenship. By mapping the intersections of these different agents and activities we can better understand what it takes to bring about change in the media, and thus in society.

When talking about organizations and individuals who are intentionally changing the image of Asian Americans in the media, there is an obvious category of activists I do not want to leave out—artists and creators from within the independent Asian American filmmaking world. From documentary filmmakers like Renee Tajima-Peña and Tad Nakamura to narrative filmmakers like Wayne Wang and Mira Nair, there is a rich history and tradition within the Asian American community of creative expression through moving images. These films are supported and screened at a wide array of Asian American film festivals across the country, with the two largest located in San Francisco and Los Angeles and smaller festivals held yearly in New York, Washington, D.C., San Diego, Austin, Eugene, Chicago, Pittsburgh, Philadelphia, Houston, and other locations. Despite the importance of these films and their impact on the way the community is portrayed and represented, there is a well-developed body of research on this particular aspect of Asian American media activism. An extensive anthology of essays written by artists within the independent Asian Pacific American media arts movement from 1970 to 1990, edited by the UCLA Asian American Studies Center and Visual Communications, describes these artists' work in their own words (Leong 1991). *Screening Asian Americans* (2002), a collection edited by Peter Feng, tackles the same subject matter from a more distinctly academic perspective, with essays on topics such as the history of Asian American Media Arts Centers to specific investigations of Filipino/a American, Chinese American, and Korean American women's cinema. Glen Mimura's *Ghostlife of Third Cinema: Asian American Film and Video* (2009) additionally considers the perspective of international and queer cinema in its exploration of Asian American independent media, while Jun Okada's (2015) book *Making Asian American Film and Video: History, Institutions, Movements* examines the institutional history that undergirds the creation of such films.

Asian American artists and filmmakers have made incredibly important contributions to the way that Asian American bodies and identities have been inscribed, and their contributions to representational change have been well documented in the works mentioned above. Yet in many ways, the productions described in these works remain sequestered within the niche market of Asian American film festivals and Asian American Studies classrooms, seen only by patrons of these events and those who belong to the Asian American independent cinema scene. It is rare for even the most popular, award-winning films screened at Asian American film festivals to find mainstream distribution, which means that everyday film-going audiences almost never have the opportunity to see such work playing at their local theater or even being available for rental. It is not necessarily the size of the audience that limits such works but the low level of accessibility, since much of the work of Asian American independent filmmakers is only available to privileged audiences in specific geographic locations for a small amount of time. Thus I briefly theorize the connection between Asian American independent media and online videographers in chapter 5, but I do not explore independent film in any detail. In this book I investigate the organizations and individuals who set their sights on improving mainstream media and other forms of media that are widely available and accessible to general audiences. These activists hope to take part in a broader social justice movement that extends beyond Asian American audiences to impact the way that Asian Americans are perceived and treated as cultural citizens.

The Research Process

This project is based on a three-year ethnography of Asian American media activism organizations in Los Angeles, as well as in-depth interviews with individuals who were associated with such activism.[3] Research began in the fall of 2008 when I started attending the general meetings for the Media Action Network for Asian Americans. Although I identified myself as a researcher who studied the representation of Asian Americans in the media, it was clear that the boundaries between participant and observer would be indelibly blurred in my relationships with members of the organization. I became a regular participant within the business of the organization and eventually was asked to serve on its board of directors, which I did for almost two years. When I returned home from my meetings I would jot down field notes and transcribe the observations I had scrawled in the margins of my meeting agendas, but I would also take on the regular work of the organization—editing drafts of letters to movie studios, creating and updating the organization's blog, and offering my opinions and suggestions whenever called for.

This book is not wholly ethnographic; I did not spend significant time in the field studying some of the organizations profiled in this study, such as the advertising agencies and policy centers. For those chapters, my analysis relies on a combination of interviews, archival research, attendance at events, and brief visits to their offices. But it was my time with MANAA from 2008 to 2011 that is at the heart of this study, as it was through MANAA that I became well-acquainted with the other subjects of my study and was able to fully immerse myself in the world of Asian American media activism. Leaders from the fledgling organization Racebending.com started attending MANAA meetings in the fall of 2009 to present their case for protesting the casting of *The Last Airbender*. After meeting and working with them, I began closely following their online communities, communicating regularly with the leaders online. Members of MANAA's leadership were also among the select few invited to meet with the television networks as part of the Asian Pacific American Media Coalition (APAMC) and engage with the policy work that overlaps with that of the Asian American Justice Center. In the fall of 2010, I was invited to attend the annual network meetings with ABC, NBC, CBS, and FOX because of my status as a board member. Although I conducted formal interviews with members of these organizations and told them that I was studying organizations like theirs for my research, it is safe to say that they did not see me as an objective or neutral participant in their cause—they understood that I was an activist alongside them, even if I was occasionally presenting my thoughts about their work at academic conferences or publishing papers about them in academic journals.

Within ethnographic work, there has been much debate and discussion about the advantages of being an "insider" versus an "outsider" to the community one is studying. If the researcher belongs to the community he or she studies, there is often a fear of the researcher "going native," as anthropologist Bronislaw Malinowski (1922) has called it. By this he means the researcher becomes so immersed in the lives of his or her subjects that he or she loses the capacity for analysis and insight. As Duncan Fuller (1999) states, the dreaded consequences of going native include "the apparent loss of validity, integrity, criticality, necessary distance, formality, and ultimately, reputation." Moreover, Robert La-baree (2002) argues that being an insider creates a number of ethical dilemmas that can overcomplicate the research project, such as how to enter a field one already belongs to, how to position oneself in order to maintain trust with respondents, and how to negotiate friendships with informants, all the while balancing a research agenda.

While these can be valid concerns in many situations, I would argue that my research has been strengthened by the access afforded to me by virtue of my identity as both activist and scholar. Although I would not go so far as to claim that being an insider necessarily offered me a position of "epistemological privilege," as is often the case with feminist research or research on other disempowered groups (Griffith 1998), there are still many ways in which this study could not have been written had I remained outside these organizations. In particular, it would have been limiting to only be able to observe what went on during public meetings or during scheduled interviews. As a full participant in the lifeblood of these organizations, I was able to gain a much more detailed portrait of the way they functioned—including the strategic planning that occurred in instant messages online, the daily emails shared between organizational leaders, the exasperations expressed in the late hours after a meeting had ended, and the epic struggles and heartaches that would never have been exposed to anyone but an insider. On a practical level, the network meetings with the APAMC are extremely exclusive and the information discussed within them is proprietary. Because I was a board member of MANAA, I was allowed access to these rare meetings, and while participating in them I took on the role of activist, not scholar. Although I could not report any of the actual content of the meetings, my participation within them helped me to more deeply understand the kind of work that was being conducted there.

It is also worth considering how my own identity impacted my research. Within qualitative studies growing importance is being attached to the identity of the researcher, given that subjects might position their own stories differently depending on who is asking and listening. In Elizabeth Chin's (2001) ethnography of black children and consumer culture, she admits that her own racial ambiguity helped her remain somewhat outside the black/white boundaries that were so central to her participants' communities. Moreover, her status as a researcher often prompted others to see her as a "teacher" figure rather than as a threatening agent of the state or an outsider completely lacking in authority. In many ways, my own identity tends to occupy a liminal position that says more about the one identifying me than any static truth about my position as insider or outsider. When asked about my racial background, my response is that I am mixed race, Japanese and white. For some, this means that I belong wholly to the Asian American community. But many others do not ask me about my background, and it is possible that from my physical appearance I pass as white—or even Latina, given my Hispanic last name. For yet others, my racial identity is simply a question mark.

This liminality bleeds over into discussions of my identity as a scholar and activist. I was often asked to take on leadership positions within the various organizations I interacted with, but they were also interested in using my academic work as evidence of their own legitimacy and significance. In these examples it becomes clear that there can be important overlaps between activists and scholars, even within the same work—scholarship can be seen as activist and the work of scholars can be seen to contribute to activist efforts. Within the fields of cultural studies, Asian American Studies, and even media studies, the position of siding with marginalized communities and attempting to use scholarly works to have a positive impact on their realities is a heartily championed position. As George Lipsitz (2008) describes it, "scholar activists have been disseminating the situated knowledge of communities in struggle for many years" (90), including individuals from fair housing movements, prison reform movements, environmental justice movements, AIDS research, international antiviolence coalitions, labor organizers, and queer theorists. In each of these projects, academics have been able to call attention to the work of these activists in ways that create new kinds of knowledge and lead to social mobilization. Cultural studies theorists have also long implored scholars to impact the power structures that they study. As Jennifer Slack and Laurie Anne Whitt argue, "cultural theorists, consciously and emphatically, aim not merely to describe or explain contemporary cultural and social practices, but to change them, and more pointedly, to transform existing structures of power" (Slack and Whitt 1992, 572). For myself I hope to embrace the challenge of creating a work that "does something," rather than simply standing on the sidelines describing what I see, even if that makes my position as a researcher more complicated and demands more careful introspection.

Ethnography is the work of the researcher "being there," spending significant amounts of time immersed in the social world, observing and absorbing everyday cultures. It is immersive and messy, involving critical examinations, but also bodily engagements. Although ethnography has traditionally been considered the central methodology of anthropologists seeking to understand foreign peoples and cultures, researchers from cultural studies and countless other fields have now taken up the practice of ethnography as a way of understanding their own cultures of everyday life. By undertaking an ethnography of these organizations as a participant who was not afraid to take a stand and get dirty in the trenches alongside the other participants, I hope to be in a position to reveal insights about the realities of media activism that accurately portray those most closely involved, but also useful to those still in the field trying to make a difference. If this book seeks to make sense of the struggles in which these individuals have been engaged by applying the framework of cultural citizenship to Asian American media activism, I hope that the knowledge produced in doing so will assist future media activists in a way that continues to positively contribute to justice and equality for Asian American communities.

The Structure of the Book

This book is structured around specific sites of media activism that deploy different understandings of what cultural citizenship looks like in activists' fight to impact media practices. I move from groups that are most easily identifiable as media activists, such as MANAA and the APAMC, to groups that take more untraditional positions in the fight for representation. I begin by presenting a cultural history of media activism in Asian American communities that originated with actors in Los Angeles in the 1960s. This history provides the context for examining the work of MANAA, one of the most long-standing contemporary organizations engaging in Asian American media activism. By examining some of their campaigns, we can begin to take a deeper look at the traditional tactics that media activists use. As with all Asian American politics, media activists are faced with a changing landscape both in terms of who constitutes Asian America, what citizenship entails, and what kind of representation they are most interested in impacting. For the members of MANAA, cultural citizenship is based on the idea that Asian Americans need to be treated "just like everyone else." This results in a set of strategies that demand the expulsion of all stereotypes and negative depictions of Asian Americans in film and television, and pushes toward a strict definition of Asian America as being bounded within national borders. Yet this exploration of their strategies shows that the assumption that cultural citizenship is predicated on assimilation has served to limit the purview of their activism. By laying out some critiques of the way traditional advocacy organizations operate, we can see that there is a call to investigate other potential sites of media activism and rethink the possibilities for impacting change on a systemic level.

Chapter 2 examines media activism at the level of policy and governmental intervention. My interviews with individuals at the Asian American Justice Center and the APAMC show what an important tool media policy has been in shaping the idea of cultural citizenship as part of a system rather than simply an individual experience. By taking a more systematic perspective I am able to highlight the different ways that Asian Americans have fought for change at the level of media industries—creating relationships through the APAMC with the television networks, through the rise and fall of Asian American cable channels, the merger of Comcast and NBC Universal in 2010, and changing the way that the Nielson Company measures minority viewers. Each of these policy battles demonstrates that the Asian American consumer-citizen has a voice in speaking up for the policies that shape the way the community is represented, and shows the different ways in which Asian Americans have worked to voice their concerns to these powerful bodies.

Chapter 3 begins to more explicitly explore the connection between the project of Asian American media activism and consumer movements. Given the reality that media images are commercial products and that those who produce them are motivated by financial incentives, it is important to position Asian Americans as more than simply cultural citizens—they must be seen as powerful consumer citizens. This chapter focuses on the work of Asian American marketing and communications firms like IW Group, AAAZA, and other members of the Asian American Advertising Federation (3AF). These companies work to strengthen and promote the idea that Asian American consumers are a target audience for corporations. This reframing of how Asian Americans should be viewed, as well as their work in producing images and advertisements that feature Asian Americans, is clearly connected to the larger project of Asian American activism as described in previous chapters. Yet this chapter also begins to refine the definition of "media activist," given the goals that often motivate advertisers in this kind of work. In assessing the different strategies of those who hope to impact media industries, we can begin to see that nonactivists play an important role alongside the avowed activists described in chapters 1 and 2.

Chapter 4 continues to challenge who it is that we might consider part of Asian American media activism by looking at some of the most popular Asian Americans on YouTube. Indeed, Asian Americans are often perceived as being on the forefront of adopting digital media practices, with their high rates of internet and mobile phone usage. The lively community of Asian Americans using online social media can be seen to be participating in shaping new spaces for the creation and dissemination of Asian American imagery. In many ways these participants are simply following in the footsteps of Asian American independent filmmakers who saw self-representation as an important mode of cultural citizenship. Yet I argue that the affordances of online media also provide a different kind of platform for users to engage with Asian American media. First, we can examine the way that online media has contributed to the development of an Asian American celebrity culture surrounding its most popular participants. These individual celebrities use the online networks facilitated through new media to connect with one another in an act of transmedia branding, creating bridges between online media and the mainstream realms of film and television. Their doing so leads to the emergence of an Asian American popular culture that plays an important role in furthering the goals of Asian American media activists by echoing the work of advertisers who seek to reify a collective identity for Asian American audiences.

Chapter 5 follows up on this investigation of the use of online tools and social media by looking explicitly at activist and political projects. I begin with an analysis of hashtag activism on Twitter, where Asian

Americans have developed the ability to call attention to issues of importance to them by means of digital participation. The widespread interest of news media outlets in the phenomenon of Asian American hashtag activism—particularly in #NotYourAsianSidekick and #CancelColbert—clearly demonstrate the way that Asian Americans are fighting for recognition, better treatment, and belonging as a collective. These two campaigns also emphasize the centrality of media representation in realizing these desires. Although the high percentage of Asian American participants on Twitter clearly played a role in facilitating this dialogue, this kind of visibility is not always reliant on numbers—individuals also must have an affective connection to the issue at hand, and feel that their contributions matter. I conclude this chapter with an exploration of the media activism surrounding *The Last Airbender*, which relied heavily on fans of the Nickelodeon television show. In examining the tactics of the activists who sought to protest the discriminatory casting of M. Night Shyamalan's 2010 film we can begin to see how media activism is shifting in a new media environment.

This investigation of different sites for media activism shows that many different communities are working toward improving the image of Asian Americans in the media beyond traditional activist organizations. Some of these communities have yet to fully embrace their connection to activist movements and ideologies while others continue in an unbroken activist tradition stretching back to the 1970s. Together their work must be recognized for its role in shifting the way that Asian American cultural citizenship is imagined, desired, and achieved.

1

The Limits of Assimilationism within Traditional Media Activism

In the summer of 2009, a board member for the Media Action Network for Asian Americans (MANAA) was watching television and happened to catch a special promotion on CBS's show *Big Brother*. Guest star Jeremy Piven was making an appearance so that he could reveal the trailer for his latest film, *The Goods: Live Hard, Sell Hard*, in which he plays a silver-tongued car salesman. The trailer focused on his rallying speech, where he yells, "Don't even get me started about Pearl Harbor . . . Never again! Never again!" Together the other salesmen join in the chant, including Asian American actor Ken Jeong, who looks nervous. Suddenly an older white man who had been eyeing him yells, "Get him!" and the men begin beating Jeong.

Incensed by the portrayal of anti-Asian sentiment and the racially motivated violence that was played for laughs, members of MANAA, including founding president Guy Aoki, immediately sprang into action. Aoki contacted the vice presidents at CBS, communicating the group's concern about the inclusion of such an offensive scene in the trailer. The VP of Diversity responded by saying that although they did not condone the content of the trailer, they would not apologize. MANAA's members then began contacting the film's producers at Paramount Pictures, various local media outlets, and fellow Asian American activists. Soon the issue was being reported on news channel KTLA's blog, while colleagues at the marketing firm IW Group, the Japanese American Citizens League (JACL), and the American Jewish Committee of New York echoed their support of MANAA. Hearing nothing from Paramount Pictures, they began to plan a protest outside Paramount's gates. The next day, over forty members of various Asian American community groups gathered together to chant and wave signs on the street. That afternoon, the president of Paramount emailed the president of JACL. In his letter, he apologized to the Asian American community for the

In 2009, Asian Americans held a protest outside Paramount Pictures because they were upset about a scene in *The Goods: Live Hard, Sell Hard* in which a racially motivated beating of an Asian man is played for laughs.

"hurtful, racially disparaging language" and stated that they "genuinely regret the use of this language in the film." Further, Paramount discontinued use of the trailer that focused on that scene and offered to meet with Asian American leaders to discuss the issue in person.

In many ways, this moment of Asian American media activism can be seen as an instructive model—through community partnerships, quick decisive action, and a clear argument they were able to communicate their message to both the studio and the news media and garner a positive response. But this story is not an isolated incident; on the contrary, this mode of media activism with regard to Asian American portrayals has existed in nearly the exact same form for decades. By examining the history of Asian American organizing around the issue of media representation, we can begin to better understand the tactics traditionally utilized by media activists. By connecting this work to the fight for Asian American cultural citizenship, we can go further in our analysis and see that the theory of change being utilized here is one of assimilation to the mainstream—that traditional media activists want Asian Americans to be seen as "just like everyone else." With this as the goal, cultural citizenship will become possible because Asian Americans will not constantly be treated as "the other." But as the cultural history of Asian American media activism groups from 1969 to the present shows, the contemporary media and sociopolitical landscape have shifted beneath them, particularly with regard to the way cultural citizenship intersects with mediated representations. Thus, by focusing on the work of the Media Action Network for Asian Americans from 2008 to 2011, we can see that many traditional media activism strategies are in need of updating. These include the emphasis on stereotype analysis rather than allowing for interpretive variation, the importance attached to national boundaries to the exclusion of transnational notions of the citizen, and attending to broadcast media and film rather than expanding to include new media. By historicizing the efforts of Asian American media activists today and identifying these moments of contradiction and rupture in activist organizations' methods, we can open up a space for considering alternative, and potentially more effective, tactics in the fight to impact Asian American media imagery.

The History of Media Activism

As Katherine Montgomery (1989) argues, "all forms of mass media have been targets of advocacy groups at one time or another" (5), including everything from books and newspapers to comic books and movies. As early as 1915, the NAACP was already creating headlines with its national boycott of *Birth of a Nation* for its overtly racist themes, including the glorification of the Ku Klux Klan and depictions of African Americans as violent and primitive (Stokes 2007; Wallace 2003). Although the silent film directed by D. W. Griffith has been heralded in the history of cinema for its groundbreaking techniques and epic budget, members of the NAACP were incensed by its message of white supremacy and of blackness as threatening. They petitioned the National Board of Censorship as well as hundreds of individual theaters, seeking to prohibit screenings of the film and the excision of the most offensive scenes. They argued that the film was a threat to public safety because of its potential to incite racial violence. When their efforts to enforce censorship failed, they launched a nationwide protest that included picketing outside movie theaters, writing scathing reviews in dozens of newspapers, and even buying tickets so that they could throw eggs at the screen (Lang 1994). The NAACP was not the first organization to complain about the derogatory effects of filmic racism, but its well-publicized efforts were important in conveying the power of media activists to the public. This kind of protest, designed to curtail the impact of such a film upon mass audiences and decrease the earning power of the movie for the filmmakers and the studio can clearly be seen as a form of censorship. Indeed, one of the NAACP's first efforts included bringing its concerns to the National Board of Censorship, an industry organization founded in 1909 that reviewed films and made recommendations for cuts or the suppression of inflammatory material. The battle over *Birth of a Nation* started a conversation across the country about the balance between state censorship and the freedom of speech for filmmakers to create and distribute their products freely.

One consequence of the desire to impact society through film was that censorship boards at both the state and national levels often represented an alliance between conservatives and progressives. Conservative activists were interested in banning the portrayal of topics like abortion, birth control, and other sacrilegious activities, while progressives "welcomed moving pictures as a means to develop a new cultural consciousness, mediate between social classes, and thereby blunt social conflict" (Rosenbloom 2004, 373). The National Board of Censorship included a diverse membership from organizations such as the Women's Municipal League, the Children's Aid Society, the Charity Organization Society, and the Federation of Churches (Grieveson 2004). Both sides agreed that if films could serve to uplift society, then portrayals of obscenity, "crime-for crime's sake," suicide, violence against women, drunkenness, and the ridicule of the insane needed to be curtailed (Rosenbloom 1987). Despite this alliance, progressive reformers have simultaneously struggled with the reality that any kind of censorship is a potential infringement on the right of free speech. This includes the efforts of industry censors and their voluntary suggestions, government censors, and the censorious demands of citizen groups. Charles Lyons argues that although the work of pressure groups like the NAACP can rightfully be categorized as censorious, their work should not be unilaterally condemned—on the contrary, it can actually play a part in upholding the idea of a healthy democracy. As he states, it is better to risk pressure groups becoming censorious than "in any way to limit groups' right to 'peaceably gather' and protest" (Lyons 1997, 1).

Although specific films have caused much uproar over the past century, there has been no bigger media target for pressure groups than television. Since the birth of television, advocacy groups have pressured television broadcasters to change various programs according to their community's needs. Groups made up of interested citizens have brought together women, gays and lesbians, racial minorities, the disabled, and other disenfranchised communities seeking inclusion and more nuanced representation. Other pressure groups hoping to impact television have included religious groups seeking plotlines that accord with their morals and values, antiviolence groups hoping to curtail the graphic depictions of violence on television, and educational groups hoping to push their particular messages. According to Montgomery (1989), the reason television was such a central target was its enormous popularity and prominence in the homes of Americans as the medium through which they received news, entertainment, and information about the world.

Racially motivated groups were among the very first to protest television's imagery as well. When *Amos 'n' Andy* premiered in 1951 on CBS, the NAACP immediately organized to call for its cancellation. The television show was based on a radio program of the same name that followed a handful of African American men through comedic foibles. The radio show, performed by its two white creators Freeman Goshen and Charles Correll, aired from 1928 to 1960 and was wildly popular with white Americans. In 1931, an African American editor at the *Pittsburgh Courier* began criticizing the show, both for its offensive portrayals of the African American characters and because its white creators were reaping all the financial gain (Barlow 1999). He called for the show's cancellation, collected the signatures of nearly 750,000 African Americans, and began a national conversation about the portrayal of African Americans in the media. When the television show premiered in 1951, it featured an all-black cast for the first time on network television. But for those familiar with the previous incarnations of the program, it clearly relied on the same belittling stereotypes—the Uncle Tom, the crook, the mammy, the buffoon. The NAACP was prepared for the television show's premiere and promptly followed through with a letter-writing campaign to the show's sponsors that called for a nationwide boycott.

The efficacy of the NAACP's actions is debatable, as the show continued for two seasons before it was eventually shelved. It was also broadcast through syndication for the next decade. Montgomery calls this result unsuccessful and remarks that "black activists were particularly disturbed by their powerlessness in keeping the offensive series off the air" (Montgomery 1989, 15). Others argue that "the campaign without a doubt affected the status of the show" (Nelson 1998, 82), and that it caused "blacks to question the image of the race projected by the entertainment industry and even by Afro-American periodicals" (Shankman 1978, 249). Indeed, in many ways we can think of media activism as an important force in constructing racialized identities. In calling attention to the patterns of stereotypical portrayals of African Americans in the media, activists are participating in the act of defining who or what it means to be African American.

When one examines the history of actions taken against media images, a model for traditional modes of media activism emerges. If a problematic image is in need of attention, a media activism group can take one of five possible actions (or sites of action):[1]

1. Contact the *creators* of the offensive image and lobby for change. This can take the form of letter-writing campaigns, phone calls, or attempts to organize meetings with media producers or executives.
2. Educate *consumers* and encourage them to boycott the media in question.
3. Convince *advertisers* to pull their advertising money, or use their financial leverage to make demands such as hiring changes or an increase in diversity.
4. Move the cause to the court of *public opinion* by using news media to influence public support for the activists' position.
5. Threaten *legal* or *governmental* intervention or regulation by suing the company, or by petitioning the Federal Communications Commission (FCC), the Equal Opportunities Commission (EOC), members of Congress, or state elected officials to look into the issue and take action.

The efficacy of each potential tactic depends on a complex configuration of factors. These include the kind of image being protested, the kind of group initiating the protest, and the cultural and legal landscape surrounding the production and distribution of the image, among others. For legal or governmental intervention, the possibilities have shifted due to media policy changes over the years, including the legal power of censorship boards as well as legislation impacting the authority of the FCC, such as the Fairness Doctrine. Likewise, the viability of convincing advertisers to pull their support or of an impactful consumer boycott depends on the perceived or real market strength of the offended parties. Despite the complicated interplay of these moving parts, this model has proven remarkably stable over the last century in outlining the options available to pressure groups as they attempt to use whatever means possible to create change in the media—and the same has been true for Asian American media activists.

The Asian American Battle for Representation

When examining the history of Asian American media activism, we must begin with the theater. Although dramatic productions before an intimate live audience are not part of the mass-mediated world that contemporary Asian American media activists hope to impact, many of the first media activists were born within the Asian American theater. This makes sense when we recognize that complaints of stereotypical roles, yellowface, or Asian Americans being held back from leading roles are not limited to film and television—each of these forms of representational discrimination existed on the stage long before they ever made their way to the screen. This kind of discrimination was foundational to the movement for creating all-Asian American theater companies such as East West Players, Asian American Theater Company, Northwest Asian American Theatre, and Pan Asian Repertory Theatre. These companies shared a common goal, namely, creating a space for the development and expression of Asian American theater. But additionally they also represented a clear response to the way Asian American actors were being mistreated within mainstream theater. As Esther Kim Lee (2006) explains, popular representations of Asians in mainstream theater were stereotypical or overtly mocking of Asian culture, and nearly all Asian roles were given to white actors. As a result, "every Asian American actor [had] an anecdote about being told by producers and directors that they were not 'real' as 'orientals' or Asians" (24). After decades of Asian representation being commandeered by white actors in yellowface, the idea of "Asianness" itself had been reduced to an over-wrought amalgam of prosthetic eyepieces and heavy accents—so much so that it was not even considered realistic for an actual Asian actor to play such a role.

In addition to the growth of Asian American theater companies, the late 1960s also saw the beginning of dedicated advocacy organizations for actors.[2] The first of these was a group called the Oriental Actors of America, which held its first meeting in March 1968. This coalition of Asian American actors in New York was dedicated to combating these discriminatory employment practices. They were particularly focused on ending the practice of yellowface and ensuring that the Actors Equity Association—the leading theater union—auditioned Asian actors for Asian roles. In a letter to the Actors Equity Association articulating these demands, they closed with this statement: "It would be wonderful if one day all actors including the oriental actors will be able to play various types of roles disregarding the racial differences, but that day is far from reality for the oriental actor. We can't even audition for oriental parts." This statement, written in 1968, marks a sense of panethnic solidarity on the cusp of the Asian American Movement—and even the term Asian American itself. The term "Oriental" was eventually rejected for its negative connotations and for its history of differentiating the "East" from Occidental Europe, which was considered the center of the world. But the names of "Oriental" advocacy groups indicate that the desire to form advocacy organizations predated a more general awareness of the concept of "Asian America."

In 1970, members of East West Players, the oldest Asian American theater company in the United States, joined together with other actors of color to advocate for minority actors and artists. In the spring of 1970 they first called the group ETHNIC, but by June they had changed the name to BOA, or Brotherhood of Artists. BOA was described as "a unified council of organizations dedicated to the advancement and protection of ethnic minority artists in America." After their first meeting they recruited fifty dues-paying members at $5 per year, including actors from Latino theater organizations like Nosotros as well as Asian American theater professionals. BOA's statement of purpose reads, "BOA (Brotherhood of Artists) was formed out of the realization that rich cultural resources which exist in America's minority communities continue to be overlooked and ignored." As a result, they came together to promote what they believed were more authentic depictions that did not rely on stereotypes and to combat the misrepresentation of minority groups. They also encouraged minority actors to choose careers in the performing arts and related areas and served as a collective voice for disenfranchised minorities in the entertainment industry.

One of the first issues that BOA took on alongside Oriental Actors of America was the casting of the Los Angeles Civic Light Opera Association's 1970 production of "Lovely Ladies, Kind Gentlemen," a musical version of "Teahouse of the August Moon." The role of Sakini, a Japanese man, had been given to a white actor named Kenneth Nelson—a decision that aligned with all the previous white actors who had played the role, including Marlon Brando. Members of BOA were particularly incensed because they believed no Asian American actor had even been considered for the part. As they stated in letters soliciting support from other artistic organizations,[3] there were three reasons why they thought the production should be boycotted:

1. No Asian was interviewed or auditioned for the lead role of Sakini before it was cast by a white actor.
2. While the producer of the show Herman Levin conducted "fair" auditions, chorus roles were cast in view of how whites could double as Japanese rather than the reverse which actors felt should be the case for a show set in Japan.
3. Asians have been continual victims of stereo-types which often is rooted in the continual use of whites in parts calling for Asian artists. (Mako 1970)

They called on theatergoers to return their tickets and explain to the producers that they were doing so in support of the Asian community.

In response to these attacks the play's producer, Herman Levin, wrote multiple letters to the activist organizations, claiming that Asian actors had been auditioned for the role and that in fact twelve Asian actors had

Activists from Brotherhood of Artists (BOA) protested the Los Angeles Civic Light Opera Association's 1970 production of "Lovely Ladies, Kind Gentlemen" because white actors in yellowface were cast instead of Asian actors.

been cast in the play, including the lead female role. In a letter responding to the Council of Oriental Organizations, he wrote:

> The depiction of a racial minority with "honesty, integrity, and authenticity together with the theatricalism that an artist naturally brings with him" is an objective which depends for its success on only one factor—the talent of the actor. His race, creed, color or national origin is irrelevant. My casting of "a" (as you rather snidely put it) Kenneth Nelson is not only good casting artistically but in no way violates any of the tenets of good citizenship.

His coproducer Edwin Lester wrote a similarly outraged response letter, claiming that BOA and other organizations were trying to impinge upon their artistic freedom. He wrote, "Nothing could be more discriminatory than the insistence of our Oriental Americans or other group that the producer and authors should be barred from selecting a Caucasian if they think that he is the best man for the role." He added that the role of Sakini had gone to a man who was half-Spanish, and thus the activists were "actually discriminating against a citizen from another minority group." The combative, defensive, and frequently sarcastic tone of their response letters revealed that the directors were resolute in their casting decisions and could not be convinced that they had made even the slightest error. In fact, they seemed determined to turn the accusations of discrimination onto the activists themselves. The play continued with the cast unchanged in spite of the controversy, and the activist organizations moved on to newly developing issues.

The efforts of these activist organizations are clearly centered on the values of cultural citizenship, as they simply want to be allowed access to participate in this cultural form. In their requests they point to the injustice of being denied the ability to audition and be included in the process from the outset, in addition to the outcome of having non-Asians take on yellowface in the final casting. Such actions contribute to the entire world of theater and dramatic performance being denied to individuals of certain racial or ethnic backgrounds because it is assumed that they are not talented enough. Here Asian Americans are not even being allowed the opportunity to audition for the role of someone of their own race. This exclusion from a cultural practice provides a very straightforward example of the way that cultural citizenship operates—while these individuals are not being denied their political or legal rights to belong to this country as citizens, they are being denied entry into a cultural institution that would allow them to participate as equals, and they are further being excluded from sharing their participation and performance with theater-going audiences. The example of theater helps us to see how cultural citizenship is denied to individuals—as it is individuals who are denied the opportunity to audition or denied a role because they are deemed not talented enough—but the consequences impact the larger collective of all Asian American actors as well as all those who attend theater performances and must witness actors in yellowface or the absence of Asian American performers.

Although most of BOA's campaigns were focused on the theater, some of their later campaigns also included television and film. For instance, they met with CBS television about a television version of the movie *Anna and the King of Siam* called *Anna and the King* because they worried about the recurrent theme that Western culture was superior to the inferior and backward Thai culture. They also contacted NBC when they heard of plans to make a Charlie Chan movie starring the white actor Ross Martin—a role that would be played by white actors time after time. Many of the actors who got their start in the theater and were part of BOA later went on to form the Association of Asian/Pacific American Artists (AAPAA) as they moved on to more roles in mainstream media. Founded in 1976, AAPAA was formally established as "an artistic, educational organization with an emphasis on promoting interracial cooperation and understanding." More informally, during one of its board meetings in 1979 it formulated a list of goals:

> Serve as an advocate group; Work with studios about casting; Create a better image of Asians; Promote Asian talent; Work closely with community organizations; Show ourselves in one or two high quality productions; To educate ourselves and to educate the general public; Get some of our people in decision making positions.

Although AAPAA was an advocacy organization, it is important to note that like BOA, it was composed entirely of actors and industry professionals. This meant that when AAPAA members met with studios to address their concerns about issues like the scarcity of Asian Americans in their casting and hiring, they were putting their own jobs at risk. In one meeting they discussed the fact that their organization was "perceived as being anti-employment because they are against all stereotypes, especially the villainous one and that was threatening to them as artists because they are called upon to do so much of these roles." In order to combat the idea that they were antiemployment and only engaged in critique, they began having yearly awards programs where they honored members of the industry who promoted positive Asian Pacific American images. Rather than reward the actors who were "lucky enough to land these jobs," they rewarded producers, writers, and directors whose work opened up more jobs for Asian Americans. Despite the threat to their careers, AAPAA members nevertheless continued to contact movie studios with their complaints about the use of white actors to play Asian roles in films like *Blade Runner*, discrimination and racist comments made on set, failure to cast minority actors, anti-Asian defamation within the media, stereotypical portrayals in films like *16 Candles*, and the hypersexualization of Asian women.

The efforts of organizations like BOA and AAPAA intersected with many other like-minded organizations. A group called the Chinese Media Committee started doing advocacy work in the Bay Area in 1969, including making arguments to the FCC that Chinese had been misrepresented in television programming. Another group called Asian Americans for Fair Media was founded in Los Angeles in February 1974. Some of its battles included pushing for Asian American representation on the board of the FCC, protesting the use of a stereotypical karate figure in a Von's advertisement, and sponsoring an "Asian Media Day" designed to educate the public about its work. In 1981, a professional organization for journalists called Asian American Journalists Association (AAJA) was founded. As of 2015, the AAJA continues to serve as an educational and professional association, helping Asian American journalists in their work but also contributing to media advocacy efforts as they pertain to news media. Following this wave of different organizations coming together, a number of ad hoc organizations also arose in response to specific movies or offensive images. As mentioned in the Introduction, protests against the movie *Year of the Dragon* contributed to the birth of many media advocacy organizations for Asian Americans in 1985, while in 1980 an organization called Coalition of Asians to Nix Charlie Chan protested the use of yellowface in yet another Charlie Chan movie.

Sorting through the history of Asian American media activism is a piecemeal endeavor at best, as there were a number of different groups whose work overlapped in both the projects they took on and their general goals. Many groups formed in reaction to specific images as they were developed and broadcast, and they dissolved or died out when the image had run its course or if they failed to bring about change. Nearly all these organizations consisted of volunteers who were not paid for their efforts—in fact, many leaders within these groups worked within the media industry, meaning that their volunteer efforts jeopardized their careers. More generally, many of these groups were simply too small or informal to sustain themselves beyond a few years.

C.A.N. CHARLIE CHAN!

COALITION of ASIANS to NIX CHARLIE CHAN

c/o 1031 N BROADWAY LA 90012

680 4462 • 226 9581

Throughout the history of Asian American media activism, many organizations have sprung up to protest specific casting choices or offensive images. In 1980, the Coalition of Asians to Nix Charlie Chan organized to protest the casting of a white man as the star of *Charlie Chan and the Curse of the Dragon Queen*.

In 1991, when all these groups had fallen by the wayside, yet another group of politicized Asian Americans came together to fill the void in advocating for better media representation. This time, the impetus for political organizing centered around the fiftieth anniversary of the bombing of Pearl Harbor. Los Angeles news organizations began running stories that revisited old antagonisms between Japan and the United States, rehashing false rumors and old prejudices. These stories coincided with the vandalism of the homes and businesses of several Japanese Americans. This targeting of the Japanese American community caught the attention of a number of Japanese American activists who had worked together on the Redress and Reparation Movement in 1988. They were not actors or industry professionals, just concerned Asian American citizens who had a history of political activism. This meant that there was no conflict of interest when they asked media producers to hire more Asian Americans; they could position themselves as simply community advocates who had no desire for personal gain.

Together they decided to establish the Media Action Network for Asian Americans.

The Work of MANAA

When I started attending the general meetings for MANAA in 2008, they followed a consistent pattern. On the third Thursday of every month—save December, when meetings were held on the second Thursday so as not to interfere with holiday plans—members of MANAA met in a small room on the second floor of the Chinatown Public Safety Association building. Their choice of meeting space reflected the fact that they did not have any budget for renting space, so they relied on in-kind contributions from supporters for all potential expenses. The room in Los Angeles' Chinatown was used because one of the longtime board members also served on the board of the Chinatown Public Safety Association, and thus could use the room for free. As attendees settled into their metal folding chairs, they were offered hot tea and a selection of muffins, also donated by a board member.

MANAA's meetings were open to the public and could be attended by anyone interested in issues of Asian American media representation. As a result of this open invitation, most meetings consisted of half a dozen core members who had been involved for many years, and a few first-time attendees who were there just to learn about the organization. Members included many individuals from media industries—directors, actors, writers, and people who worked on the business side of the industry. Although there were formal membership dues of $50 a year ($35 for students) for those who wanted to receive the yearly newsletter and be eligible for board positions, most participants were simply recognized as active members when they began to help out with organizational business. This could include everything from being assigned to monitor and report back on specific TV shows or movies, to more demanding work such as drafting letters to media organizations, making educational presentations to local colleges, or helping to plan protests. During periods of organizational growth, the meetings swelled to fifteen to twenty attendees per month, while during a lull there would be no more than a dedicated few for months on end.

Members of the Media Action Network for Asian Americans meet in Los Angeles' Chinatown for their monthly general meeting, where they discuss organizational business and recently viewed images of Asian Americans.

Regardless of how many members were currently involved, the business of the organization was to monitor and work to improve the representation of Asian Americans in the media. In keeping with its mission of "advocating balanced, sensitive and positive portrayals of Asian Americans," it kept tabs as best it could on the way Asian Americans were represented within the entertainment media. While I was volunteering with MANAA from 2008 to 2011, it was the only dedicated watchdog organization for Asian American media representations. Yet its work reflected the long tradition of Asian American media activism that had come before it, and was the product of many generations of Asian American community organizers coming together to strategize about how to most effectively impact such representations. Thus although my investigation of MANAA was made possible by my intimate relationship with the inner workings of this single organization, none of its actions can be seen as its alone—it was simply following in the footsteps of all the organizations that have undertaken this kind of work, including BOA, AAPAA, the Chinese Media Committee, Asian Americans in Fair Media, AJAA, and the others previously discussed in this chapter.

One of the most critical functions of every media activism group is deciding when to take action once an image has been brought to its attention. At almost every monthly meeting, someone would bring up an image that he or she felt was problematic. Either a member had noticed the image or an outsider had emailed the organization. After consulting with those who had seen the image in question and striving to make the image available to all members, the group had to decide what action to take. At the most basic level, members' available options were to ignore the image and perhaps write an email back to the original complainant, or to respond in some way, usually by reaching out to the creators of the image. In extreme circumstances where the creators could not be reached or refused to respond positively, MANAA has waged all-out war by organizing rallies, protests, or boycotts of offensive films and TV shows. Alternatively, if the original image was positive, MANAA could praise the producers. Like AAPAA, MANAA has also produced a series of award shows over the years, which were designed to reward producers of exemplary imagery and raise the profile of Asian American actors and industry professionals.

In general, MANAA's response to an image was based on four factors—emotional response, achievability, allocation of resources, and past precedent. Since most people who attended MANAA's meetings were Asian American, group consensus on the offensiveness of an image was often reached simply by asking if anyone was personally offended by it. Emotional responses such as feeling proud, embarrassed, insulted, angry, amused, or pleased were all seen as valid reasons for the group to make a decision. If the members of the group decided that the image was offensive and should not be ignored, they began to consider the achievability of impacting change. There was quite a bit of industry knowledge within the group, given that some members of MANAA were actors or worked in some capacity in the media industry. Also, there were many who attended yearly meetings with the television networks and film studios, and thus considered themselves industry insiders from the close connections and relationships made in those meetings. From this history and knowledge, the group generally had a sense of the stages of a project in which things like scripts or actors could still be changed, the way movies are marketed and written about in the press, and how to target the end product in a way that would have the most impact. However, because of their closeness with certain members of the industry, group members also had a strong desire to take a proactive stance and work with the image's creators, rather than to continually burn bridges or deliver threats when the media producers had made a mistake.

This desire to maintain positive relationships with media producers is a common attribute of activist groups whose main goal is to impact representations in mainstream media outlets. In her investigation of GLAAD, Kristen Schilt found that it was "more productive to employ educational campaigns that provide information for altering future LGBT representations than to use hostile tactics, such as boycotts, that tend to only effect the immediate issue at hand" (Schilt 2003, 184). This is based on the belief that defamation is more commonly the result of ignorance than malice. Hence cooperative tactics can actually be productive in preempting future incidents as well. One example of this was when MANAA learned about a film being made in which Chinese people were cast as the enemy threatening to take over the world. They contacted the producers to explain that this image relates to the systemic notion of a "Yellow Peril," wherein the U.S. government actually has historically created policies to subjugate Chinese Americans because they were seen as a threat. By taking this action, the group hoped not only that the information would impact the movie in question, but also that it would prevent such images from being re-created in the future. In fact, these educational moments do not always impact the representations in the targeted film. But MANAA hoped to contribute to a growing discourse about systemic racism in the media and the way stereotypes can contribute to anti-Asian sentiment.

Another factor is the resources that can be allocated to the project, which include concrete factors like manpower and more intangible ones like time and effort. One board member stated, "You pick battles that are worth fighting and that you are able to commit resources to. Pursuing an issue takes people power and follow-up. There are some issues that we think sound interesting or it would be nice to look further into, but we just can't because no one has the time." The group's most common methods of protest were writing a letter or email to the image's producer, issuing a press release condemning or praising the image, or trying to set up a meeting with the producers. While all these activities take time to carry out, they also take writing skills, experience, and more importantly, willingness and persistence.

MANAA's model of traditional activism has brought it many successes over the years, not the least of which includes simply sustaining momentum for over two decades. It has taken much talent, loyalty, and dedication for an all-volunteer organization like MANAA to remain vibrant. Most of these qualities are embodied by Guy Aoki, a founding president of the group who has remained one of its most active board members. Through his long commitment to the issue of Asian American representation, he cultivated many close connections with those who worked in entertainment media, news media, and other activist organizations that could help to get a campaign off the ground. His fearless and confrontational style was rare among his colleagues—particularly those who were afraid of risking their jobs to speak out—and offered an important means of bringing discussions of racial politics into the popular media sphere. Further, he was well known for tackling personalities like Sarah Silverman and Adam Carolla on the air for making jokes that offended Asian Americans. Silverman had used the word "chink" in a joke while performing on the Conan O'Brien Show in 2001, and Carolla included a skit on his radio show in 2006 that mocked the Asian Excellence Awards by saying that all the presenters said was "ching chong ching chong." This kind of racist language—using the word "chink" and joking that all Asian language sounds like "ching chong"—was exactly what MANAA wanted to remove from public discourse. The members of MANAA felt that having white comedians use such language to make Asian Americans the punchline of a joke was indelibly harmful, as it propagated the idea that the use of such derogatory terms was acceptable in spite of their histories of slander. Although both comedians later maintained that they continued to disagree with Aoki about his understanding of comedy, his blunt arguments and often humorous critiques clearly had a lasting impact—Silverman included a subsection in her memoir called "Guy Aoki: Heart in Right Place, Head Up Wrong Place," while Carolla frequently agonized about Aoki years later on his humorous podcasts.

Guy Aoki, the founding president of the Media Action Network for Asian Americans, is a well-known spokesperson for Asian American media issues.

Beyond Aoki's media appearances and the success of the protest of *The Goods: Live Hard, Sell Hard*, MANAA has made numerous successful interventions into the world of Asian American media representation since its founding. In 1994, MANAA led a nationwide protest of the film *Rising Sun* because it feared that the film's negative portrayals of Japanese as violent and ruthless businesspeople trying to take over the United States would lead to a backlash against Japanese Americans. With protests in New York, San Francisco, Chicago, Seattle, and Los Angeles, MANAA and its collaborators (among them Nosotros, the Gay and Lesbian Alliance Against Defamation, the American-Arab Anti Discrimination Committee, the Japanese American Citizens League, the National Coalition for Redress and Reparations, and the Women's Organization Reaching Koreans) counted their success in the impact of their protest on national media coverage of the film. Aoki described the outcome as follows:

> In all the interviews I saw on T.V., all the comments the stars made were in answer to our accusations. . . . They weren't able to talk about that

lightweight stuff; they had to spend all their time defending the film. So, I think we won the public relations battle: even though Fox spent millions to publicize *Rising Sun* and we didn't have a budget, we controlled the spin on the film. (Aoki 2009)

MANAA has protested a number of films over the years, each time weighing the success of its actions by the amount of media coverage that its protest draws, or in cases like that of *The Goods*, in a positive or conciliatory response by the studio, although this is admittedly quite rare.

These outward displays of disapproval and calls for boycott belie much of the behind-the-scenes work in which MANAA engages. With regard to the *Rising Sun*, members of MANAA contacted the studios on numerous occasions, giving them ample opportunity to enlist their help in improving the film and potentially avoid the entire situation. It was the organization's general policy to always contact the studios and producers as soon as they heard about a potentially problematic project and try to impact change from within, a strategy that has often proved effective. In 1997, members of MANAA heard that there was to be a remake of CBS Television's series *Hawaii Five-O* and immediately went to work pressuring the network to cast an Asian American in a lead role. Although CBS had planned to cast a white actor in the role of Nick Irons who takes over Five-O, members of MANAA met with CBS President Leslie Moonves to argue that the show should more accurately reflect the Asian population of Hawaii. After much conversation, Asian American actor Russell Wong was cast in the lead role, making it the first time that MANAA was able to affect the racial makeup of a series before the casting decisions had been completed. Unfortunately, the pilot was not approved by network executives and the show did not air. But in 2011 when the show was again rebooted with an entirely new cast, two of the four leads—albeit the two lesser leads—went to Asian American actors Daniel Dae Kim and Grace Park. These small victories, even over the course of many years of work, reflect the tremendous impact organizations can have when they build positive relationships within the studios.

These examples constitute only a small fraction of the work that MANAA has accomplished over the years; members were frequently called upon to speak on panels or give interviews to the mass media, and they participated in a number of educational outreach events at col-

leges and community festivals each year. They were also given the opportunity to speak directly to media producers and gatekeepers in yearly
meetings with the top television networks, which I discuss at length in
the next chapter. Despite these successes, it is important for community
groups to constantly evaluate their surroundings and their positioning
in order to continue to be effective, and there is always room to grow
with regard to finding new ways to educate and bring about change.
During my time with MANAA there were a number of areas in which
its collective struggles for cultural citizenship were potentially limiting
or restrictive, rather than allowing for the flexibility and fluidity that has
long characterized Asian America.

Focusing on Stereotype Analysis

On MANAA's website it states that the group "was formed . . . to address
the negative stereotypes long perpetuated by the media which detri-
mentally affects all Asian Americans, hurting not only their self image,
but how non-Asians treat them" (About MANAA n.d.). We can see that
stereotypes are one of the foundational issues that such groups face. Further, one of the resources that MANAA created and relied upon is a
document called "Restrictive Portrayals of Asians in the Media and How
to Balance Them." The document explains that MANAA does not want
to limit creative imagination, but to "encourage Hollywood's creative
minds to think in new directions." For instance, instead of portraying
Asian cultures as inherently predatory, MANAA lists a stereotype buster
of "Asians as positive contributors to American society." Instead of portraying Asian Americans as restaurant workers, anchorwomen, martial
artists, faith healers, or prostitutes, it suggests busting the stereotype
with "Asian Americans in diverse, mainstream occupations: therapists,
educators, U.S. soldiers, etc." This list of stereotype busters has been routinely handed out at meetings with media producers and is indicative of
a commonly deployed discourse on stereotypes.

Yet this notion that stereotypes must necessarily be avoided or possibly protested is a somewhat limited way of interpreting racialized imagery. It is clear that roles for Asians fall into an embarrassingly limited
set of caricatures—Asian women are seen as sexual objects or dangerous
villains (the Lotus Blossom and the Dragon Lady), while Asian men are

emasculated and nerdy, the karate master or the evil villain. Asian actors are always subordinate to white actors; in the case of Asian women, the result of an interracial romance can be dangerous and potentially fatal, and the Asian man can never compete against white dominance. In general, Asian actors and actresses are consistently portrayed as ignorant foreigners, despised model minorities, or cartoonish enemies.[4]

But beyond pointing out the harm that can be inflicted by these limited representations, we should also consider the complicated and nuanced ways in which viewers might read and interact with any kind of imagery, as well as how specific images are being deployed. Theorists like Ella Shohat and Robert Stam (1994), Michele Wallace (1990), Herman Gray (1995) and many others have pointed out the fallacies inherent in stereotype analysis and the related call for "positive images." If the problem with racism is that racialized bodies are categorized as inferior, then by calling for more positive imagery we seem merely to be saying that we want to reverse that equation and put racialized bodies in a superior position. This, of course, would do nothing to alter racist ideologies and structures. Also, when we talk about what these so-called positive attributes are, in many ways we are simply reifying the dominant culture, saying that cultural markers such as certain types of clothes, or occupations, or lifestyles are inherently better than others. Despite a general desire to "uplift" racial minorities through filmic representations, this kind of binary discourse leads to an essentializing of both whiteness and of the racialized bodies who are called upon to reproduce those qualities.

Ella Shohat and Robert Stam (1994) argue that although the work of stereotype analysts has been indispensable, a stereotype-centered approach nonetheless leads to some serious problems. These include ahistoricism, essentialism, moralism, and individualism, all of which cause analysts to flatten our reading of the image at hand. To elaborate upon each of these categories, let us look at the example of the character Saito, played by Japanese actor Ken Watanabe in the film *Inception*. Saito's character in the fantastical thriller is a powerful Japanese businessman who pays a team of criminals to enter a competitor's mind so that his business won't be overtaken. If we are to contextualize this role within known tropes such as the yellow peril or the Asian villain trying to take over the world, we might contend that this character is thus stereotypical. His Japanese accent clearly marks him as an Asian foreigner and his actions are often violent and threatening, as in the scene where Saito tortures and possibly kills a member of the team in order to find out where the team leader is located. Such characterizations would seem to firmly lodge Saito in the camp of the "bad guy" or the "negative representation." Yet in watching the film, it becomes clear that the moral system of this imaginary futuristic world is unclear, and we know very little about Saito's true motivations or background. His character is as richly developed and acted as any of the other primary characters. To label him the yellow peril simply because he is Asian would be to fall into the trap of essentialism—to assume that his attributes are indelibly connected to his racial identity—as well as ahistoricism, since these labels match a racialized body to a concept that may have outgrown its usefulness or gained new meaning in its contemporary context. To condemn his character's actions as "bad" would be to fall into the trap of moralism, as we cannot definitively ascertain what actions and characters are right and wrong. Indeed, movie producers so feared this outcome—that Saito would be seen as the "bad guy"—that they specifically reached out to Asian American bloggers and community organizations with free tickets and promotional merchandise to ensure that Asian Americans would support the film.

Celine Parreñas Shimizu (2007) has also critiqued stereotype analysis in *The Hypersexuality of Race*—a text that reads from the margins to show how even the most seemingly "negative" images of Asian American women in pornography can be mined for their productive potential. Shimizu allows for the possibility of a pornography that is politicized and redemptive, and by speaking with female producers, spectators, and critics is able to identify many different forms of protest and critique within these oft-disparaged roles. Similarly, in Peter Feng's (2000) examination of Nancy Kwan, he looks to independent films made by Asian American women as a way of recontextualizing and reinvesting spectatorial pleasure in *The World of Suzie Wong*—where Suzie Wong plays the quintessential Asian prostitute with a heart of gold. Feng seeks a middle ground between claiming that the film is either racist or anti-racist, arguing that meaning is dependent on readings by the audience, locating pleasure at the intersection of the closed narrative structure of the film and the polysemy of Kwan's star discourse. In each of these

Adorno *representation* (handwritten margin note)

works, theorists admit that even "bad texts" can be pleasurable and that textual meaning can be interpreted in multiple ways, particularly by Asian American audiences and viewers. Shimizu and Feng also redeem the actors who take on stereotypical roles, interpreting their actions and performances as resistant despite the fact that they often knowingly embody stereotypical roles.

Asian American activists who rely on a straightforward conversation about positive and negative stereotypes are at odds with such analysis. Indeed, activism against stereotypes leaves no room for spectatorial pleasure or any resistive process of reading and playing with images. It is clear why some activists would take this stance—if the problem at hand continues to be a lack of general knowledge of the ways that Asian Americans have been unfairly forced to fit into a prescribed mold of submission by media producers, even the most simplistic education about the stereotypes that have come before would have to remain a primary goal. Yet I would also argue that activists stand to gain a great deal by incorporating different reading strategies into their understanding of the way media imagery operates. Although viewers might find a certain image stereotypical and fear that mainstream audiences will sharpen their cartoonish mental image of Asians as a result, there is no reason for conversation to stop at this level. Indeed, rigid binaries wherein all images are categorized as good or bad, praised or protested, stereotypical or stereotype-busting, can serve to alienate and distance activists from actual Asian American audiences who might find pleasure in being fans of Jet Li's martial arts villainy or who think that Lucy Liu's dragon lady portrayals are subversive and empowering. In some cases, performers have even been seen to deliberately employ stereotypes as a means of skewering them, or to appropriate stereotypes through camp in order to mobilize and call attention to their cause.

Comedienne Margaret Cho, a longtime queer feminist activist and the first Asian American woman to star in her own sitcom, poses a challenge to this hard stance against stereotypes. In her performances, she frequently mocks her parents by using an exaggerated Korean accent and teasing them about their immigrant ways. In one of her bits she mocks Asian foreign exchange students, assuming an affected accent and the deferential bow. But as Rachel Lee (2004) argues, Cho's bit is not meant to skewer Asians, Asian Americans, or Asian immigrants in her foreign exchange student act. On the contrary, "Cho theatricalizes white civility—precisely what passes for whiteness everyday—by Orientalizing it, exaggerating the colored person's response toward such civility, and finally holding that civility suspect" (108). That is, Cho uses yellowface and self-Orientalizing gestures to illustrate and critique racial inequality through her comedy.

Adhering to a straightforward condemnation of all things stereotypical can leave a group like MANAA unequipped to deal with satire and comic portrayals like Cho's that might actually help communicate its message about social injustice. To combat this blind spot, activists might find it productive to partner with individuals, organizations, and communities who celebrate a more active interpretation of the relationships individuals create with their media. In later chapters I will explore more of these possibilities.

Fighting for Citizenship through Assimilation

These distinctions about what constitutes a stereotypical representation of Asian Americans help to reveal the interconnectedness of representation with identity and citizenship. Asian American media activists have long argued that if we can increase the visibility of Asian American bodies and stories in the media, then Asian American audiences will begin to recognize themselves in media images and the mainstream viewing public will begin to understand a diversity of experiences outside their own. However, in deciding what kinds of images are acceptable in depicting Asian America, a very particular definition of cultural citizenship is at work—to be seen as fully American, Asian Americans must portray themselves as "just like everyone else." This is what motivates a condemnation of Asians being marked through difference, such as an Asian character being good at karate or speaking with an accent. Although an extreme version of this desire might be read as a desire for postracialism wherein racial difference is thought not to matter at all, MANAA's position does not demand the complete erasure or recognition of race as a salient category. On the contrary, it is because of its belief that race has mattered historically and continues to matter today that it persists in fighting for racial equality and the improved treatment of Asian Americans. Yet underlying its rigid denunciation of stereotypes is an adherence to the political value of assimilation, or the desire that Asian Americans not stand out as different in any way.

However, the shorthand phrase "just like everyone else" that I use here to describe an assimilationist position must be problematized for its implication that Asian Americans are the only ones suffering from representational inequities. While it might be more accurate to specify that MANAA wants Asian Americans to be unmarked in the same way that white, male, middle-class, heterosexual, Christian, or otherwise hegemonic bodies are understood within media representations, I intentionally use a less specific characterization in order to remind us that such a desire is always fraught with impossibility—there is no identity that remains unmarked, and there can be no perfect representation that would satisfy all demands. Nevertheless, Ella Shohat and Robert Stam remind us of how stereotyping functions:

> Stereotypes of some communities merely make them uncomfortable, but the community has the social power to combat and resist them; stereotypes of other communities participate in a continuum of prejudicial social policy and actual violence against disempowered people, placing the very body of the accused in jeopardy. (Shohat and Stam 1994, 208)

Although no community can escape the process of stereotyping or unwanted characterizations, minority groups suffer from a lack of power that could be used to combat and resist the social impact of such representations. When deploying a definition of cultural citizenship that calls out for assimilation or assumes that some positions do not suffer from negative representation, media activists may be failing to correctly identify the source of social injustice at work.

Another way we can more clearly see this particular definition of cultural citizenship is by observing how MANAA negotiates the national boundaries of what and who are included in the category of "Asian American." Throughout its project of deciding what images to take on, MANAA's leadership has often been forced to draw firm national boundaries around its own Asian identities. One of the organization's oft-repeated stances is that because Asian Americans are not the same as Asian nationals, media representations must disavow any connection between Asia and the United States. For example, after the 2011 earthquake and tsunami in Japan, MANAA received emails condemning some of the anti-Japan messages they had seen propagated on Twitter. In response, a MANAA member wrote to the rest of the organization:

> We don't defend foreign countries, Asian or otherwise. And it's a fact. Are we going to be asked to defend call centers in India which also take away jobs from Americans? I understand they are worried about the impact on Asian Americans but unless someone makes anti-Asian sentiments in general, it's not our "jurisdiction" to comment.

This statement represents an extremely common sentiment within MANAA—it doesn't want to intervene in issues that focus on Asia because it is important to make a distinction between "Asians" and "Asian Americans." Given that Asian Americans have historically been denied the basic rights of American citizenship, including everything from the right to immigrate, to naturalize, to own property, to vote, or in the case of internment, to be free from unjust imprisonment, it makes sense that activists interested in the broader notion of citizenship would want Asian Americans to be viewed as full-fledged Americans. Yet I argue that this definition of assimilation as the defining marker of cultural citizenship reveals a desire for the national boundaries of the United States to fully enclose Asian American identities. This particular definition of cultural citizenship can be read as a denial of the existence of transnational identities, as well as a reification of whiteness as the norm or the ideal. MANAA uses the term "jurisdiction" as if it were useful to designate certain issues on which it has the authority to speak, but in fact this statement cuts it off from a diversity of issues and communities that it might find beneficial to include in its work.

Although MANAA has been fighting the same battle since its creation in 1992, in many ways the landscape surrounding it has changed. During one general meeting, an interaction between participants helped illustrate some of the ways that this discourse around stereotypes can become a conversation about national identity. MANAA's general meetings provide a space for members to discuss how they feel about recent images in the media. Members are routinely asked to monitor specific television programs and then report back on the kinds of roles Asian American actors are given. At this meeting, actor Tim Kang was celebrated because he was cast in a "typical tough cop" role in *The Mentalist* on CBS, as opposed to the nerdy computer tech role that Asian men are usually given in procedural dramas. Some long-standing members of the group agreed that seeing the Asian cop chase after a runaway suspect, hit him with a two-by-four, cuff him, and say "You're busted buddy," was a victory because it was the type of role usually written for white men. However, at this meeting a newcomer challenged this view, saying, "I didn't like seeing the Asian guy act like a white cop. It bothers me when you see Asian people trying to act white on TV." In response, the MANAA members asked how an Asian cop would act differently. Would he use martial arts? Would he speak with an accent? Essentially, would you have him act stereotypically to mark his Asianness? These rhetorical questions seemed to be critical of the use of stereotypes, but actually they indicate MANAA's deep investment in assimilation.

For the long-standing members of the group, it was of critical importance for Asian Americans to be seen as no different from white people. This kind of desire of course presupposes that whiteness is something that can be attained, rather than acknowledging that whiteness is just as much a social construction as Asianness or any other racial identity. The specific nature of the clip being discussed also illuminates some of the problems implicated in this desire. First, the show was praised for offering a role where an Asian American man was a member of the police, and this character was praised for enacting violence on another man. Although the victim of violence was purportedly a criminal, for Asian Americans to aspire to be in a position where violence, racial injustice, and the abuse of power are systemic is quite problematic. In *Pedagogy of the Oppressed*, Paolo Freire warns about the dangers of striving for liberation in a way that leads to the oppressed becoming oppressors or "sub-oppressors" themselves. He finds that "almost always, during the initial stage of the struggle . . . their ideal is to be men; but for them, to be men is to be oppressors. This is their model of humanity" (Freire 1970, 45). Moreover, Celine Parreñas Shimizu's theorization of Asian American masculinities reminds us that we should not take hegemonic white masculinity as the ideal, but should instead aspire for representations of ethical manhood (Shimizu 2012).

In assessing the conversation surrounding Tim Kang and others, we can see that these views embraced some of the more limited ways of viewing the concept of assimilation. As it functions here, assimilation can be characterized as the inevitable process through which minority groups adapt to life in the United States by discarding their previous culture and embracing the dominant Anglo-American, Protestant, middle-class culture (Alba and Nee 2003). This one-sided ethnocentric view elides the reality that the mainstream U.S. culture itself is changed by the influx of immigrants and the diversity of cultures within the country. Further, assimilation is not necessarily a linear form of adaptation, but rather a complex and fluid process of negotiation and creation. Cheng's (2001) critique of these expectations of traditional assimilation offers a helpful way of looking at the case of Asian Americans. She argues that while assimilation is idealized in the so-called American Dream, it is actually impossible for Asians because "the standard of assimilation, 'Americanness,' denotes whiteness" (69). Cheng's portrait of the United States is one where racialization gives way to a melancholia that is deeply internalized and often unexplored. Cheng argues that "the double malady of melancholia for the racial-ethnic subject is the condition of having to incorporate both an impossible ideal and a denigrated self" (72). Further, Cheng sees assimilation and mourning as intimately connected, and worries that it is wrongly assumed that one can potentially "get over" the experience of loss and racial grief. Since assimilation requires a complicated process of incorporation and introjection that can last a lifetime, the grieving process is in reality continuous: "there is no such a thing as 'just' letting go" (97).

Beyond what Cheng sees as the melancholia of assimilation, expectations of the positive impact of assimilation also serve to reify the dominance of normative "American" culture, since it implies that all other groups must necessarily change their own ways to fit in. In this way of thinking, the dominant culture seems to represent an idealized version of the world that needs no modification. Activists who rely on this paradigm remain trapped within a fixed binary in which Asian Americans are seen as either detested outsiders or as assimilated white Americans. Rather than relying on this binary, activists could more productively seek out a middle ground or a mode of representation that more fully encompasses what Lisa Lowe (1996) famously refers to as the "heterogeneity, hybridity and multiplicity" that truly mark Asian America. Perhaps instead of praising actors for taking on roles that would usually be given to white actors, they could begin to imagine roles uniquely suited to Asian Americans and the complicated histories and cultures encompassed within this community. While their own perspective on cultural citizenship requires that Asian Americans assimilate to a white (or hegemonically masculine) norm, they could embrace a definition of cultural citizenship that demands that the "mainstream" culture within the United States shift to accommodate and accept practices of difference.

The diversity of the community is also important to consider, given that another problem traditional Asian American media activism organizations have yet to face up to is that the demographics of those encompassed by the term Asian American are always changing. As mentioned earlier, MANAA has resolutely stood fast to the argument that Asians should not be caricatured as perpetual foreigners because they are actually American-born and native English speakers. To that end, the organization criticizes representations in which an Asian American actor is made to speak with an accent, since the accent becomes a symbol of the Asian as foreigner. Yet its failure to tackle issues taking place in Asia also reveals its perception of national boundaries as concrete when the reality is that they are becoming more porous than ever, particularly between Asia and America.

For instance, an episode of *Desperate Housewives* was brought to MANAA's attention when the character Susan asked her doctor, "Can I check your diplomas because I want to make sure they're not from some med school in the Philippines." The Filipino American community was outraged by the criticism of the quality of education in the Philippines, but MANAA refused to take a stand. Since the derogatory comment was made about the Philippines but not the United States, MANAA felt it was not within its scope. This stance is particularly unfortunate given the strong presence of Filipino professionals within the American medical community, particularly in California where it is estimated that one-third of all nurses are Filipino American. Indeed, the invisibility of this population of professionals would actually be directly within the purview of an Asian American media activism organization. As an online petition from Filipino Americans stated, "Many of the hospitals in major metropolitan areas of the U.S. (and the world) would not be able to operate without its Filipino and Filipino American staff members" (Filipino Americans demand for apology from ABC and Desperate Housewives n.d.). But MANAA's organizational position is also problematic because it fails to recognize the true diversity of Asians in the United States. For instance, over 59 percent of all Americans of Asian descent (74 percent of all adult Asian immigrants) are first-generation immigrants, meaning that English is not their native language, and they are likely still battling to become citizens (Pew Research Center 2012).

While members of MANAA are frustrated by the fact that Asian Americans are stereotypically depicted as the perpetual foreigner, such representations reflect the reality that many Asians have difficulty attaining citizenship in a country that consistently views them as "the other." MANAA's pleas for representations of assimilated, English-speaking Asian American characters possibly reflects the composition of MANAA's membership, which includes many second- and third-generation Asian Americans, as well as a predominant number of Chinese Americans and Japanese Americans. Given the unique histories of Chinese and Japanese immigrants in the United States, including anti-Chinese sentiment as a result of labor conflicts and the Japanese American internment during World War II, among many others, these ethnic and generational subsets of the Asian American population have specific sociohistorical reasons for seeking such treatment. Although the laws against Asian immigration led to a disproportionately high number of immigrants from Japan and China who had already settled in the United States in the first half of the twentieth century, when these restrictions were lifted in 1965 the composition of Asian immigrants shifted rapidly to include a much higher percentage of first-generation immigrants from Vietnam, Korea, Cambodia, Thailand, Laos, India, Pakistan, and the Philippines. Beyond ethnic differences, this more heterogeneous Asian American formation also views its relationship with the United States differently than earlier generations. Many post-1965 immigrants possess dual citizenship in the United States and in their country of origin and identify primarily as members of a diaspora rather than as belonging within the United States. These Americans of Asian descent have a wide diversity of relationships with their country of origin, both linguistically and culturally, and in our transnational era of global capitalism many of them navigate between continents for financial reasons. Given these realities, it is likely that the Filipino Americans insulted by the comment about medical schools in the Philippines saw the issue as one that was close to their own community or their personal experience.

MANAA's limited way of viewing Asian America also makes it difficult for traditional media activists to even have a vocabulary for many within the film industry, such as actors Jackie Chan and Ken Watanabe, or director Ang Lee—who are difficult to categorize as either Asian or American, since their identities are clearly fluid and contextual. Such stars are increasingly important to consider, given that movie studios have become so interested in the international market that they frequently employ well-known Asian actors who are then introduced to domestic audiences. For instance, the role of the Green Hornet's Asian sidekick was given to Jay Chou, a famous singer/songwriter-turned-actor from Taiwan. The blockbuster marked Chou's first foray into American cinema, and he needed to learn English to prepare for the film. Although members of MANAA expressed disappointment that this role and others went to international talent rather than promoting Asian American talent, it is clear that the marketability of an international cast is becoming an undeniable influence in Hollywood.

Asian American Studies scholars have long argued that Asian America has a complicated relationship with Asia and the rest of the world. The foundation of Asian American Studies itself coincided with anti-war movements and the desire for Asian Americans to unite with their Asian brothers and sisters who were being killed in Vietnam. Early activists who came together as part of the Yellow Power movement or who united to form Asian American studies programs saw deep connections between their plight in the United States and the battles that were being undertaken overseas—even in countries that they had never set foot into or that did not match their own ethnic heritage. As Maeda (2009) found, Asian American activists in the 1970s were building alliances across racial and national boundaries as a way of contributing to antiracist and anti-imperialist efforts across the globe. Although some of the work that MANAA undertakes is based on identity formations that reach back to the Asian American Movement, in many ways contemporary media activists are also disregarding these important imperatives for broader arguments against the nation and its imperialism. At the time when MANAA was first beginning its protests and community building efforts, Sau-ling Wong (1995) proposed in the pages of *Amerasia*

Journal that the field of Asian American Studies was entering a distinct mode of denationalization, and warned scholars how they might do so more carefully. She characterized the shift toward a diasporic rather than domestic perspective and the growing permeability between "Asian Asians" and "Asian Americans" as productive, but warned that scholars needed to historicize these transitions so that myths of nation could be sufficiently complicated.

These concerns continue to be salient in the field of Asian American Studies, despite the fact that media activists consistently uphold the narratives of nation and the importance of national boundaries in defining their own sense of citizenship. Kandice Chuh's (2006) arguments urging that Asian American Studies be seen as subjectless are similarly connected to concerns about upholding the project of U.S. nationalism. For Chuh, this means that we should not assume that there is such a thing as Asian America; rather, versions of Asian America are created within difference and contextualized relations of power. As she states, "reconstituting Asian American studies in difference helps us to recognize that Asian Americanist critique must be consistently and insistently critical of both U.S. nationalism and its apparatuses of power." (13) In this mode of what has been called strategic antiessentialism, postessentialism, or anti-antiessentialism, Asian American Studies looks to its position within the globalized world in order to more effectively impact justice and social change. Indeed, it is difficult to imagine Asian American media activists abandoning their collective identities as American citizens in order to change the way the entertainment media portrays their largely disenfranchised and marginalized community. Still, it is important that Chuh's injunction that we recognize that there are different ways of identifying Asian America, ones that can include a more global perspective, be taken into consideration.

Neglecting New Media

The final area in which traditional modes of activism may have become outdated is the choice of what media to target. Members of MANAA have traditionally preferred to tackle issues originating within network television rather than any other medium, with film and radio as sites of secondary interest. This preference is based on the fact that the group is interested in what can be considered "mass media," and network television is believed to reach the largest audience of American viewers. Also, given that MANAA annually sends a contingent of board members to meet with the networks, these conversations can be both effective and efficient. In contrast, trying to contact movie studios or other media producers can be difficult if not downright impossible without inside connections, thus becoming a waste of time and energy. When MANAA was asked to respond to an offensive video on YouTube, a board member sent the following email:

> One of the problems with YouTube posts and other kinds of internet sites is that they do not have a general media aspect to them. If you do not click onto the YouTube post or do not visit the internet site, you will not be assaulted by the offensive language and/or images. In regular broadcast media (or even basic cable), people are assaulted by what is on without actively seeking it out, so that is why we target those kinds of outlets.

The same reasoning has also been applied to offensive books and novels, websites, podcasts, and tweets. However, there are a number of problems with this reasoning, beginning with the fact that consumers seek out broadcast television much the same way as they seek out internet sites, either directly choosing a program or site they are interested in, or else clicking through a number of choices sort of aimlessly—and in both cases there is the definite possibility that they could stumble upon unwanted or offensive material. MANAA's strategy of focusing on prime time television to the exclusion of other forms of media also reveals a failure to recognize that we are no longer in the network era, when it could have been assumed that network television was among the few options available to audiences.

To understand the limitations of this kind of thinking, we can look to the changing structure of television and the different ways that meaning and representation are constructed in our increasingly mediated world. As Amanda Lotz (2007) explains in *The Television Will Be Revolutionized*, we are now living in a post–network television era. Understanding the nuances of this term can help us better understand the impact of the media. She characterizes the network era, between 1952 and the mid-1980s, as one in which the three top networks (NBC, CBS and

ABC) dominated the airwaves and commanded mass audiences. There was very little choice about what to watch or how to watch it, and most programming was created with a white middle-class audience in mind. Shows like *I Love Lucy* and *The Beverly Hillbillies* garnered 90 percent of the viewing audience when they aired during their scheduled time slot. In the 1980s, the proliferation of cable channels and technologies like video cassette recorders and remote controls began to give viewers more choices as to both content and viewing experiences. Lotz calls this era the "multichannel transition," as targeted, niche audiences began to grow in importance. Our contemporary era of television, called the post-network era by Lotz and the neo-network era by Michael Curtin, is characterized by a number of constantly changing factors. First, viewers can now interact with television by "pulling" content—from the internet and websites like Hulu, from TiVos and Digital Video Recorders, from DVD boxed sets and Netflix streaming or rented discs—to be watched on their own schedule. Nor is content restricted to the television screen; it is available for view on cell phones, computer screens, iPads, and a multitude of other viewing devices.

As Curtin (1997) argues, advocacy groups may have traditionally maintained the goal of "[challenging] the concentration of media ownership and [struggling] for control over prime time television," (68) but this strategy is a relic of the "high network" era of television from the 1950s to the 1980s when there were far fewer options for viewers. In our contemporary era, television no longer consists exclusively of programs and advertisements for the mass market; instead, offerings are increasingly diversified, fragmented, and transnationally minded. As Curtin argues, the neo-network era

> features elaborate circuits of cultural production, distribution, and reception. . . . [T]he key to success is no longer the ownership and control of a centralized and highly integrated medium-specific empire but the management of a conglomerate structured around a variety of firms with different audiences and different objectives. (71)

As a result, he suggests that advocacy groups move away from a strategy that focuses solely on impacting gatekeepers at the networks and instead look to promote alternative media venues, develop more alternative resources, or create particular brands based on political synergies within the choices of citizen-consumers (74). Moreover, the different market structure of online media actually opens up new opportunities for Asian American media activists. Their battles over prime time television are often constrained by the network's need to satisfy mass audiences, but on the internet there is much more flexibility and opportunity for experimentation without such well-defined economic controls.

The ability to address online representations is particularly important for Asian American communities, given the explosion of representations of Asian Americans on the internet as well as the high number of internet users within Asian American households. Not only are numerous offensive images propagated on blogs, internet videos, and websites—an issue that activists need to find a way to adequately address—but the internet also provides a space for Asian American artists and media producers to create and distribute their own creations. Countless Asian American individuals and groups have bypassed the conventional gatekeepers to media access and skyrocketed to online fame and fortune, and media advocates would do well to keep their eye on these innovations. Although I discuss internet representations of Asian Americans more fully in later chapters, here I simply want to acknowledge that new media is an important site for investigation, and point to the difficulty of making the argument that broadcast television remains the most pressing target.

Conclusion

The strategies and tactics that I have described reflect a very traditional sense of media activism that has remained static since the 1970s. Thus, although I point to some ways in which Asian American media activism groups could benefit from more flexibility and adaptability in their choice of targets and tactics, these criticisms are not specific to MANAA alone. On the contrary, this case study of a single organization is reflective of a long history of similar tactics that have provided activist organizations with a strong stable of strategies and tactics that are effective in many cases. Yet by looking more closely at some of the rhetoric used to justify their strategies and the specificities of their individual decisions, we can more carefully identify potential improvements in the more general paradigm of media activism among Asian Americans. For instance, responding to offensive images online can be difficult and indeed demands a new set of strategies to contact the producers, engage in education and message construction, and implement change. Yet in our highly fragmented world of niche media and transmedia storytelling that stretches far beyond the realm of television, new forms of media activism are needed that can be flexible and nimble enough to adapt to each new scenario.

In the next chapter, I delve more deeply into the arenas of media industries and media policy in order to explore the new strategies that could be adopted to move forward into a new media era. It is clear that a media activism strategy wherein organizations keep their ear to the ground with regard to the complicated face of representation in all its many forms may be the only way for interest groups to have an impact. For Asian Americans, this means pushing past the overly simplistic binaries of "positive" and "negative" images to embrace the way viewers actually respond to images, and educating audiences about the history of discrimination and stereotyping without limiting their own interpretive capabilities. It also means returning to the transnational alliances in which the Asian American Movement was rooted and seeing the category of Asian American as fluid and constantly changing, rather than rigidly nationalistic. Although these tactics may lead to small victories, and indeed over the last fifty years this kind of activism has had a very positive impact, a broader perspective on both the history of media activism and the momentum within Asian American Studies can build on these successes.

2

Leveraging Media Policy for Representational Change

In the battle to reform representational practices, media monitoring organizations like MANAA clearly play an active role in policing and restructuring the discourse around Asian American imagery. Yet individual organizations can only do so much, given their limited resources and largely reactionary protocols. Responding after an image has already begun to circulate in the media is an ad hoc strategy that can be difficult to sustain over time. In this chapter I explore the many ways in which media activism has become more proactive, systematized, and even institutionalized over the years through an engagement with regulatory policy. The word "policy" can be traced back to its roots in the word "police" in France, where the government and the police force were more integrated than they are now (McGuigan 2003). Yet if we consider the fact that media institutions and products fall within the realm of culture, the question remains of who can and should police culture. I argue that from a variety of different vantage points and cultural sites, activists are actually regulating corporations as a way of impacting the media—two institutions that are, at their core, inextricable.

Activist interventions into regulatory policies provide a means for outside bodies beyond activist organizations to hold cultural producers accountable and threaten consequences if they fail to comply with their agreements. I begin by exploring how the media has historically been regulated through governmental policies, and the intersection of those policies with the agendas of activists. But I also look beyond governmental regulation to examine the way activists are working to regulate privately owned media corporations—from the national networks (NBC, ABC, CBS, and FOX), to the Nielsen Company, to cable channels. Through memoranda of understanding, the institution of advisory councils composed of noninterested parties, and by filing petitions with the FCC to either support or deny rights to broadcasters, the work of media corporations has been policed by those interested in the representation of minorities in a number of ways.

We can think of policy that specifically interacts with cultural institutions as "cultural policy." Jim McGuigan (2003) emphasizes that "cultural policy raises questions of regulation and control but its meaning should not be restricted to an ostensibly apolitical set of practical operations that are merely administered and policed by governmental officials" (24). Rather, cultural policy makes it clear that politics are always already integrated throughout culture, particularly within the arenas of aesthetics and artistic expression. Media productions and other creative endeavors are largely (though not completely) unregulated by the government, but given their significant political and cultural impact there are still many ways in which they can be pressured to respond to demands for greater democratization and diversification.

It is important to investigate these kinds of interventions, given that cultural studies and media studies have long been critiqued for failing to address or adequately contribute to policy considerations. Cultural studies practitioners like Meaghan Morris want scholars to produce work that interacts with the institutions and power structures that inform culture, rather than remaining locked in an endless cycle of textual analysis (Morris 1988). With regard to the representation of Asian Americans in the media, there is clearly an opportunity for the intervention of cultural studies in cultural policy. Although cultural studies encompasses an exceedingly broad range of topics and subject matter, it is safe to say that issues of media representation, textual studies, identity, and difference fall well within its purview. Cultural studies can show the important role of cultural policy in regulating and influencing the public by the way it polices these issues—by educating the public about stereotypes, protesting offensive images, and promoting minority media producers. Further, in seeking out ways in which the image of Asian Americans in the media can be impacted by cultural policy, we can continue to articulate the connection between representation and cultural citizenship. As Justin Lewis and Toby Miller (2003) state, "cultural policy is . . . a site for the production of cultural citizens, with the cultural industries providing not only a realm of representations about oneself and others, but a series of rationales for particular types of conduct" (1). Beyond the laws and statutes that can allow or deny immigrants the status of citizen, media representations continue to uphold and develop different notions of citizenship through a much broader lens, including customs, language, and consumer behavior, among others.

In this chapter I also explore the complicated interplay between regulatory policy and censorship. As described in the previous chapter, deciding whether a role is stereotypical or offensive, and thus whether it should be permitted or protested, is incredibly difficult. An important question remains—how can Asian American media activists promote positive representations of their community without becoming censorious and negative? Can Asian American media activists find effective ways to use policy to impact the way images are created, and is policy work necessary or essential to their movement? In this chapter I explore the different ways that cultural policy has historically limited the ability of Asian Americans to intervene in the way their community has been represented, as well as the ways in which activists are now poised to use policy to bring about positive change. I argue that the history of the relationship between pressure groups and media policy shows that conservative and progressive activists have entered into many—perhaps surprising—alliances in their efforts to impact the creation, distribution, and ownership of media content. However, in the current legal landscape it is difficult for Asian Americans to continue in this vein of broad media reform. Instead, their efforts to regulate and work with corporations have become a new site for enacting cultural citizenship—though as always, they have to guard against the threat of making counterproductive or even dangerous alliances.

Censoring Film

The last chapter examined the wide variety of steps activist groups have taken to influence the images and messages propagated within the mass media. I briefly discussed the national debate about legal or governmental oversight of film and television with regard to the film *Birth of a Nation*, but there have been many other efforts to control the content and distribution of media productions throughout the history of the United States. In the early 1900s there were no established guidelines for government censorship of films, but a number of states began to shape standards on an ad hoc basis. In 1911, women's groups in Portland,

Oregon, persuaded their City Council to create a Censor Board to review the content of all motion pictures shown in the city. The Council eventually passed an ordinance stating that it could refuse to approve any film that showed obscene, indecent, or immoral content (Erickson 2010). In Ohio, a censorship board created in 1915 successfully rejected the screening of *Birth of a Nation*. In the landmark case *Mutual Film Corporation v. Industrial Commission of Ohio*, the U.S. Supreme Court decided that films were commercial products and therefore could not be protected under the First Amendment, unlike the press, art, or other sites for public opinion, which could (McEwan 2008). Although the ban on the film was eventually overturned, the case set a precedent showing the power of the state to censor and control imagery. By 1926, many states had enacted laws to create such censorship boards—including Pennsylvania, Ohio, Kansas, Maryland, New York, and Virginia—and over a dozen bills had been introduced in Congress attempting to create federal censorship boards charged with licensing all films before they could be allowed in interstate commerce. Individual cities across the country continued in this vein, establishing their own processes for viewing and containing images that they deemed inappropriate for the public (MacGregor 1926). These state-level censorship boards often simultaneously represented the interests of conservative and progressive activists, both of whom sought to control imagery for the greater good of promoting societal uplift. Although their vision for a more prosperous society may have looked slightly different, they found mutual strength in the force of their censorious demands.[1]

Given the clear threat of federal censorship by the government, the motion picture industry hastily took on the task of self-regulation. In 1922, Will Hays was named president of the Motion Pictures Producers and Distributors Association. Largely responsible for the task of public relations, Hays set about trying to improve Hollywood's image and assuage the fears of the burgeoning state censor boards. In 1924, he established a set of guidelines called "The Formula," followed up with a list of "Don'ts and Be Carefuls," both of which recommended that films not show nudity, profanity, miscegenation, and sexual perversion, and be careful about showing arson, sedition, and seduction, among other things. Despite the fact that these guidelines were not enforced and depended on voluntary compliance by the movie studios, Hays's work was successful in staunching the tide of censorship in state legislation. However, with the advent of sound technology in the late 1920s, states again began organizing for governmental control (Vaughn 2005). Their agitating, coupled with pressure from the Catholic church, led to the creation of the well-known Hays Code, or the Production Code, in 1930. From 1934 to 1952, members of the Production Code Administration headed by Joseph Breen had the power to change scripts and ban movies, which they regularly utilized.

This kind of censorship continued until 1952, when the case *Joseph Burstyn, Inc. v. Wilson* challenged the constitutionality of film censorship with regard to Roberto Rossellini's film, *The Miracle*. When the film was shown in New York, there was an outcry by churchgoers about its allegedly sacrilegious plot, which depicted the impregnation of a woman who believed she was the Virgin Mary. When the New York State Board of Regents banned the film, distributor Joseph Burstyn appealed the decision. The Supreme Court sided with Burstyn, arguing that movies were entitled to freedom of speech. Its ruling specifically reversed the ability of the state to censor films for being "sacrilegious," and subsequent rulings stated that films could also not be banned for being "immoral," "sexually immoral," "inciting to crime," or "harmful"—in effect, this ruling ended the banning of movies (Harris 1954).

We can see that throughout history, activism at the local level—whether through women's groups agitating to create citywide censor boards, religious groups attempting to shut down a screening at a particular theater, or African American groups protesting a racist film in the local press—has effectively intimidated the motion picture industry into changing its ways. The institution of the Hays Code marks a profound restructuring of the way moviemaking was conducted, and represents a dramatic power shift from the filmmakers to the censors in the early years of cinema. Again, we must question whether or not progressive, antiracist activists today would seek to use such strategies of censorship and the prohibition of free speech, or even collusion with filmmaking industries, in order to bring about social change. Yet it is important to note that throughout the history of media activism, citizens with messages to promote have risen up against media producers, and media industries have responded by changing their own structures to contain and squelch these critiques.

Regulating the Airwaves

While Hollywood's Hays Code and state censor boards had set their sights on the motion picture industry, radio and television have been governed by a different set of concerns. Film was the target of activism because of its impact on moral character, but radio and television have been seen as important public institutions that need to be available to the masses. In particular, there has been a focus on protecting the instrumentality of radio and television as a vehicle for providing non-entertainment news and public affairs programming to the public. The Federal Radio Commission (FRC), established in 1927, granted licenses to those seeking to broadcast on a certain spectrum, but ownership remained "in the public" and was meant to be used in accordance with "the public interest" (Baxter 1974). The Federal Communications Commission (FCC), which replaced the FRC in 1934, has the mission to

> make available so far as possible, to all the people of the United States, without discrimination on the basis of race, color, religion, national origin, or sex, rapid, efficient, Nation-wide, and world-wide wire and radio communication services with adequate facilities at reasonable charges. (Communications Act of 1934)

Historically, this included a mandate to regulate content to ensure a diverse set of viewpoints and "fair" coverage of controversial issues. Due to the scarcity of broadcast frequencies, the Communications Act of 1934 mandated that broadcasters give equal time to opposing viewpoints on controversial issues, among other requirements. This requirement, known as the Fairness Doctrine, also included a restriction on "personal attacks," requiring that individuals or groups be given a chance to respond if an attack was made on their honesty, character, or integrity. Although the precise meaning of this mandate has been vague since its inception, the threat of revoking or failing to renew a station's license has provided complaining parties with significant power in motivating stations to comply with their demands.

Like the motion picture industry, the television industry also responded to this fear of governmental regulation by developing its own form of self-regulation. As Katherine Montgomery (1989) outlines, the

National Association of Broadcasters in 1951 developed a "Code of Good Practices" as a means of shielding the industry from critique. Unfortunately, a scandal erupted around quiz shows in 1959 when the outcomes of popular competition shows like *Twenty-One* and *The $64,000 Question* were found to be rigged. As a result, scrutiny over the networks intensified. In particular, the relationship between advertisers and the content of shows was called into question, as the outcome of the quiz shows was blamed on advertiser strategies to maintain viewership. Television stations created positions like the Head of Broadcast Standards and entire standards and practices departments to serve as middlemen between pressure groups and the networks, but the power of the consumer to make demands continued to grow.

In particular, African American civil rights groups made the strategic move to hold the FCC accountable for racial discrimination. Steven Classen (2004) details the efforts of activists who sought to revoke the station licenses of television and radio stations in Jackson, Mississippi, for discriminatory practices evidenced in the failure to hire African Americans. They argued that station owners had intentionally cut the signal when African Americans were being featured, interrupting the programming by feigning technical problems, and that they had failed to adequately present African American perspectives on the topic of integration. Members of the NAACP began petitioning the FCC to deny license renewals on the grounds that the stations were not abiding by the Fairness Doctrine. The FCC first responded in 1962 by issuing a public statement reminding stations to include black perspectives on the issue of integration, and to give opposing voices the opportunity to speak out on controversial issues. But in 1966, the courts ruled that the listening public had been aggrieved, and for the first time citizens now had standing to legally challenge the renewal of licenses.

Classen argues that the case was groundbreaking because the FCC was forced to address questions such as, "who were the consumers of television, and what rights, if any, did these consumers have? . . . who should have direct access to, and thus power within, the station licensing process?" (Classen 2004, 63). Consumer-citizens now represented an important constituency which regulatory agencies were forced to recognize and respond to. In a 1968 ruling, WLBT was granted a probational short-term license, admitting that it took the issue of race relations into consideration and that the station needed to resolve the questions raised. As a result of this ruling, the tactic of filing complaints with the FCC to revoke licenses became what Montgomery calls "a powerful weapon of intimidation. The rare instances in which the FCC granted short-term licenses as the result of a pressure campaign were chilling reminders to the industry that no station was really safe, now that political advocacy groups had legal power" (Montgomery 1989, 25).

Despite the important role that the FCC and other governmental bodies have historically played in elevating the voice and power of everyday consumers, a number of legislative changes have drastically reduced these abilities. First, although the Fairness Doctrine was resolutely upheld in a 1969 Supreme Court decision, its power has gradually been eroding ever since. The legislation had always been based on the complicated and even contradictory notion that citizens should be free to voice their opinions freely and without government oversight, while also allowing—and possibly demanding, under threatened penalty to do otherwise—that multiple viewpoints and perspectives be represented. Moreover, the means and methods for upholding this delicate balance have always been deliberately vague, and it was unclear whether or not the Fairness Doctrine actually encouraged the proliferation of opinions or had the opposite impact, a "chilling effect," on controversial speech (Hazlett and Sosa 1997). Under the Reagan administration in 1987, the FCC decided to stop enforcing the Fairness Doctrine, arguing in its 1985 "Fairness Report" that as there were now sufficiently diverse outlets for opinions government oversight was no longer needed. Although the actual wording was not removed until 2011, this decision in the 1980s to do away with the Fairness Doctrine was representative of larger shifts toward government deregulation on a national level that had begun a decade earlier.

Throughout the history of broadcast media, regulatory agencies have ostensibly served the role of providing technical oversight in order to safeguard the public interest. Yet it has also always been the case that broadcast media constitutes a for-profit industry that cannot be removed from corporate interests, and moreover it is unclear exactly what is encompassed by the term "public interest." For instance, the FCC sought to promote a diversity of ownership in an attempt to promote a diversity of programming that was thought to be good for the public. Yet, as Horwitz argues, "the same economic opportunities and pitfalls confront any owner, and induce that owner to air programs which will attract the largest possible audience. Programming, therefore, tends to be imitative and seeks to be inoffensive" (Horwitz 1989, 174). Despite this general desire to see a diversity of content, in the early 1980s the FCC removed nearly all its content regulations. Guidelines requiring nonentertainment programming, coverage of community issues, news and public affairs programs, informative children's programming, and even political debates were all rescinded. Rather than regulating television in the name of the public interest, the FCC "sought to let the market prevail" (246). Under the logic that television was nothing but a business, "anti-siphoning" regulations that had sought to give the public access to important televised programming were lifted as well, and the cable industry began to proliferate.

As Horwitz points out, the regulatory reform movement that led to this drastic reduction of government oversight on mass communication included a remarkably diverse set of parties. On the one side, free market conservatives sought to liberate their economic enterprise from governmental oversight and take on a more laissez-faire approach to regulation. But left-leaning political interest groups also had a stake in deregulation, seeking to end corporate power and bring back participatory democracy (265). For those seeking to fight for the public interest, regulation appeared to protect those who benefited financially from media industries, dampening the possibility for actual competition and diversity. Thus the fight for deregulation offered yet another opportunity for a natural alliance between groups that usually seek to oppose each other—free market economists and public interest groups. Unfortunately for the public interest groups, deregulation of the telecommunications industry increased the ability of media corporations to consolidate their power and uphold the status quo. Although the proliferation of cable networks offered new opportunities for diverse programming, the prevailing free market logic most often meant that there was little incentive to chase down minority market shares, and even less opportunity for minority ownership.

Forming the Asian Pacific American Media Coalition

Another way public interest groups such as Asian Americans have tried to systematically impact the media industries has been through the court system. In the case of poor or harmful representation, it would seem that defamed groups should be able to sue media producers when their portrayals are derogatory. Yet as Heinke and Tremain (2000) point out, the courts generally refuse to allow groups to sue for defamation when their number is larger than twenty-five. As a result, interest groups and minority spokespeople have been unsuccessful in their attempts to influence content through lawsuits or other legal proceedings. Since this makes it necessary to find a sole party impacted by discrimination, Asian American actors and actresses should be able to prove that they are the victims of employment discrimination when they are denied roles based on their race. Unfortunately, the fear of being blacklisted for taking such an action and ending one's acting career is generally too large a risk for an actor to take. This issue is also complicated by the legal language in Title VII of the Civil Rights Act of 1964, which states that it is illegal "to fail or refuse to hire an individual . . . because of an individual's race, color, religion, sex, or national origin." This means that it is just as illegal to fail to hire a white person as a black person in any position or role, and that race is simply not a pertinent factor in one's ability to do a job. But in the case of the entertainment industry, an additional memorandum states that "a director of a play or movie who wished to cast an actor in the role of a Negro, could specify that he wished to hire someone with the physical appearance of a Negro" (Onwuachi-Willig 2007). This language evades racial discrimination by noting that casting might call for a specific "physical appearance," while simultaneously invoking First Amendment rules protecting creative freedom (Robinson 2007). In effect, media producers are free to cast as many white people and deny as many people of color as they want. This reality is compounded by a liberal integrationist move toward "colorblind casting"—a practice that in reality often leads to the erasure of roles for people of color rather than serving to counter discriminatory casting, as an insistence upon the insignificance of race only serves to reify the normative value of whiteness (Pao 2010).

If lawsuits and public policy have waned in their ability to impact the representation of Asian Americans, the other possibilities for the policing and regulating of media industries exist within the private sector, or within media corporations themselves. One organization that has been at the forefront of efforts to address both these aspects of representation is the Asian American Justice Center (AAJC), which was headed by Executive Director Karen Narasaki from 1992 to 2012. With a mission to advance the human and civil rights of Asian Americans and build and promote a fair and equitable society for all, the AAJC maintains that "Media Diversity" is one of its core issues. As Narasaki stated,

> The popular media affects how other Americans see or don't see Asian Americans. They have the opportunity to either enforce or negate stereotypes. Since we work on hate crimes and discrimination, we see this kind of work as preventative because it leads to a less ignorant population. (Narasaki 2011)

This statement clearly marks the work of the AAJC as activist, since it shows the clear definition of a social problem and the connection between this problem and the work undertaken to alleviate it. Due to the AAJC's work in this kind of media activism, Narasaki was appointed to a number of advisory and oversight boards, including the Federal Advisory Committee on Diversity for Communications in the Digital Age. This committee is charged with making recommendations to the FCC regarding policies and practices that will further enhance the ability of minorities and women to participate in telecommunications and related industries. But Narasaki was also instrumental in working on issues of representation in entertainment media as chair of the Asian Pacific American Media Coalition (APAMC). By examining the work of the APAMC, we can better understand some of the potential for impacting change through policy, as well as some of the challenges that arise in attempting to do so.

One of the first ways in which Asian American media activists laid the foundation for becoming more institutionalized was through the formation of the Asian Pacific American Media Coalition in 1999—a coalition that is largely focused on policy-oriented issues. Although a number of black, Latino, and Asian American organizations had separately been working on issues of representation for years, they came together as a national coalition as a result of events that transpired in 1999. That spring, the NAACP made headlines when it called attention to the fact that no regular roles had been given to people of color in the entire new lineup of fall shows on the four top TV networks (ABC, NBC, CBS, and FOX). NAACP president Kweisi Mfume teamed up with a coalition of black, Latino, Native American, and Asian American activists and threatened a "brown out," or consumer boycott, as well as a lawsuit if the situation was not addressed. The Multi-Ethnic Media Coalition was formed to serve as an umbrella organization for the NAACP,[2] the National Latino Media Council, American Indians in Film and Television, and representatives of a number of Asian American media groups that came together as the APAMC.[3] The goal of the coalition was to enter into written agreements with the networks, getting their assent to a variety of demands. The coalition also appointed former members of congress for each group—including Kweisi Mfume for African Americans, Norman Mineta for Asian Americans, and Esteban Torres for the Hispanics/Latinos (there was no Native American representative)—in the hope that the congresspeople would lend weight and send the message that their demands were serious.

Their invisibility in the entertainment arena tied the different groups together, creating a collective voice that was powerful and could not be ignored. They were able to explain their frustrations together, raising the volume on their concerns and fears. Alex Nogales, president of the National Hispanic Media Coalition and Secretariat for the National Latino Media Council emphasized the importance of seeing minority populations represented accurately in entertainment programming:

> When you don't see them, then the perception is that they don't exist, or that they're not part of the workforce. That's crazy. I know that [TV and film are] make-believe, but when that perception moves public policy, when that perception makes people love you or hate you, when that perception is an obstacle to your child's well-being in terms of self-esteem and success, it matters. It's important. (Nogales 2011)

After intense negotiation, the coalition was able to successfully create memoranda of understanding (MOUs) with each of the networks. In the MOUs, the networks agreed to increase minority representation through greater recruitment, contribution to pipelines of minority talent, and the establishment of a senior vice president of diversity who would be in charge of instituting these changes. They could not include specific numbers or quotas to be reached due to employment discrimination laws, but as Narasaki reasons, "In most cases you're starting from zero, so to say increase was not that much of a stretch." These signed documents mark an important step toward holding the networks accountable for responding to the demands of the activists—they were forced to improve the diversity of their workforce and create representations that more accurately reflected a multicultural reality.

The networks also agreed to provide regular statistics on how many minorities were hired behind and in front of the screen,[4] and to meet face to face with the activist organizations every year. These meetings are of critical importance, as Guy Aoki argues:

> In the past if MANAA or any other organization was upset there would be a big stink in the media for a few days and then we'd go away. Now we have ongoing meetings and statistics and they have to answer to us about why they went down or why it got better. They have to report back to us and be responsible to us. (Aoki 2009)

The meetings include everyone from the president of the network and the vice presidents to the casting directors and heads of every division. When the networks hired their senior vice presidents of diversity, these individuals served as organizers for the meeting and also collected and distributed the annual statistics. The Multi-Ethnic Media Coalition also began awarding yearly "Report Cards" to each network based on these statistics, with separate grades in categories such as Actors in Primetime Scripted Shows, Actors in Reality Programming, Writers and Producers, Directors, Program Development, Procurement, Entertainment Executives, and Network Commitment to Diversity Initiatives.

In 2000, the first year when report cards were awarded, the results were disastrous—all the networks earned either a D or an F overall. As the coalition reported, "the four major networks by and large have not significantly followed through yet on agreements signed with the coalition last year to increase the number of minorities in both the business and creative divisions" (Braxton 2000). The next year things were not much better, as the highest grade—awarded to NBC—was a C (Braxton 2001). Despite criticisms from the networks that the coalition refused to acknowledge their progress, the coalition continued year after year to use the report cards to criticize the networks and their failure to comply with their promises.

In 2003, the organizations finally began to note an improvement in the visibility of blacks and Latinos, but the numbers of Asian Americans and Native Americans began to slip. In later years, the networks settled around a C average in reports from the Asian American community, with not a single network ever earning greater than a B- overall.

TABLE 2.1. 2010 Asian Pacific American Report Card on TV Diversity

	ABC	CBS	FOX	NBC
Actors: On-air Prime-time Scripted Shows	C	C+	B-	B-
Actors: On-air Prime-time Reality Programming	B	C-	C+	B-
Writers and Producers: Prime-time	B-	C-	B-	C-
Directors: Prime-time	C-	C+C	D-	C
Program Development	B-	C-	C+	B-
Procurement	B	A	C+	A
Entertainment Executives	B-	B	B+	B
Network Commitment to Diversity Initiatives	B+	A-	B-	A-
Overall	B-	B-	C+	B-

The 2010 Asian Pacific American Report Card on TV Diversity shows great improvement from years past, but clearly demonstrates the lack of opportunities for Asian Americans in all aspects of network television. Source: Angry Asian Man Blog

Although the report cards eventually disappeared from the public record as activist organizations began to utilize the data and the network meetings to strategize around different goals, Narasaki argues that the awarding of report cards was effective because of the media coverage it produced. The yearly awarding of report cards at a joint press conference gave the news media a hook for reporting on the TV season, as well as concrete measurements for gauging progress in categories beyond acting. Although the news media eventually lost interest in covering the announcement of the report cards given that the story was largely the same each year, Narasaki still felt they were important.

I could tell they cared because I would get calls where they would be yelling at me about how we came up with their grades, or they would lobby

Alex Nogales from the National Hispanic Media Coalition, Sonny Skyhawk from the American Indian Coalition, and Guy Aoki and Marilyn Tokuda from the Asian Pacific American Media Coalition met in 2011 to discuss the network report cards.

me in advance about why their grades should be higher. They cared because it was an external measurement of their program, and largely based on the data that the networks themselves were generating. (Narasaki 2011)

Moreover, the report cards offered an opportunity for the different minority groups to structure new and detailed arguments each year, rather than simply hammering out the same generic complaints and pleas year after year.

Although these initial agreements were the result of a coalition built across race and ethnicity, the different minority groups have not always worked together to advocate for improvements in representation. Rather, each individual group was promised time for their own individual meetings so they could convey their own messages every year.[5] This is an important point, given that each group faces a distinct and unique representational challenge. For instance, Latinos have succeeded in creating shows like *The George Lopez Show* that feature their own community, but they are rarely integrated into the fictional worlds of shows outside these specifically Latino-themed ones. African Americans have also made great strides in the number of actors being hired, but they are often confined to channels like FOX and the WB/UPN. In contrast, Asian Americans have succeeded in being given roles as side characters like Sandra Oh in *Grey's Anatomy*, Archie Punjabi in *The Good Wife*, or Aziz Ansari on *Parks and Recreation*, but they are rarely given the chance to star in their own show or have an entire show built around an Asian American cast. When *Fresh Off the Boat* and *Dr. Ken* premiered in 2015, they served as a reminder that there had been no shows focused on an Asian American family for the past twenty years, and there has still yet to be an hour-long drama featuring an Asian American cast. The methods for bringing about change also needed to be different, reflecting the different histories and cultural realities of each community. During the meetings, each activist group has the opportunity to explain the specific cultural nuances of its own community so that the networks can begin to consider how minority characters and storylines can be worked into new projects, as well as to convey criticisms or suggestions for currently existing programs.

To some extent, the impact of these meetings can be seen in the numbers. As the AAJC states on its website, there has been "more than a 20 percent increase for both regular and recurring roles for Asian Pacific Americans on prime-time television shows" (Asian American Justice Center n.d.) since the meetings and report cards began. But participants in the meetings also report that the networks' attitudes have undergone a major shift in the past decade. As Guy Aoki describes it, "Even after they signed the MOUs, I think each network had a difficult time. When they looked at how they would have to change the way they did business to meet these goals, they were surprised" (Aoki 2009). Others similarly report that communication was incredibly difficult in the early years because each one's guard was up and no one was really listening to anyone else. In some cases, coalition members ended up in angry shouting matches with network executives. But as the years progressed, the conversations took on a more collaborative and solution-oriented tone. "Sometimes people who work on diversity issues for the networks are just liaisons. They're there to say no," said Marilyn Tokuda, who joined the APAMC in 2002 when she took on the job of Artistic Director of East West Players and later served as a cochair of the coalition. "But we have seen them really evolve. Now they are really thinking about diversity and trying to change the culture of the companies" (Tokuda 2011). Members of the APAMC also noted that many of the Asian American activists who were invited to meet with the network executives struggled to overcome their cultural upbringing that emphasized being deferential, avoiding being a troublemaker, or rocking the boat. Indeed, it can be incredibly intimidating to meet with the president and vice presidents of the largest television companies in the nation. But members of the coalition have found their own way to participate because they believe in the cause. As Tokuda states, "The meetings are really important because we go in there and are evaluating and criticizing and having face to face meetings with decision makers, and putting pressure on them" (Tokuda 2011).

Despite the long-term progress the television companies have made, further conversations are always needed. The report cards generally showed little change year after year—and sometimes backsliding—despite the improvement in the relationship between the activists and the networks. In some cases the networks even inflated their numbers to some degree. For instance, a show with a single episode that took place in Chinatown might employ a number of Asian American actors as guest stars, resulting in what appeared to be a spike in hiring. But those guest roles were sure to evaporate, and they were usually brief. Similarly, many Asian Americans would be listed as regulars, but they were given significantly less screen time and fewer lines than their non-Asian counterparts. In a study commissioned by the AAJC in 2004, researchers at UCLA found that Asian American regulars had consistently smaller roles than their fellow actors (National Asian Pacific American Legal Consortium 2005). Narasaki explains, "This meant the Asian American characters didn't have much impact. They weren't well-rounded characters. They couldn't have families or back stories or romances—they were a sidekick" (Narasaki 2011).

During their meetings with the networks, members of the APAMC have the opportunity to probe the statistics and to have a conversation about the quality of the roles given to Asian Americans. They can praise characters that they feel are exemplary and criticize the roles they think were handled poorly or the shows in need of revision. Such conversations have to be handled carefully, as the activists realize that television consists of creative content. As outsiders to the industry, telling the networks exactly what decisions should be made might seem to infringe on their creative control as artists and producers, and might negatively impact their ability to have such conversations at all. For instance, the coalition often examines the new lineup of shows with regard to location, since cities like San Francisco, Los Angeles, or Honolulu have an unusually high percentage of Asian Americans. Similarly, shows that take place in hospitals are often desperately in need of more Asian roles, given the high percentage of real medical professionals who are Asian. But rather than demanding that such shows reach a specific quota of Asian American actors, activists appeal to the artistic work of creators by arguing that the show will seem more realistic if it incorporates more Asian American actors to reflect the diverse racial makeup of those cities and workplaces. There are also economic arguments that can be made, given that shows are more popular with minority and mainstream audiences when they have diverse casts.

Beyond these conversations and opportunities for feedback, another result of working with the networks has been the successful implementation of a number of diversity initiatives, such as minority writing programs. These include the ABC Scholarship Grant Program, the ABC Daytime Writing Program, the CBS Diversity Institute/Writers Mentoring Program, the FOX Writer's Initiative, and the NBC Diversity Initiative for Writers. As Narasaki argues, television is a writer-centric business—unlike film, which is more focused on directors. For a series to be successful, the writer must be able to craft the entire narrative. As Narasaki says, "Writers write from their own experiences. So if there's no Asian writers, there's no Asian stories. We won't get a scripted Asian American show until the writers we put into the pipeline become more senior" (Narasaki 2011). Fortunately, the writers' programs have been in existence for many years and the number of writers has continued to improve steadily. In fact, there have been more improvements in the number of Asian American writers than actors. But members of the APAMC worry that simply employing Asian American actors does not necessarily mean that stories about their community will be told. For one thing, not all Asian American writers strongly identify with the Asian American community, particularly if they grew up in mostly white areas. As with any minority group, it is dangerous to assume that bodies can be collapsed with identities, since hiring minority writers offers no guarantees of shifts in content or storylines. But an additional concern is that even if writers from diverse backgrounds want to write about their backgrounds, they will be afraid to do so for fear of being pigeonholed as an "Asian American writer." To combat this, members of the APAMC request that the networks specifically encourage writers to write on the basis of their own experience, and make it clear that they are hoping to see diverse stories rather than the same mainstream stories over and over.

The Plight of the Asian American Show

The fear that Asian American storylines are risky or offer particular challenges is not completely unfounded, given the poor track record of Asian American programming. Although the first season of *Fresh Off the Boat* was celebrated by critics and fans, its predecessors did not fare so well. The ABC sitcom *All-American Girl*, starring Margaret Cho, premiered in 1994 and focused on the humorous intergenerational conflicts and culture clashes within a Korean American family. Cho played a thoroughly assimilated valley-girl punk rocker, while veteran actors Jodi Long and Amy Hill played her strict Korean mother and wacky grandmother. Despite its avowed intention to create representations that were authentic, relatable, and positive, the show quickly came under fire for its portrayals of Asian Americans. As one article reported, "several [critics] complained that Grandma's speaking about how things are done in 'the old country' and Mom's pushing Cho to date only Koreans were stereotypical and unflattering portrayals of Asian-Americans" (McMahon 1994). The Asian American community also had an extremely polarized reaction. Many Asian viewers immediately expressed their anger over details of the show ranging from the accents of the non-Korean actors, to cultural inaccuracies in the food and home décor, to the fact that familial relations were being mocked (Kang 1995) and declared that they would rather remain invisible than suffer such insulting portrayals. In contrast to this criticism, MANAA awarded *All-American Girl* numerous honors at its 1994 Media Achievement Awards for the show's groundbreaking work and frequently praised it in conversations with ABC.

When the show failed to capture a sizable audience, the network responded by making major changes. It cut all but two of the Asian American actors and tried to refocus the story on Cho's non-Asian roommates. In 1995, the show was canceled altogether. Later Cho revealed her struggles for creative control, including the fact that she was told to lose weight and to act "more Asian," despite the fact that the entire show was created around her star persona (Cho 2001). Media activists worried that the sour taste left from the failure of *All-American Girl* would discourage the networks from experimenting with Asian American storylines and characters any further, and given the twenty-year absence of Asian American families on television, this did seem to be the case.

In 2010, NBC premiered a new show called *Outsourced* that signaled a different sort of intervention into the world of Asian American representations. Instead of focusing on Asian immigrants or second-generation Asians in the United States, *Outsourced* traveled all the way to South Asia to tell the story of a white American who must move to India to run a call center for an American novelties company. While struggling to learn about Indian culture, he befriends a kooky but lovable cast of Indian coworkers and hijinks ensue. The show offered a somewhat conservative foray into the world of "the Other," allowing mainstream viewers a safe and familiar set of eyes through which to view the hilarity of the Indian workplace. On the one hand, the show followed in the footsteps of *All-American Girl* by focusing on a largely non-white cast and employing many Asian American actors and writers. Yet the show could not be considered "Asian American" in any way, given its international setting and white protagonist, and it relied heavily on juvenile pranks such as potty humor and physical pratfalls rather than sophisticated storytelling.

Before the show premiered, NBC invited Los Angeles-based Asian American and South Asian media activists (some of whom were part of the APAMC) to screen the pilot and provide feedback. For the most part, the activists invited to the screening agreed that the Indian workers were warm and funny, and that the show brought a desperately needed familiarity to the accented voices most Americans only encountered through call centers. But the show was far from perfect—audiences were clearly meant to identify with a white male protagonist rather than the somewhat silly Indian side characters; jokes were made at the expense of Indian customs, religions, foods, and names; and the modern metropolis of Mumbai was portrayed as an exotically backward village. Behind

The short-lived NBC sitcom *Outsourced* focused on the experiences of a white American man who moves to India to manage an outsourced call center.

the scenes, the activists struggled to decide what they should report to NBC, since a laundry list of complaints might make it look like they didn't support the show or want to see it succeed. The network had finally given them what they wanted—a show starring people of color—and they didn't want to seem ungrateful or risk their relationship to the network. In the end, they emphasized a need to be careful not to make the white protagonist the only star and perhaps to include an Indian American storyline as well in the interest of promoting dialogue about the differences between Indians and Indian Americans.

When the show premiered to the public, Asian American bloggers and online reporters were not so strategic with their criticisms. The show was accused of promoting xenophobia and racism, and one reporter wrote that the show "managed to singlehandedly piss off every Indian who made the mistake of thinking that in the 21st century, television may slowly be phasing out the stereotypes" (Sinha-Roy 2010). The show's ratings slowly began to plummet, and after it was placed in the unpopular timeslot of Thursdays at 10:30 p.m., its prognosis was negative. Although the waning viewership coupled with charges of racism might give the impression that the show had been wholly abandoned by Asian American audiences, a group of largely South Asian fans rallied at the last minute to demonstrate their support alongside the show's cast and crew. Moreover, the suggestion by activists to include an Indian American character seemed to be honored with the episode "Take This Punjab and Shove It," whose plot included competition over a talented Indian American hire. But all to no avail—after only one season the show was canceled.

The Ratings Game and Asians on Cable TV

Although the activists discussed thus far have long fought for the creation of an Asian American show, it is clear from the outcome of their efforts that the pressure to create a single show that can appease the capricious interests of critics, mainstream audiences, Asian American audiences, and activists is an impossible task—each of these different audiences has a different set of needs, a different set of complaints, and different understandings of what it would take to appease them. Rather than try to create the perfect show, another way of opening up an institutionalized space for the creation of Asian American images is an Asian American cable channel devoted to a range of original content. There is no shortage of talented Asian American filmmakers who traverse the Asian American film festival with their feature films, documentaries, shorts, and serial programs, but without a venue such as a cable channel it is virtually impossible for these media producers to distribute and screen their work. Although there are far fewer cable channels devoted to Asian and Asian American audiences than there are for African Americans and Latinos, there have been a number of notable attempts to address the Asian market over the years. Among the first were ImaginAsian TV which went on the air in 2004, and AZN TV which did so in 2005. The channels were similar in their programming, featuring content largely imported from Asia and shown with English subtitles. As journalist Jeff Yang describes AZN, the content included "Variety shows and news from Hong Kong. Japanese animation. Soap operas from Korea. Bollywood movies. Valuable content, but nothing groundbreaking—and nothing targeted specifically at Asian Americans" (Yang 2005). Producers at AZN did attempt to create some new

Asian American programming produced in the United States which featured domestic talent, such as the documentary *Ivy Dreams* that followed four Asian American high schoolers through the stresses of their college application process. AZN also created a show called *Cinema AZN* that went behind the scenes of Asian American film productions and interviewed stars and creators, and a magazine-style show called *NBA Timeout* featuring Asian American basketball fans at a time when Yao Ming was the only Asian player in the NBA. The channel was also home to the Asian Excellence Awards held from 2006 to 2008. Still, the dominant programming on both AZN and ImaginAsian TV brought international content to American audiences, leaving it unclear as to whether the show was for immigrant families or second-generation Asian Americans.

L. S. Kim argues that the existence of these networks and the concept of Asian American television brought a number of questions to the fore, including what "Asian America" might look like—why is there not an African America, or a Native America, she asks—and who might belong to it? As Kim states,

> part of the discourse reminds Asian Americans of their (or their parents' or grandparents') foreign status as some are more "acculturated" than others, and moreover, as they stand apart from the "non-Asian" viewer, i.e., American and white. Is this a schizophrenia linked to the larger social and discursive struggle to define Asian American—as 'American' *or* 'Asian'? (Kim 2005)

Perhaps because of this schizophrenia and inability to define their audience, almost immediately after they began both networks started to struggle financially. AZN was located on Comcast, which gave it wide distribution. But after only eight months, employees were drastically reduced and the programming was slashed to only the most limited offerings (Caramanica 2006). In April 2008 the channel was canceled. Some accounts claim the channel "suffered from low advertiser interest and limited distribution; with other cable companies declining to carry the network, AZN only manages around 13 million subscribers, a marginal sum against the 100 million average for Comcast's networks" (Wang 2008). But others feel that the channel failed because

Comcast did not take it seriously and did not give it enough staffing or advertising support. With little to no advertising for the channel or its programs, Asian American audiences could not have known that it existed.

But there is another major challenge facing owners of minority cable channels—the lack of accurate data on audiences of color. The size and composition of the television audience has always been of central importance to the television industry, as ratings play an important role in determining which shows are aired or canceled, what storylines or content should continue, and where advertisers will buy their spots. All this is based on the fact that the television industry is supported by the purchasing of ads, and the price of advertising is determined by the number of eyeballs the advertisements reach. As Ang states, "the ratings firms occupy a key position in this corporate transaction because it is their product, the ratings information, that forms the agreed-upon standard by which advertisers and networks buy and sell the audience commodity" (Ang 1991, 54). Given that consumer research would be suspect if it originated from either television producers or advertising companies, ratings have historically been measured by an uninterested outside party. In the United States, the A. C. Nielsen Company has long held an unregulated monopoly on television ratings. Founded in 1923, Arthur C. Nielsen's company began conducting consumer research for companies like General Electric and Bausch & Lom. In 1942, Nielsen turned to media audience measurement with the invention of the Audimeter, which collected information about how a radio was being tuned and allowed for the start of the Nielsen Radio Index. In 1950, Recordimeters began collecting data on television viewership, and Nielsen also began measuring and interpreting the viewing habits of 1,200 radio and television consumers (Wood 1962). Although the Nielsen Company continues to engage in a wealth of consumer research, its name has become synonymous with television ratings and audience measurement.

Despite the importance of determining who constitutes an audience, the Nielsen Company has only recently begun to measure the race and ethnicity of television viewers. As Narasaki explains, when the different coalitions threatened a "brown out" in 1999, the lack of viewership data would have actually made the impact impossible to track: "At the time Nielsen was not adequately sampling minority communities to do the ratings. That meant you could stop all minorities from watching, but it wouldn't have necessarily affected the ratings. They just weren't asking a sufficient number of minorities what they were watching" (Narasaki 2011). Although Nielsen has slowly been improving upon this issue, problems arose in 2005 when Nielsen announced that it would be switching to a new television ratings system. It had previously measured viewing habits by mailing diaries to families in select cities and asking them to self-record what shows they watched. This method was slow and potentially inaccurate since it relied on memory and selective reporting. To combat these problems, it began moving to a system called "local people meters" that would be installed directly into the television sets of Nielsen families in their largest markets. But in their preliminary tests, viewership for Fox-run UPN affiliates in New York that carried many shows geared toward black and Hispanic audiences saw the number of viewers drop significantly. An advocacy group called Don't Count Us Out formed to protest these results, arguing that minority audiences were being undercounted by as much as 25 percent (Maynard 2005) due to problems with the people meters. Although Nielsen contended that the error rating was true of all metered sampling and was better than the previous methods, the discrepancy between minority households and the general market could not be ignored. Nielsen instituted a Task Force on Television Measurement and appointed a diverse contingency of community, business, and media leaders to investigate the issue of minority audience measurement and make recommendations for improvement.

There were a number of positive outcomes from the task force's work on this issue—most importantly, that Nielsen was urged to finally address the issue of minority viewership and the challenge of collecting accurate data from diverse communities. The task force recommended solutions such as providing training in languages other than English, recruiting field operations staff and representatives who were ethnically and linguistically diverse, educating the staff about local cultures, installing phone lines in sample households that did not have them, and oversampling minority populations to ensure adequate numbers of participants. When Nielsen decided to create a set of more permanent advisory councils, the first to be instituted was the Asian Pacific American Advisory Council. The eleven-person council consisting of business and civic leaders helped to tailor Nielsen's research and outreach efforts to more effectively measure Asian American viewers. The creation of this advisory council was significant given that Nielsen had not previously attempted to measure Asian viewers in any meaningful or reliable way.

Although there are still many shortcomings to the way that Asian viewers are recorded, Nielsen's forays into the Asian market steadily improved due to the oversight of the advisory council, which led to new data and insights. For instance, the ratings for the top television shows in Asian American households clearly show that Asian Americans do not have exactly the same viewing patterns as the general market, as had previously been assumed. The top ten shows might be similar but the order is often different, and as Narasaki has found, this often reflects an increased interest in programs that have Asian American participants or actors. For instance, a study of television viewership in 2008 revealed that the top three broadcast shows for Asian Americans were *Heroes* (which starred Masi Oka, James Kyson, and Sendhil Ramamurthy), *NFL Sunday Football*, and *Grey's Anatomy* (which starred Sandra Oh), while *Heroes* did not make the top ten list for any other racial group (Nielsen Company 2009). This shows that the institution of advisory councils and the subsequent improvement in the measurement of Asian American viewers can offer substantial improvements in the ability for Asian Americans to stand up for their community and the way it is represented.

The Comcast/NBC Universal Merger

Despite the fact there are now more measures for assessing minority audiences and that Asian Americans have more voice in advising and regulating media industries, there remains another problem for media activists who are concerned with diversity—the shrinking and consolidating of media ownership. When the mass media is controlled by a smaller and smaller number of firms due to deregulation, the marketplace for ideas shrinks, as "those firms are capable of affecting public opinion, the national agenda, democracy itself, and global culture" (Noam 2009, 9). In particular, under FCC chairman Michael Powell, the Telecommunications Act of 1996 opened the door to further media consolidation. Although the Act had many components, one of the most significant elements was that it lifted the limit on the number of properties one television or radio company could own. For television, the total percentage of national audience reached has slowly been increasing from its original cap at 35 percent. This greatly increased the potential market power of media companies like AOL Time Warner, AT&T, or News Corp (Chambers and Howard 2006). Although the 1996 Act specifically contains language promising to increase female and minority ownership of broadcast licenses and facilities, there has been little actual progress toward this goal. In 2006, ten years after the implementation of the Act, women owned a scant 4.97 percent and racial minorities owned 3.26 percent of all commercial broadcast television stations (Turner 2006)—a clear failure of the Act's ability to increase diverse ownership.

The debate over media consolidation intersected with the interests of Asian American media activists in 2010, when Comcast, General Electric Company, and NBC Universal sought to merge in a joint venture. The merger proposed to combine NBC's news and entertainment programming that included channels like USA, Bravo, SyFy, CNBC, and MSNC; Universal Studios' film interests, theme parks, and cable channels; and Comcast's internet and cable services, which included channels such as E! Entertainment Television, Style Network, and the Golf Channel. In order to do so, they had to first receive FCC approval that the merger benefited the public.

Opposition to the merger was extremely vocal, with minority groups such as the National Coalition of African American Owned Media and the National Hispanic Journalists Association filing petitions to deny it. They argued that both firms had failed to do business with minority-owned media or place minorities in executive positions, and called for the FCC to deny the merger. The Greenlining Institute, an advocacy organization for the protection of consumer interests, also testified against it, arguing that doing so would diminish opportunities for diverse voices, undermine democracy, and cut jobs. In his testimony, Sam Kang stated, "Comcast and NBC both say they are serious about diversity, but the truth is, both struggle when it comes to the number of minorities within their workforce and management who actually have the ability to hire or influence content" (Kang 2010).

Given that the APAMC had been meeting with NBC for years and knew its track record on minority hiring and minority influence on content, it seems it would see an ally in Kang and the Greenlining Institute. But instead of openly criticizing the company for its poor track record and joining with the chorus of opposition to the merger, members of the APAMC saw an opportunity to use policy to leverage an updated agreement with the company just as it was growing even larger and more influential. Knowing that Comcast and NBCU would be eager to avoid having a coalition of minority representatives blocking the merger, the APAMC began drafting memoranda of understanding for their communities in exchange for their support. This move marks yet another dangerous alliance between progressive interest groups seeking to diversify representation and the free market conservatives whose policies often end up homogenizing the media and shutting minority voices out. In this sense, the APAMC's support for the merger mirrors the support of procensorship legislation by progressive activists in the early days of cinema, as well as efforts to deregulate media industries in the 1970s. In each of these cases, the strategic use of public policy led to important gains for minority communities and grassroots community activists. But it is important to consider the costs of allying with a coalition that in other respects exists in opposition to the goals of a progressive, activist organization seeking to bring about an increase in opportunity and a decrease in discrimination for its disenfranchised community.

Regardless of the potential negative consequences, Asian American activists, supported by Congressional Asian Pacific American Caucus chairman Mike Honda and Rep. Judy Chu, chairwoman of the caucus's economic development taskforce, filed a statement in support of the merger. In a press release following the merger, the Asian American Justice Center stated, "AAJC had asked the FCC to approve the acquisition after reaching an agreement, on behalf of four other Asian American organizations, with the two companies about increasing diversity and the presence of Asian Americans on the airwaves" (Asian American Justice Center 2011). In the MOU the AAJC explicitly outlined what part Asian Americans would play in the future of the corporation's work. Its requests were similar to those that had already been established with African American and Hispanic organizations. The sixteen-page document first established that the newly merged companies would honor their previous diversity commitments, which included the annual meetings with the APAMC and the disclosing of statistics about minority hiring and other diversity initiatives. The rest of the agreement focused on five areas: corporate governance; employment/workforce recruitment and retention; procurement; programming; and philanthropy and community investments. The MOU also supported a new video-on-demand channel called Cinema Asian America that was set to launch in December 2010. The channel featured Asian American film and video largely from the film festival circuit, providing a much-needed venue for Asian American content that had often struggled to find distribution. More importantly, the MOU stated that Comcast would commit to carrying a new Asian American channel. Knowing the mistakes that were made with AZN TV, the APAMC added a demand that the channel needed to be supported with advertising so that the community had a chance to know about it.

Asian American Media in the Digital Age

With this new MOU in place and increasing reliability in assessing Asian American audiences, the potential for a successful Asian American cable channel is now greater than ever. But beyond these improvements, there have also been noteworthy changes in the social landscape that could contribute to different outlets for representation. The population of Asians in the United States has only continued to grow in the last decade, and to spread from beyond the coasts to encompass a vast array of cities across the nation. Also significant is the fact that the stakes for starting up a new cable channel are now much lower due to changes in television technology. In the move from analog, to cable, to our current era of digital television, the spectrum for carrying cable channels has become exponentially greater. When AZN TV was started, cable channels had a much higher bar for achieving success. In the digital televisual world, the cost and risk associated with new cable channels are lower because there are fewer limitations with regard to how many channels can exist. Of course, the threat that any channel could fail if it has no viewership continues to exist. As Narasaki explains, "You can leverage policy into opening doors and leveling the playing field, but then we have to show that it was a profitable decision" (Narasaki 2011).

Already, Asian American channels like MYX-TV and MNet America have quietly ventured into what might be considered a transnational digital television space. Both channels are 24/7 English language networks available via satellite (and cable television in larger markets) that explicitly target Asian American audiences. While both their parent companies are in Asia—MYX TV is a subsidiary of ABS-CBN, an entertainment company in the Philippines, and MNet's parent company CJ Group is in Korea—the channels make a concerted effort to reflect Asian American pop culture and sensibilities. Their programs largely focus on the K-Pop music scene, but also include a variety of original programming that features young Asian and Asian American talent. For instance, in April 2014 MYX TV premiered a docu-series called *I'm Asian American and . . .* that explored a wide sampling of Asian American stories. Each of the ten episodes focused on a single Asian American and his or her unique passion in life, including a dating coach for virgins, a living doll, a triplet whose siblings have autism, and a lawyer who fights human trafficking. While this show centers on Asian Americans, MYX TV also has a show called *Supermodelme: Femme Fatale*, a modeling competition show in the vein of *America's Next Top Model*, which was shot in Singapore and features Asian models from all over the world. MYX TV is partnered with Soompi, a popular English-language internet community for Korean pop culture (Ocampo 2011). This partnership helps to sustain interest in the channel's programs and its pop idols, and gives fans a forum for meeting other viewers and discussing pop culture.

MNet America was launched in 2010 when CJ Group purchased the majority of the Asian American cable company ImaginAsian, which was based in New York. With CJ Group's focus on the Asian global market, MNet America was poised to reframe the role of the cable provider from a focus on Asian America domestic content to delivering Asian content to the North American market. Ted Kim, who served as CEO and president of MNet until 2014, saw these two goals as overlapping: "The idea is that we want to be a place where all things that are cool in terms of the Asian content world can exist here. We want to service our community—the people who consume our content and like our point of view" (Kim 2009). Although Kim greatly admired the work of Asian American filmmakers like Justin Lin, his vision was to expand

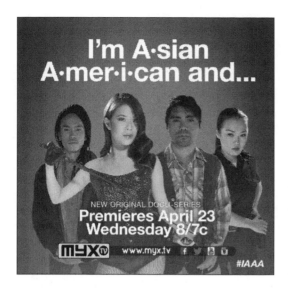

The MYX TV docu-series *I'm Asian American and . . .* presents a diverse and eclectic array of lifestyles, including a dating coach, a living doll, a performance artist, and a lawyer.

the purview of Asian America to include a more global perspective—to connect to fans of Korean dramas or Japanese anime from all over the world. With a focus on youth audiences aged 13–24, MNet's strategy also includes a focus on content distribution through digital and wireless platforms, including mobile phones, personal computers, and tablets.

Companies like MYX-TV and MNet are important given the increasing flexibility between Asian and Asian American culture, as well as Asian Americans' greater access to satellite channels from Asia in addition to American ethnic media. Immigrant and first-generation families in the United States now have access to more media options than ever before, and the expansion of the kinds of programming they consume in their homes and communities has an effect on the larger Asian American culture. Brian Hu's (2010) investigation of English-language online fan communities for Korean dramas traces a powerful affective connection within the Asian diaspora that offers a new space for articulating racialized identities. In particular, there is an active community of 1.5 and second-generation Asian American youth who maintain an interest in Asian pop culture, sometimes across ethnic or linguistic boundaries. Their participation in the diasporic media community helps them to retain a sense of cultural rootedness in an Asian heritage even as English remains their primary language and they are fully assimilated into American life. These flexible identities challenge the prevailing thinking in white U.S. society about the way Asian American audiences interact with both domestic and international media, and offer new possibilities for considering the way general audiences view and interact with Asian and Asian American media. The route toward capturing these audiences is by no means obvious; as Aswin Punathambekar (2009) describes it, all MTV's efforts to capture diasporic audiences with programming geared toward South Asian American youth (MTV-Desi), Korean (MTV-K), and Chinese American youth (MTV-Chi) were canceled when they failed to attract their target market. Punathambekar argues that the programming on MTV-Desi did not adequately intersect with the "decidedly transnational, hybrid, and increasingly digital youth culture" (Punathambekar 2009), but there are plenty of digital media companies poised to do just that.

Cultural Citizenship and the Nation

These kinds of relationships between Asian Americans and the Asian culture industries complicate our picture of cultural citizenship. In the vision of social justice drawn by the activists discussed throughout this chapter—Karen Narasaki and others at the AAJC, Hispanic and Latino media activists, members of the APAMC—the media industries are seen as an important site for increasing minority participation because who we see in the media impacts how we think about ourselves and our communities. If we see Asian American bodies and stories, then we can begin to include those bodies and stories within the imagined borders of our nation. Even as the centrality of primetime television wanes due to convergence culture and post-network media consumption patterns, we cannot ignore the systematic erasure of Asian Americans (and other people of color) on network television. This is why the activists described in this chapter have worked to use policies and other kinds of long-standing contracts or agreements as a means to claim cultural citizenship. For them, it is only through these more official and legitimized discourses that Asian Americans can gain recognition as full members of American society. In many ways, this strategy of media activism relies upon the nation as a site for citizenship—as with legal citizenship, it is recognition of one's legitimate position within the borders of the United States that marks one as a cultural citizen.

But recognition of the relationships that Asian Americans possess with countries outside the United States may pose a challenge to this struggle to fight for a specifically American kind of citizenship. It is certainly important to claim this understanding of cultural citizenship, particularly for those Asian Americans who were born in this country and do not have any kind of identification with other nations or cultures beyond the United States. Yet as mentioned in the previous chapter, if we examine the way Asian Americans are interacting with global flows of media, other visions for cultural citizenship begin to emerge. Through cultural production and consumption, many Asian Americans are constructing a kind of cultural citizenship that transgresses and disrupts national boundaries, offering a new ethics of intercultural interaction and understanding.

For instance, second- and third-generation Indian Americans have begun attracting attention as a lucrative market for Bollywood films, music, fashion, and dance cultures. As Jigna Desai argues, "the impact of the Bollywood film and music industry in the 1990s has created a new language of cultural identity and affiliation among second-generation youth in the United States" (Desai 2005, 56). As a result, Bollywood filmmakers now create storylines with this specific diasporic audience in mind, tracing cultural connections between Non-Resident Indians and Indians in India in the hope of reincorporating the larger community of diasporic Indians into the imagined community through cultural engagement. Similarly, a *New York Times* article in March 2012 called attention to the trend of a "Korean Wave," or *hallyu*, wherein South Korean cultural imports like soap operas and musical groups have found popularity and fame in the West due to online social media. With Korean music industries now focused on digital distribution and touring, K-pop bands and artists like Wonder Girls, Super Junior, Jay Park, and Skull have been able to develop fan bases in the United States, making movies on the TeenNick channel and appearing on David Letterman's "Late Show" (Sang-Hun 2012).

These examples of the flexibility of Asian American cultural citizenship help us to better understand the kinds of relationships Asian Americans might have to their country of origin or ancestry, and expand our notion of cultural citizenship beyond the borders of the United States. But within these examples there are more identities at play than simply those of Indian Americans and Korean Americans. Bollywood film is popular in far-flung locales such as the Middle East, Africa, and East Asia, and the term "Korean Wave" was originally applied to the spread of South Korean culture throughout East Asia, including Indonesia, Japan, Taiwan, Vietnam, Hong Kong, and China. If we can expand upon these two examples, the kind of cultural citizenship illustrated by the sharing, creating, and consuming of Asian and Asian American culture could more accurately be illustrative of an Asian American cosmopolitanism than of diasporic nostalgia or the precise matching of ethnicity or language to cultures of origin. Cosmopolitanism, when used in the realm of culture, encompasses the idea that one is a "citizen of the world," appreciating cultural forms such as music, food, and artwork outside their home culture. The idea of cosmopolitanism often stands as a challenge to national identities, as illustrated by these cases of Asian American cosmopolitanism. But cosmopolitanism is also a moral worldview—not merely describing the aesthetics of enjoying other cultures, but claiming that one ought to engage with others and learn about their cultures. In fact, the basis of cosmopolitanism is the idea that humans share certain characteristics that transcend cultural and societal difference, and therefore we must seek out these universal traits by engaging with different societies and peoples (Appiah 2006). Although we must be careful not to neglect relevant power differences, particularly at the nation-state level, that color our cultural differences and cannot always be transcended (Roberts 2011), theorizing the flow of media cultures between Asia and the United States within the ethics of cosmopolitanism can help us understand the importance of using cultural citizenship to transform national boundaries.

Conclusion

Although Asian American media activists have already taken a position on the NBC/Universal merger with Comcast that allies them with those who seek to consolidate media ownership and close down opportunities for minority ownership and participation, there are still numerous opportunities for policy intervention that can continue to strengthen the representation of Asian Americans. It is clear that their strategy of partnering with NBC/Universal rather than standing in opposition positioned the Asian American community to have a continued voice in the company's business, just as they positioned themselves as advisories to the Nielsen Company when it became clear that Asian Americans had been left out of the ratings game. In recognizing the existence of multiple Asian American cultural citizenships, as well as the idea of a global or cosmopolitan Asian America, we can again see opportunities for diasporic and transnational media endeavors that engage Asian American audiences and provide opportunities for Asian American artists, actors, producers, and media professionals. The increasingly productive relationship that Asian Americans have developed and maintained with powerful media industries could very well open the door to encouraging and supporting this kind of transnational media production.

Throughout this discussion of the way Asian American activists have intervened in the television industry there is always the looming presence of the "Asian American audience" or the "Asian American consumer." In each of these strategies for policy interventions into the way representations are shaped, shows are created, ratings are measured, and channels are expanded, there must always be fundamental considerations about the media corporation's ability to make a profit from the decisions that are made. The television networks, the Nielsen Company, and cable providers are unlikely to be persuaded to change their ways unless there is a financial incentive to do so. Yet we must not forget that television programming is not the product being sold. Rather, it is the selling of the audience to marketers that funds and sustains the industry of television. Thus, it is important to know who the Asian American audience is—how many consumers belong to this category, what their viewing habits look like, and how they spend their money. It is difficult to consider making an argument for the potential of Asian American television, whether for entire cable channels or single Asian American characters and storylines, without this data. But it is not only media creators who research this data. Other important bodies to consider are the multicultural and Asian American advertising agencies that create and rely upon the Asian American market in order to exist. In the next chapter I focus on the interaction between Asian American advertising agencies and media companies to see how the representations of Asian Americans must also be understood as intimately connected to marketing and advertising.

3

Social Change through the Asian American Market

In the previous chapters we have seen Asian American media activists relying on ethical motivations for impacting change. They argue that minority communities should be represented accurately and fairly, that discrimination should be decreased and diversity increased in the entertainment industries, and that their own community should be included within the larger national citizenry as visualized in the media. The work of convincing both media producers and audiences that these issues deserve their attention involves highlighting the starkness of injustice and inequity that surrounds them. But there are also ways in which this kind of work engages and relies upon the notion of consumer activism, wherein change comes about through consumer groups collectively impacting the sales and profits of powerful corporations. Given that media production is a business that relies on selling a product, advocates do well to emphasize the salability of a product that aligns with their community's needs—and its converse, the threat of boycott when a product fails in the eyes of the community or is outright offensive. Although it is possible to convince audiences and producers to simply "do the right thing," activists also realize the strength of strategically positioning themselves as citizen-consumers, arguing that listening to their demands is a financial necessity for the media industries that produce those images.

This recognition of the power to impact the profitability of a show, a channel, or a media corporation has long played a part in the strategies of traditional media activism groups. Efforts to boycott a movie or theater for showing an offensive program were clearly aimed to financially impact movie producers and distributors. In the early days of television when programming was tied to a single sponsor, pressure groups could effectively exert influence over the show by convincing the advertisers to either pull their financial backing from the show or to demand a change in the contact. This kind of activism was most effective in the 1950s when shows had single sponsors, and those sponsors had significant control over the programming (Montgomery 1989). As the funding model changed in the early 1960s to spot advertisement or the "magazine" format, with different advertisements mixed in alongside the programming, this tactic became less effective. With this change in formatting, power over the content of a show shifted from the sponsor to the networks, and advertisers exercised much less influence over either scheduling or content. Further, if a sponsor came under pressure from an interest group and decided to pull its advertising, another advertiser could simply replace it. Nevertheless, even as advertising continues to diversify and there are fewer direct connections between sponsors and programming, activists still see advertising agencies and corporations as important allies in their efforts to alter content. After all, the financial model for television is still solely based on selling audience eyeballs to advertisers, and advertisers still want the high price of their investment in programming to contribute to an increase in their bottom line. Given this relationship, advertisers do retain some power in their relationships with television networks, and media activists can take advantage of this relationship in furthering their own goals.

If advertisers play an important role in influencing media producers, then positioning a community as a collective of powerful consumers is essential to convincing advertisers to pay attention to demands of any sort. Asian American media activists have done just that, emphasizing the strength of their own spending power in attempts to woo advertisers to their point of view. In 2010, the Affirmative Action and Diversity staff at the Screen Actors Guild commissioned a report called "From Dollars and Sense to Screen: The Asian Pacific Islander Market and the Entertainment Industry," outlining both the ethical and fiscal imperatives for industry professionals hiring more Asian Americans. As the report states, "Like other consumers, APIs respond best to products and advertisements that seemingly understand and cater to their individuality and culture. Consumers like to see themselves in media and will consume products to which they can relate" (Screen Actors Guild Affirmative Action and Diversity 2010, 11). In this report and in similar presentations to media executives, Asian Americans do more than request advertisers to learn about their culture—they also position themselves as one of the fastest growing and wealthiest base of consumers who cannot be ignored. This portrait of Asian America is in stark opposition to the image of the poor, working-class Asian Americans who suffered from discrimination in Chinatowns during the height of the Yellow Power movement. By invoking a new set of images and characterization of Asian Americans, activists hope to change the way representations are conceived and produced, rather than simply reacting to—or worse, accepting—the images that are presented to them.

This kind of consumer activism is of course not separate or disengaged from politics; on the contrary, as Lawrence Glickman (2009) argues in his history of consumer activism, American politics have always been intertwined with the demands and activities of consumer society. From antislavery campaigns in the 1800s to the long-standing use of boycotts to convey a social message, the powerful impact of consumption on politics is far from revolutionary or new. In the previous chapter I argued for the productive potential within media policy and interventions by regulatory bodies. In contrast, this chapter's exploration of the marketplace as a site for social change might seem to be reflective of a neoliberal landscape wherein the enterprising individual is thought to be capable of governing him or herself. Consumer activism is often based on the idea that an individual's everyday choices of what to purchase and how to consume are deeply social and political acts that can have long-term consequences. Yet here I draw discourses of consumption back to this idea of the collective by examining the ways Asian Americans are participating in consumer activism.

When Asian Americans strategically come together to affirm their power as a collective consuming body, they demonstrate an understanding of cultural citizenship as consumer citizenship. Of course these terms are not wholly identical; as we have seen in previous chapters, there are many other ways that Asian Americans have claimed cultural citizenship outside the consumer realm. Yet this is certainly one understanding of the way that cultural citizenship gains meaning and power—given that citizenship in the United States is often explicitly tied to the buying power of any group of individuals, the acknowledgment of Asian Americans as a distinct group of consumers is connected to their recognition as citizens. As Lisa Sun-Hee Park (2005) explores in *Consuming Citizenship: Children of Asian Immigrant Entrepreneurs*, many Asian Americans openly connect their feelings of identification and recognition as Americans to the products they consume and to financial success. The desire to deploy consumer identities in this way is specifically connected to experiences of racism and to the hardships of their immigrant parents. In this chapter, I investigate the way Asian American consumer culture has been deployed to align with the other kinds of media activism that also works to produce cultural citizenship.

At the center of this conversation about the creation of the Asian American marketplace, recognition of the strength of Asian American consumers, and the subsequent intervention in discourses of cultural citizenship, are advertising agencies. Alongside the steady rise of the multicultural advertising business, including those focusing on the African American and Hispanic markets, numerous agencies have been created since the 1980s in areas like New York, San Francisco, and Los Angeles specifically to target Asian Americans. Working with clients of every size—from McDonalds and national insurance agencies to small community organizations and projects—these agencies serve to bring brands, products, and messaging into Asian American communities that are largely informed by ethnic media. This includes placing ads within television programming, community newspapers, and public spaces where information is primarily conveyed "in-language," or in non-English languages. The dominant segments targeted by Asian American advertisers include Chinese, Korean, Filipino, Indian, and Vietnamese. Other ethnic groups, such as Japanese, Cambodian, Laotian, and other Asian American communities are only targeted for specific campaigns.

By investigating the work of such agencies, we can gain important insights into the relationship between Asian American consumption and citizenship. Further, advertisers also work to create and insert the image of Asian Americans into the media. Advertising agencies do more than direct campaigns and shape brands; they are also media producers themselves, creating everything from print and video media to immersive brand experiences that utilize Asian American actors and professionals. This chapter focuses on the work of these agencies in creating and reifying the idea of an Asian American market that can be sold to their clients, and the resulting images that are created to invoke and entice such an audience. Based on my interviews with industry professionals, visits to the offices of advertising agencies, attendance at the annual Asian American Advertising Federation's Marketing Summit, and analysis of various ad campaigns, I analyze the critical role that marketers can play in the world of media activism. I first consider why the creation of such a market is problematic, since it seems to rely on stereotypes and generalizations that belie the actual diversity of the Asian population in the United States and are reminiscent of the myth of the model minority. Moreover, given that advertising is based on the idea of commodifying identity into a product that can be sold for profit, there is also a question of how politically beneficial the creation of this kind of market can be for a disenfranchised community. I then go on to consider some of the ways in which advertisers can avoid these problems, and further, how they are contributing important efforts in the fight for more representation and better representation of Asian Americans in mainstream media. In doing so, they recognize the power of Asian Americans as consumer-citizens and open up new possibilities for the politicization of Asian American media.

Consumer Culture and Citizenship

Before delving into the use of consumer culture and minority advertising agencies for political purposes, I want to discuss the importance of the role of advertising in our society. Although marketing ostensibly exists to sell products and brands, advertisements also work to indelibly associate mass consumption with aspirational lifestyles and values that align with dominant ideologies. Advertising's plethora of repeating images and competing signifiers crowd the visual arena, continually confirming hegemonic ideals and norms. As Stuart Ewen (1976) argues, advertising creates the illusion of a homogeneous national culture of plenty that can be attained through consumer culture and leisure. He traces the construction of this illusion back to the 1920s, when workers' lives were becoming increasingly industrial and feelings of alienation and the loss of community began to grow. In contrast to this collective loss of power, "the basic impulse in advertising was one of control, of actively channeling social impulses toward a support of corporation capitalism and its productive and distributive priorities" (Ewen 1976, 81). But in upholding the system of capitalism, advertising effectively conceals social inequalities and disparities, suppressing any attempts to challenge the status quo. The promise of happiness as a result of consumption serves to replace the desire for the satisfaction of fair wages, political power and participation, social equality, or other desirable improvements in the lives of ordinary citizens. From this historical overview of the way advertising was deliberately utilized in the dampening of resentment over the loss of power by laborers, we can already begin to understand some of the critiques of the marketing industry. But when we turn to the way advertisers specifically focus on minority communities, their profit-oriented motives seem even more dangerous.

Advertising and consumer culture have always played an important role in creating and defining social identities such as those related to race, gender, or sexual orientation, just to name a few. The advertising industry operates by segmenting populations into different demographic or market categories so that its messages can be tailored to specifically appeal to these target audiences. But the act of creating these distinct identities as market segments constitutes those identities for consumers as well; through the work of advertising, ideologies and identities become inextricably bound. Robert Goldman argues that the meaning of a commodity is not determined by its use-value, but by the combination of product and image that emerges out of the social practice of advertising. Products become so deeply associated with the signs attached to them that they can no longer be disengaged, and the consumer becomes transfixed by the process of drawing "pleasure from the image-making process itself, the glorification of the product by associating it with important social qualities becoming our satisfaction too" (Goldman 1992, 19). Advertisements to women for cleaning products and to men for powerful trucks, to girls for pretty dolls and to boys for construction sets, all clearly teach consumers about the normative rules of gender in our society—and offer the acquisition of goods as the means for successfully achieving these social identities and relationships. In this sense, the business of selling products cannot be separated from the politics of identity.

This relationship between the construction of commodities and identities is of critical importance for communities who suffer from the imbalance of power inherent in capitalism, and for those whose visibility—or lack thereof—has real political consequences. Katherine Sender (2004) finds in her examination of gay marketing that "even a cursory look at contemporary marketing activity reveals that the separation of business endeavors from their political effects is spurious" (4). On the contrary, the place of gays and lesbians within the marketplace is deeply connected to their social and political struggles. Although the recognition of gay, lesbian, bisexual, and transgender (GLBT) consumers as an attractive market can serve to demonstrate affirmation and acceptance, activists within the GLBT community have worried that this carefully constructed visibility might also have negative effects on their fight to gain political power. This is particularly worrisome given the potential for promoting an assimilationist politics within grassroots organizations, and the tendency to skew visibility toward only the more secure segments of the community, such as white male professionals. Arlene Davila (2001) is similarly concerned about the impact of the advertising world on Latino identities and politics. As she argues, the advertising industry's "political economy, history, and composition are directly implicated in the global processes and transnational bases that sustain commonplace understandings of Latinos as a 'people' and a 'culture'" (3). When Hispanic advertising positions the community as unified and depoliticized, or as falling into patterns such as being culture-bound, family-oriented, and brand-loyal, these characterizations are solidified as meaningful and salient, removing any possibility for competing or contradictory narratives. For all minority groups, advertising agencies— among a host of other social forces—constitute identities as inherently generalizable, homogeneous, and thus manageable. In doing so, identities can be manipulated and contained, serving to increase the profits of both advertising agencies and the corporations who hire them to improve their brand and sell more products.

If advertising and consumer culture serve to silence resistance and gloss over social injustices, it seems that the growth of multicultural advertising industries would be implicated in these problems. Indeed, the commoditization of identity within different spheres of the advertising world deserves close examination and critique, as Sender and Davila have done. But I also want to consider the way that everyday practices of consumption can be productively constitutive of citizenship, and what political possibilities that relationship entails. Consumption and citizenship are often closely related in popular discourse—one need look no further than the post-9/11 injunction to stave off the terrorists by continuing to go shopping to see that a citizen is one who participates in upholding the American economy by consuming goods and products. But the arena of consumption can also be connected to the idea of participation in political life, since one's buying power can be seen as a political act. Nestor Garcia Canclini (2001) argues that "when we select goods and appropriate them, we define what we consider publicly valuable, the ways we integrate and distinguish ourselves in society, and the ways to combine pragmatism with pleasure" (20). Although consumption can be caricatured as a system in which dehumanizing corporations work to deceive the masses into blindly buying into a system that oppresses them, in many ways the picture is much more complicated than this— the act of selling and buying can be interactive, and consumers can have agency by contributing to the way that society values or defines certain objects and practices. Although the idea that consumers have a "choice" is debatable, one can argue that through the act of choosing one product over another they communicate what is important to them, and vote with their dollars for a system of cultural values that accords with their own.

Lizabeth Cohen (2008) traces the history of the relationship between citizenship and consumerism in the creation of what she calls the Consumers' Republic—"an economy, culture, and politics built around the promises of mass consumption, both in terms of material life and the more idealistic goals of greater freedom, democracy, and equality" (Cohen 2008, 7). Cohen sees mass consumption as one of the defining aspects of American society, seeping into every corner of politics and culture. She is particularly interested in the way individuals have developed politicized identities as consumers—the "citizen consumers" who organize to protect the rights of consumers, the "purchaser consumers" who use the positive effects of their own purchasing power to assert themselves, and the "purchaser as citizen" who contributes to the maintenance of a national economy with his or her personal purchases. In each of these formations, citizenship is expressed through one's behavior as a consumer—either by becoming civically engaged or simply by upholding the cultural ideals of the nation through consumption.

Although individual acts of consumption may seem to be self-interested and thus have no bearing on the nation as a whole, Cohen reveals how individuals become part of a collective consuming body that can wield political power. In the early consumer movements, individuals banded together to fight for things like fair pricing and product quality. Disempowered groups like women and African Americans also had the opportunity to demonstrate their opinion through consumption, strengthening their collective voices through boycotts and consumer activism, and legitimating themselves as important political constituencies. In Cohen's assessment of the Consumers' Republic, "a dynamic mass consumption economy [expected] not only to deliver prosperity, but also to fulfill American society's loftier aspirations: more social egalitarianism, more democratic participation, and more political freedom" (Cohen 2008, 403).

The connection between practices of consumption and citizenship must also be recognized in the context of minority communities, such as African Americans. Robert Weems (1998) argues that the recognition of African Americans as a legitimate consumer group at the turn of the century helped blacks develop the ability to protest offensive advertisements, support the growth of black-owned businesses, and use their collective spending power for political gain. In fact, Weems characterizes consumer activism as the most "potent nonviolent strategy employed by African Americans" during the Civil Rights Movement, which drew strength from a long history of boycotts such as the "Don't Buy Where You Can't Work" campaigns in the 1930s and the promotion of "Double Duty" patronage of black-owned stores. We can see through these examples that a group's collective behavior as consumers can have a serious impact, and that consumption can be an empowering act of citizenship.

But Weems also warns about the dangers of going too far in conflating consumption with political action, since it can also have negative consequences. Once marketers realized that their sales would increase when they targeted black audiences, they set their sights on alcohol and cigarettes, promoting products that negatively impacted the health of the black community. Blaxploitation films similarly showed the potential dangers of becoming a marketable audience. Films showcased the talents of black actors and actresses, but contained "extra doses of the film industry's unholy trinity of sex, violence, and crime. Thus, the term 'blaxploitation,' while not grammatically correct, does accurately convey the fleecing of African American moviegoers during this era" (Weems 1998, 83). This "fleecing" was further compounded by the fact that few African Americans actually made money off these films, given that the theaters were largely owned by white businessmen and the profits from the cheaply made films went to their white producers. As with Cohen, Weems argues that there is always a drawback to the elevation of consumption as a means of political participation. While African Americans may have become active citizens in their fight for consumer rights, their increased visibility as a collective made them a target for harmful campaigns. Once they had become a visible consumer group, advertisers and corporations wanted their spending money at any cost, obviously without regard to the social implications of their advertising or the harmful impact of their products—all they wanted was to increase their own profits.

These are important issues in the constitution of a new consumer audience, particularly one that is already marginalized or oppressed. As Elizabeth Chin (2001) notes in her exploration of black kids and consumer culture, "consumer consumption [is] a sphere of inequality where differences in consumption are the result of processes beyond that of the accretion of individual desire" (8). Differences and inequalities are not decreased in the consumer world, and the same political and economic factors that saturate our everyday lives remain present. As Weems's work shows, these inequalities are both created and transmitted through the media industries—in the representation of minorities and in the economic structures that produce and distribute those images. Thus, it is of critical importance to examine the relationship between consumer audiences and discourses of citizenship when looking at Asian American media activism. Given that an important element of citizenship is the act of being represented at all, there are countless ways in which Asian Americans have been distanced from being part of the imagined nation. But by harnessing the power of their collective voice as consumers, Asian Americans have the opportunity to change their own representation.

Defining the Asian American Consumer

If consumption can help us define citizenship, political involvement, and a larger notion of representation, what exactly does Asian American consumer culture look like? Until the latter part of the twentieth century, Asian Americans were not seen as a desirable market for advertisers or media companies. As mentioned in previous chapters, this is related to the idea that a panethnic Asian American identity had not yet been clearly articulated, either within the community or as a market segment. Yet as Shirley Lim (2006) argues, there is evidence that popular culture provided a site for Asian Americans to enter the American consumer republic. In her investigation of Asian American newspapers and magazines, she finds that "examining liberal-democratic narratives shows how Asian Americans used that language within their popular culture practices to argue for an enhanced place in the American nation-state" (Lim 2006, 90). In the 1930s, Chinese Americans sought to assert their nationalism and use cultural citizenship as evidence that they did not support Japanese aggression in Asia. Employing consumer culture to do so, Chinese American women participated in a boycott of silk stockings. Over five hundred Chinese women marched through New York City, waving banners and expressing their solidarity with a number of other anti-Japanese boycotts aimed at condemning Japanese imperialism and aggression (Glickman 2005).

After the Japanese American internment ended, Japanese American magazines from the 1950s like *Scene, Nisei Vue* and *East Wind* implored their readers to Americanize themselves by performing cultural citizenship and engaging in consumer culture—to dress and fix their hair in contemporary styles, participate in traditional sororities and women's clubs, and throw parties with American food products. Despite Lim's assertion that this kind of engagement with consumer culture had the potential to reduce racism and alleviate social inequalities, the commercialization of Asian American identities in the media and other cultural practices has been controversial in the Asian American community. When the Asian American lifestyle magazine *Jade* was first published in 1974, writers from the radical Asian American community newspaper *Gidra* were extremely critical of its appropriation of Asian American identity for profit. In an article titled "Jade: Magazine for Colonized Asians," the writer argued that articles on restaurateur Rocky Aoki ("modest pimp of Asian culture"), airline stewardess Suzi Kawasoye ("promoting the travel and tourism business for the sake of American imperialism"), Congressman Spark Matsunaga ("glorifying Asians who have made it to become politicians within a corrupt system"), and Asian eye makeup ("Asian women's eyes can become more desirable to western eyes") were evidence that editor-publisher Gerald Jann was either terribly misguided or "a conscious capitalist exploiting the public just for the sake of selling a product" (Monkawa 1974). A review of the magazine *Bridge* similarly remarked that "there is no distinction between its editorial pages and its advertising pages," which resulted in a lack of journalistic objectivity as well as a reprehensible reliance on stereotypes (Shigekawa 1974).

This kind of critique bleeds over into Asian American literature as well, where Viet Nguyen (2002) finds that Asian American writers and intellectuals have capitalized and profited from a strategy of panethnic entrepreneurship in spite of an avowed desire to use anticapitalism as a force for antiracism. Nguyen teases out this contradiction, arguing that "the contemporary Asian American identity that has allowed Asian Americans to participate in American politics—frequently as an anticapitalist force—has now also become a thing, a commodity, to be marketed and consumed" (Nguyen 2002, 9). Rather than naively idealize resistance and the subversion of capitalism, Nguyen implores academics to address the complexities of both symbolic and economic capital, and the role they play in the construction of Asian American identities and political participation. Given these concerns, the existence and operation of Asian American advertising agencies is clearly a fraught space for examining the potential for media activism. Heeding Nguyen's call to critically confront the role of panethnic entrepreneurship without slipping into blanket condemnation, let us now examine the work of these agencies and their potential for improving political discourse and participation.

The Rise of Asian American Advertising Agencies

Although Asian American advertising agencies have been in existence for decades alongside other multicultural marketers, their work remains difficult to compare to their counterparts in the African American and Hispanic/Latino advertising world. Asian American advertisers are still forced to spend a lot of energy making the argument to corporations that their community deserves attention, and more specifically a dedicated budget for advertising to the Asian American market. This is in contrast to the successes of the African American and Hispanic markets, which have rapidly blossomed into multibillion dollar industries.[1] The business of selling and promoting the Asian American market[2] is held back by a number of factors. First, at only 4 percent of the U.S. population, Asian Americans represent a comparatively small slice of the general market. Second, a number of assumptions about Asian Americans provide challenges for advertisers. In an article in *Advertising Age*, Bill Imada addresses three assumptions about the Asian American market that contribute to a skepticism in taking it on. These include the issue of small size, along with the idea that Asian Americans can be reached through English general market ads, that Asian American media are dying, and that the population is too diverse to be a viable market (Imada 2007). Imada calls these three ideas misconceptions and works to debunk them by arguing that culturally sensitive ads created in Asian languages, properly placed within the vibrant Asian ethnic media, will have a tremendous impact on the 15 million Asian Americans whose population and spending capital rival countless European nations.

Yet the ease with which these excuses come to mind remains a significant barrier for Asian American agencies to overcome. Although there are plenty of corporations who now enthusiastically go after the Asian American market, an Asian American advertiser noted that even for one of their largest clients, seven years passed from the day they started talking until the day the client signed them on—and that this lengthy period was not in the least unusual. IW Group in particular has a policy in place that it will not try to poach clients from other Asian American advertising agencies. "The pie is so small, there are so few advertisers in the Asian American marketplace, the game should be about growing the pie," explained an employee. The agency's main goal is always to simply bring more new clients into the Asian American market, no matter who ends up signing them. This is particularly important given how volatile the business can be; for small advertising agencies with only one or two clients, losing a client can mean shuttering their doors. During the 2009 recession dozens of large corporations pulled out of the Asian market altogether.

Another challenge facing Asian American marketers is the lack of research and data on Asian consumers and the difficulty that agencies face in conducting their own research. The assumption that Asian Americans are not a viable market affects more than the corporations who continue to ignore the segment—it also affects the way large research companies collect their data. While most advertising agencies can pay large research firms to collect data on their consumer segment, most of these firms either do not collect data on Asians or do not differentiate by ethnicity, making the data that they do collect extremely prone to miscalculation, overly simplistic, and difficult to use. Researchers within the strategic planning departments of these advertising agencies are forced to rely on the Census as their baseline, with additional data from only a handful of infrequent research studies.

Alice Lee, vice president of Research and Development at LA 18, is acutely aware of the difficulty of collecting data on Asian American audiences. Since LA 18 is the biggest Asian language television station in Southern California, Lee has a significant budget—particularly when compared to small advertising firms—for conducting and gathering research on the Asian American market. She happily shares her data with advertising firms in the effort to collectively bring more companies into the Asian American market, but the data itself is often incredibly poor. Some research companies only conduct their studies in English and Spanish, so many Asian immigrant families cannot even begin to fill out the extensive surveys. Further, she found that a large automotive study was using last names as a marker of race, which left Asians significantly undercounted. After investigating deeper, she found that the name Lee was considered Caucasian and that all Hispanic last names were listed as Hispanic, despite the prevalence of Filipinos with Hispanic last names and Asians with the name Lee—including, of course, Lee herself. As a member of the Asian Pacific Advocacy Board for Nielsen, Lee has seen similar problems even within the largest and most trusted source of data on media consumption. For instance, in the Los Angeles area Nielsen surveys have only a thousand meters. Since Los Angeles is around 14 percent Asian Pacific American, that means that only around 140 of these families are Asian—a number that shrinks even further when differentiated by ethnicity. As a result, the data is extremely unstable and unreliable. As Lee explains it, to get an accurate portrait of the viewers of her station LA 18, she surveys between 800 and 1,000 Chinese and Koreans alone. With Nielsen surveying such a drastically reduced number of Asian American viewers, it becomes clear why most Asian American advertisers simply say that "Nielsen doesn't do Asians" (Lee 2011).

Another problem is that Asian Americans are among the highest users of mobile phones (Kellogg 2011), which makes traditional telephonic surveying very difficult, while mail surveys are slow and expensive. As a result of this dearth of data from even the largest research corporations, most agencies are left to conduct much of their own research, both in testing specific campaigns for their clients and in general baseline surveys of their population. One company explained that they essentially do one large study every year that focuses on a question they have identified as critical at that moment, such as, "How do Asian Americans use social media?" or "How do Asian Americans consume packaged goods?" For the most part researchers in Asian American advertising firms collect qualitative data from focus groups, interviews at shopping malls or on street corners, webcam interviews, and by making ethnographic visits into private homes and other spaces of consumption. Larger quantitative studies are only undertaken on occasion, given the immense cost involved in doing so.

But this kind of quantitative research suffers from a number of problems. In particular, reports from the U.S. Census that provide baseline data for these corporations are based on artificially constructed racial categories that reify racial distinctions and institutionalize difference in arbitrary but politically significant ways. Davila (2001) notes the consequences of being able to collect Census data on the Hispanic population in the United States—on the one hand, advertisers were legitimized in their work because they had the numbers to prove that their community existed. But it also served to flatten difference between Latin American and Hispanic communities. Ien Ang (1991) also calls into question the emphasis on numerical ratings in discussions of television audiences. Media industries behave as if these sought-after audiences really exist, when in fact "no representation of 'television audience,' empirical or otherwise, gives us direct access to any actual audience" (34). Rather, the notion of an audience is merely a discursive construct that serves to deliver profits to the television stations via advertising corporations. Indeed, the entire commercial television industry depends on the collection of ratings and the conversion of these statistics into advertising dollars.

Despite these contradictions as well as the empirical difficulties Asian American agencies face in coming up with good quantitative data, these hard facts and figures are precisely what they need to attract new clients and develop the notion of the Asian American consumer. From the numbers, the Asian American market looks incredibly appealing. A 2010 video commissioned by the Asian American Advertising Federation entitled "Asian Consumers—A Segment You Can't Ignore" describes the most promising highlights of the population. In the video's teaser, available on the 3AF organization's website, images of Bollywood, sushi, the Jabbawockees, yoga, Lucy Liu, and Pokemon flash across the screen while a hip, youthful soundtrack blares in the background. We learn within the three-minute video that Asian Americans are "your new growth segment." Infographics illustrate the fact that Asian Americans have billions of dollars in spending power, the highest household income of any racial group, are well educated and own businesses, are online, buy tons of luxury goods and organic food, and best yet—are growing at an unequaled rate.

Although these statistics are meant to convince corporations that Asian Americans should be taken seriously as a market segment, they do so by reifying nearly every tenet of the model minority myth. In this video, we appear to have empirical proof that Asians are not only smart and wealthy, but are poised to take over America in the manner of the model minority's threatening counterpart, the yellow peril. Identifying the parallels between these characterizations of the Asian American consumer illuminates a number of insights. First, it is clear why advertising agencies would rely on these statistics—the model minority Asian American appears to be an ideal customer. As the marketers put it, who wouldn't want to go after an audience that is so likely to spend money on their products? Moreover, all advertising agencies function by positioning their market as the ideal consumers, whether they be teenagers, women, Hispanics, home owners, or early adopters.

But constructing Asian Americans along the lines of the model minority myth reveals some of the problems that can arise in doing so. First, these statistics may capture averages or describe a segment of the Asian American population, but they conceal the true diversity of the community. There are thousands of Asian Americans who are living at the poverty level, who are political refugees, who do not speak English or are illiterate, who are migrant laborers, who are jobless or homeless, or who otherwise do not fulfill the myth of the model minority. If we return to the idea that creating a consumer audience can play a part in constituting citizenship, we can see that this idea of the model minority grants citizenship to those who are likely already fully participating in American civic life. For these ad agencies to be laboring to expand the boundaries of Asian American citizenship, they would need to push beyond the limits of the model minority and gesture to the thousands of Americans of Asian descent who become invisible within this discourse, and are treated as second-class citizens as a result. For these individuals, trying to invoke consumer culture as a means of constructing citizenship will do little to change their realities.

The Politics of Accurate Research

Yet this is only a broad caricature of the work that advertising agencies actually undertake on a daily basis. When drawing in a client they may paint the picture of an audience that consists of only model minorities, but when it comes to actually designing a campaign, they know that their success rests on creating products that are targeted, nuanced, and culturally specific to the precise demographic they are trying to reach. As one advertiser put it, "If we're talking about entering the Asian market I don't have a problem relying on the [broader] data. But when we decide to target and market you're going after the market you can serve." In fact, some advertisers were quite pointed in their critique of the term "model minority." One advertiser stated:

> I hate the term model minority. It cuts both ways. It says model on the basis of what? Commentators will say, you're Asian you don't cause any trouble. You're studious and you're quiet and not troublesome. That's annoying because it says you don't stand up for your rights. So that's something we don't advocate. It's not one minority, it's way too complex for that. And there are serious problems within the ethnicities.

When hearing about the strategies that they employ in their specific campaigns, it becomes clear that their work does not simply address "Asian America" as if such a broad categorization existed or were useful. Rather, each specific campaign focuses on a predetermined ethnic group of a certain gender, age, educational background, geographic location, and socioeconomic standing. Most of any given campaign focuses on five main segments—Chinese, Korean, Vietnamese, Filipino, and Indians—and then further differentiates from there. Although the use of a "pan-Asian" ad might be created in some circumstances, using voiceovers in multiple languages with the same nonspeaking image of an East Asian actor, this kind of work is becoming rarer.

In order to successfully know their audience, advertisers research deep into their communities with their qualitative studies that flesh out the depth and complexity of their true audience. In Los Angeles the Asian American communications agency interTrend conducted a study on the way Twitter was used in Japan after the 2011 earthquake in Tohoku. Having noticed that there was a flurry of activity on Twitter after the earthquake occurred, it invited a team of its own researchers, partners at Bassett & Company, and a select group of academics who study Japan and social media to take a closer look. The results of their study are highlighted in a brief video entitled "Twitter: The New Haiku," which is featured on the company's YouTube site. The study's most prominent findings include the observation that there was a marked increase in the use of emotive language—words like hope, sadness, and love—in tweets from Japan immediately following the earthquake. Researchers connected the proliferation of these messages with Japan's cultural connection to haiku—an ancient Japanese form of poetry that is tightly structured but allows for much emotional depth and connections between the writer and the reader. Just as haiku are limited to three lines of verse containing only seventeen syllables, messages on Twitter are limited to 140 characters. Anna Xie, who served as a research manager for the project, outlined a few outcomes of the research. On the one hand, the agency was able to learn more about how Asians were employing online social networking, which is an arena advertisers are always keen to understand better. They also tapped into a cultural phenomenon that she hoped would help the company better understand Japanese Americans and Asian Americans, given the strength of transnational cultural flows between Asia and Asian American communities (Xie 2011). Researchers at interTrend work hard to stay on top of a multitude of trends in Asia in the hope that they can capitalize on the next crossover hit, like sushi or karaoke.

But another outcome of the study was that they were able to better understand the way that Japanese people communicated their emotions.

Xie noted that Westerners often seem to assume that Japanese people are stoic and dispassionate, unable to express their feelings. Through interTrend's analysis of Twitter and their interviews with Japanese living in Japan and Japanese Americans, they were better able to understand the cultural nuances of emotional expression and move away from these somewhat derogatory stereotypes (Xie 2011). Research projects like this one thus offer an opportunity to collect data about a community that is often neglected and relegated to stereotypes, and to transform that data into representations that are more accurate, authentic, and culturally sensitive.

Advertisers often stress the importance of understanding the cultural specificities of Asian American audiences. For instance, they know that they can't use the same ad for a Filipino community that they created with the Chinese community in mind, and they must make sure that the in-language material is not just a direct translation. Years ago, when an Asian American firm translated the statement "It makes my mouth water" into Vietnamese, the statement ended up as "My saliva drips profusely" (Imada 2011). This comical mistranslation provided an instructive moment that helped to emphasize the importance of the culturally relevant use of language. As the Managing Director of AAAZA Kevin Vu stated, "We do transcreation, not translation. It's not about the literal translation from one language to another, it's about creating ideas that make sense and resonate in different contexts" (Vu 2011). This idea of transcreation, or completely re-creating an idea so that it resonates with a cross-cultural audience, offers an important model for the work of Asian American cultural producers more generally. Given the diversity of the community, it is unlikely that any single idea could be used to the same effect without this kind of rigorous intercultural conceptualization. A failure to consider the transportability of concepts across cultures often results in images that are not only culturally irrelevant, but also potentially offensive.

In the early years of Asian American advertising, advertisers used Asian iconography, such as pagodas, cherry blossoms, bamboo, or pandas, more generically than they do today. Contemporary advertisers are sensitive to these mistakes of the past and create ads that are culturally relevant to a new generation of Asian Americans. This can even lead to conflict with their clients, since advertisers create ads that do not carry the traditional visual markers of "Asianness." The client often ends up asking, "What's Asian about this ad?" Since advertisers are dedicated to creating material that truly speaks to their audience, the images they create are designed to connect on a level that runs deeper than a simple stereotype and serves to differentiate between the multiple identities in Asian America.

Advocacy and Activism through Advertising

This study shows that one way Asian American advertising agencies can be positioned as activist is through the work they do to create images of Asian Americans with a specific goal in mind—to stay true to the community, avoid stereotypes, and create characters and storylines that Asian Americans will actually relate to and believe in. This is certainly a very limited form of activism, given that it is occurring through and within a capitalistic endeavor that clearly does not attempt or even desire to radically alter the social inequalities sustained by capitalism. Moreover, those who work in advertising agencies do so in order to make money rather than to remedy a social injustice. But just as media activist groups like MANAA and the APAMC work within the existing media system simply to improve and increase representation from inside the industry without challenging the system itself, advertising agencies are also fighting for some of the same goals as traditional media activists. Thus I argue that advertising organizations are clearly contributing toward activist causes and their work must be assessed within the larger picture of Asian American media activism. Moreover, alongside more traditional activists, their work can be seen as a way of using the media to fight for cultural citizenship. As I argued earlier, their perspective on cultural citizenship is one that connects consumer culture to empowerment within capitalist society, but their way of interacting with the media industries nevertheless is constitutive of Asian American cultural citizenship.

As media producers, the Asian American advertising organizations' goals of creating accurate, relatable content can surely be seen as political in nature when we consider the larger media landscape that often aims to do none of these things with regard to Asian Americans. In fact, this goal seems remarkably similar to MANAA's goals of rejecting stereotypes, though they attempt not simply to make a list of stereotypes and then ban them but to interact with Asian American community members to learn about their actual experiences, purchasing habits, histories, likes, and dislikes. In this sense, their work moves beyond complaining about stereotypes to creating original content that resonates with Asian American audiences. Advertisers might even use an image that is considered stereotypical if it resonates with Asian Americans— for instance, the achievements of college graduates are a matter of pride among Asian families and many images of graduates are utilized to connect to this positive emotion. Advertising agencies thus do not unilaterally condemn stereotypes; they are simply more interested in resonance and authenticity than in an empty symbol of how mainstream society views them.

From a media studies perspective it might be counterintuitive to conceive of advertisers as progressive political agents, given advertising's long history of contributing to harmful stereotypes, promoting products that are unhealthy such as cigarettes and alcohol, and generally misleading consumers in service of helping a large corporation make a profit. Yet I still want to consider the fact that Asian American advertisers are media producers, and by examining their particular histories and goals as well as the images they create we can begin to frame their work within a larger conversation about the politics of representation. In doing so, we must consider the fact that consumer culture and activism have a different relationship in the twenty-first century that is increasingly flexible. My use of the term "activist" in this assessment reflects the difficult and complex negotiations we must make in a neoliberal moment in which the marketplace has become the central site for rendering identities visible and allowing capitalist endeavors to be reframed as ethical or political. While opportunities for collective action have been systematically diminished, this does not mean that there is no potential for social justice work within this system. As Banet-Weiser and Mukherjee (2012) argue, within the discursive formations of neoliberalism both consumers and corporations can participate in activism through their virtuous capitalistic undertakings. For consumers, this means practicing "doing good" through thoughtful purchasing and ethical consumption—purchasing from companies who are thought to be contributing to social change in some way, or avoiding companies whose social practices are thought to be problematic. For corporations, this means practicing "Corporate Social Responsibility" and doing business that leads to desirable social outcomes, even when it is clear that these social justice ventures simultaneously increase their own profits. Under this logic, it makes sense to consider Asian American advertising agencies as potential agents of social change, even as their first priority is always to remain profitable as a business.

One potential limit to the effects of their work on the broader population is that Asian American marketers largely create advertisements for ethnic or in-language media and are noticeably absent from the mainstream market. Thus, while many of the images they create might be innovative and commendable, it is unlikely that their impact will spread to a larger audience. Yet this is where the labor of the marketers themselves comes into play. As champions of their own media creations, they are in constant conversation with their clients, working to convince them that Asian American advertising is a priority. Once an image has been created, the corporation can choose to use the advertisement wherever it pleases, and sometimes there is a crossover between ads placed in ethnic media and the general market. Advertisers report many cases in which a company has been so pleased with a commercial or a campaign that it has decided to extend it beyond the limited range of the multicultural market. For instance, a McDonald's advertisement for strawberry lemonade that featured Asian American dance stars Yuri Kim and Victor Wong—both of whom were stars of the show *America's Best Dance Crew* on MTV—made the crossover from ethnic media to mainstream media in the summer of 2011, much to the delight of Asian American audiences.

Beyond the creation and exposure of images by Asian American advertisers, advertisers can also adopt a more deliberate role in order to make a difference. Within their own ranks, Asian American marketers often serve to police their own work and the work of their competitors. As Asian Americans, they are not immune from creating images that uphold stereotypes or offend their own community, and they are not afraid to take a stand when problematic images surface. Bill Imada from IW Group explained:

> Sometimes I look at the work of our competitors and the work we do, and I'll say, "Who created that? It really upsets me." We make a lot of

An advertisement for McDonald's strawberry lemonade, starring Asian American dancers Victor Wong and Yuri Kim, was created for the Asian American market but later transitioned to the general market.

mistakes too. One of our competitors made a brilliant ad as part of an anti-smoking campaign that was terribly culturally insensitive. I picked up the phone and called the agency and said something. I said I love this ad from a creative point of view but think about the ramifications this ad might have. Some ads might be offensive and hurt the community emotionally and perpetuate some stereotypes that are enduring that we want to shake from the mindset of most Americans about Asians in particular. There's been a lot of those kinds of ads. (Imada 2011)

Thus members within the industry help to educate and inform one another about creating better images. One advertisement in particular on which Imada has taken a stand is a series of ads for Metro PCS that features two South Asian talk show commentators who have exaggerated accents and participate in silly stunts. After consulting with his staff and South Asian colleagues, he decided that the ad was offensive because it belittled and ridiculed South Asians. Criticizing the ad, which was not created by an Asian American agency, in his blog on Ad Age, he wrote, "Perpetuating stereotypes, whether they appear harmless or not, typecasts a group of people as perpetual foreigners who remain at the fringe of American society. They set these communities of people up for constant ridicule and make recent immigrants feel unwelcome and unappreciated." His blog post received both positive and negative feedback, with many commentators arguing that the commercials were funny and that the accents were a realistic part of Indian culture. These comments illustrate that individuals in the advertising business are in a position to initiate dialogues about representation within their own ranks and with a larger audience.

Despite this demonstration by Imada of a politicized perspective, I also want to consider the place of self-identification in this discussion of activism. Very few professionals in my interviews with advertisers claimed to see their work in the communications industry as being activist in nature. Although some did consider themselves to be activists because of other aspects of their identity—serving on the board of a nonprofit, advocating for increases in Asian American hiring, or supporting particular causes in the community—they did not readily conclude that they were activists because they had convinced corporations to target the Asian American market or created images that were not stereotypical. As one person said, "I mean, to be honest we'd all love to call ourselves activists, but the truth is that we do this because the corporations hire us for their multicultural advertising." For many who work in the industry, the financial imperative behind their work and the continued demand for increased corporate profits removes the potential for politics in their daily labor. Nevertheless, I believe the term activism is flexible enough to encompass the activities of those who are laying the foundation for avowed activists like those at MANAA or the AAJC to succeed in their work. Even if advertisers do not consider themselves to be activists because of their work in promoting the products of Coca Cola or Nike, much of their work contributes positively to and supports the more explicitly political work of community organizers whose sole goal is to positively impact the lives of Asian Americans through structural change.

Increasing the Market for Film

Another way advertisers have begun to influence the larger media landscape is through the relationships they are forging with movie studios.

In 2010, Warner Brothers tackled the Asian American filmgoing audience for the first time, launching campaigns for films like *Inception*, *Harry Potter and the Half-Blood Prince*, and *Sucker Punch*. This was the first time a major studio had hired an advertising agency specifically for the Asian American market. The prevailing logic had previously been that Asian American audiences could be effectively captured through general marketing and did not need ethnic-specific targeting. But Warner Brothers decided to take a chance and hired IW Group to reach out to Asian Americans.

The result of this decision was that Warner Brothers took a close look at its films and saw value in Asian American talent, both behind and in front of the camera. For *Inception*, this meant promoting Japanese star Ken Watanabe and Dileep Rao, who is Indian American. For *Sucker Punch*, two actors were highlighted: Vanessa Hudgens, who is part Chinese Filipina, and Jamie Chung, who is Korean American. Further, the film's screenwriter, cinematographer, and editor, all of whom are Asian American, were prominently featured and made available for interviews with ethnic media, including English-language programs like *Kababayan L.A.*, and in-language news programs. In some cases they interviewed in English, but if they could speak the language of the interviewer, they did so. Marketers for these films also reached out to the Asian American blogosphere. Sites like Angry Asian Man, 8Asians.com, and Disgrasian appeal to a wide array of second-generation Asian Americans and beyond, who might not read in-language ethnic media. To promote *Sucker Punch*, marketers also worked with popular YouTube performer Jen Chae of "frmheadtotoe," a makeup tutorial expert. The Korean American performer created a video tutorial of how to wear makeup just like Jamie Chung's character in *Sucker Punch*, integrating promotional material from the film into her standard lessons on how to make eyeliner pop on Asian eyes. Although Warner Brothers has not released statistics on the success of these campaigns, an executive reported that there was a "very positive uplift with regard to the box office numbers" as a result. Given that we are entering a new era in which Asian American box office power is beginning to be calculated and acknowledged, opportunities will increase to advocate for the movie studios to not just try to repackage their current projects to appeal to Asian Americans, but to actually create projects specifically for the Asian American audience.

YouTube makeup artist Jen Chae of the channel "frmheadtotoe" re-created Jamie Chung's look as Amber from *Sucker Punch* as part of the promotion for the movie.

Of course, the idea that Asian Americans have not traditionally been seen as a reliable audience for media projects is not new. Commercial failure has long been a reality for media producers who have created media specifically for Asian American audiences—we see this in everything from the cancellation of the television show *All-American Girl* and the cable stations AZN and ImaginAsian TV, to the death of magazines like *A Magazine* and *Yolk*, to the struggles of award-winning films like *The People I've Slept With* or *Children of Invention* to find distributors and make a profit. At a 2010 event hosted by the Asian Professional Exchange in Los Angeles on the topic of Asian American media, panelists from the media industry spent the entire time addressing the question of why so many Asian American media efforts had failed to gain traction. Similarly, Asian American film director Justin Lin blogged about someone looking at his dwindling profits and stating, "For a group of people that are supposed to be good at math, you guys must be retarded to keep making Asian American films." Lin's mainstream films like *The Fast and the Furious: Tokyo Drift* and *Fast Five* have been blockbuster hits, while his significant forays into Asian American film have struggled to find an audience.

But Lin's Asian American films and their interaction with the Asian American community deserve closer examination. One of the routes by which Asian American media producers have attempted to address Asian American audiences is through political motivation—a turn that makes sense, given that the idea of a cohesive Asian American identity is rooted in a history of political coalition building rather than any natural racial solidarity. Lin's debut film *Better Luck Tomorrow*, which has been heralded as the first "mainstream Asian American film" (Hillenbrand 2008), provides a strong example of this kind of politicized audience formation. The film's opening was accompanied by a grassroots email campaign to promote the project to college students, and Asian American business leaders treated patrons to buyouts of entire screenings. As Konrad Ng saw it, "The film became an opportunity to demonstrate the commercial viability of Asian American cinema and the market impact of Asian Americans; put differently, the film became an ethical issue that spawned practices of community organizing in support of the film" (Ng 2010). In this sense, Asian American audiences are seen as consumers, but they are interpellated first and foremost as politicized subjects. The message of the grassroots campaign was clear—if Asian Americans wanted people from their community to be able to tell their own stories and find employment in the entertainment industry, they needed to show their support through their dollars.

This economic logic is similar to the imperative of the citizen-consumer that I discussed earlier, but it falls prey to the essentialist idea that Asian American audiences will respond to a common identity. As a result of this buzz and grassroots promotion, *Better Luck Tomorrow* made $3.8 million—a significant profit given its shoestring budget of $250,000. But despite its landmark status and the devotion of its fans, the Asian American community often shrugs it off as a failure. One marketer stated:

> If you go on the street and ask 100 Asian people you see if they've ever heard of *Better Luck Tomorrow*, you'd be lucky if you found 5. Even though it's "targeting Asian Americans." I think there are a lot of movies that are about the Asian American experience that don't see the light of day. I know a lot of Asian American actors who are in those movies and they go straight to DVD.

Even the blog community at "You Offend Me You Offend My Family"—a website started by Justin Lin and his friends hailing from the world of media and activism—agrees that the film was not as successful as it could have been. "Offender" Philip writes about an Asian American activist who was protesting films like *The Goods: Live Hard, Sell Hard* and *The Last Airbender*, but when asked, the activist admitted that he had never paid to see an Asian American film in the theater.

> He was talking passionately about how we need to force Hollywood to change and show respect to our community, but even he admitted he had not done much to support our artists and our work. Unfortunately, this brother's story is not isolated. And herein lies the problem—it's great that we're willing to speak out when we see something that offends us. But until Asian Americans as a whole are willing to put down our money to support the work of our Asian American filmmakers—nothing will change. We can protest all we want, but real change will not happen until Hollywood knows we are an economic force that can make a difference in their bottom line. (Philip 2009)

The relationship between Asian American advertisers and Warner Brothers is clearly a move in this direction, but as "The Offenders" argue, this message must be conveyed to the consumers as well.

Conclusion

Cultural critic Jeff Yang broached the topic of Asian American audiences in a column for the *San Francisco Chronicle* in May 2011. After bemoaning the nauseating representation of Asians and Asia in *The Hangover Part II*—a film that takes place in Bangkok, which Yang argues becomes "a bizarro realm of brute violence, grim depravity and unfettered libido, populated entirely by broad racial stereotypes" (Yang 2011)—he noted that the only reason such schlock could be created was because audiences would pay to see it. He connected this logic of supply and demand to the failure of Asian American films, which he feared now suffer from a "reverse halo—an odor of failure—that wafts around Asian American media like a Japanese horror-film curse" so that even Asian Americans will not support films produced within the community. In order to combat this bad reputation, Yang (somewhat jokingly) proposed a reboot in the form of what he dubs "The Two Percent Project," which originated in a conversation on Facebook. The title of the project was based on the industry mathematics that a CD, film, or book could become profitable if 2 percent of the one million Asian Americans currently in college purchased it. Yang was joined by Oliver Wang, a professor of sociology and popular culture, in proposing a college tour in which five independent Asian American creators or artists would show their work. In order for the event to have an impact, there would be an additional requirement:

> Although attendance at these events would be free, every attendee would have to purchase one of the five products these artists are promoting *on the spot*, while enrolling in an online community that gives the artists long-term engagement with their consumers. The goal? Constructing an independent audience. Reinventing the Asian American brand. And creating recorded proof that Asian American artists are marketable and that a market exists to sustain them. (Yang 2011)

Their proposal attempts to reify the existence of a pan-Asian American consumer market despite the fact that media artists have failed to do so for decades. Their argument is that the sheer number of Asian Americans—and specifically Asian Americans in college, who represent a particularly fertile market—is sufficient to support community art and productions. They simply need to be organized and educated about how much their spending power is worth. Yet the idea of cultivating the Asian American audience does not begin with this project, or even with *Better Luck Tomorrow*, but somewhere at the intersection between the vast and multifaceted history of consumer activism within minority communities and the work of Asian American marketers.

Although consumption can be a limited or problematic way to effectively impact the realities of citizenship and representation, media activists are nevertheless still utilizing these discourses in order to move forward. We can look to the history of women's movements, African American consumer movements, and other successful consumer movements from the past century to see that there is a great deal of power in coming together as citizen-consumers to impact change. Yet as Glickman argues, one of the significant characteristics of citizen activism during the modern era is that consumers did not have to be physically proximate in order to recognize their collective power to impact producers. As he notes, "each person, in this vision, was a node on a network that might traverse distances as small as a few city blocks or as large as a continent or an ocean" (Glickman 2009). This vision becomes even more prescient in the era of the internet, when activists often organize, educate one another, develop politicized platforms, and take action, all in a completely virtual environment without ever even seeing one another. Indeed, we can see the impact of new media technologies in many of the campaigns examined here—in the study of Twitter in Japan, in the use of a YouTube makeup artist to promote a film, in the birthing of the Two Percent Project. If we are interested in challenging the power dynamic between consumers and producers, online media is clearly an important site for study. In the next chapter I turn to a number of these creative campaigns and uses of online communities to further examine the possibilities for media activism and the construction of Asian American citizenship through media.

4

Asian American YouTube Celebrities Creating Popular Culture Networks

Since the birth of the Asian American political movement in the 1970s, Asian Americans have been picking up their cameras and recording images of their lives as a political act that asserted their cultural citizenship. By creating visual records of their experiences, editing their own narratives, and exhibiting works of Asian American art within their own communities, they were able to validate their own histories and experiences as citizens. They took control over the way they were represented and told their own stories to their community. Rather than waiting for movie studios to decide that Asian American stories were worth telling, filmmakers developed the skills and language to create their own cinema. The very idea of "Asian American film" is itself politicized; the title is not simply used for films made by someone who happens to be of Asian heritage creating moving images in the United States, but for films made by those who identify as Asian American that deliberately focus on telling Asian American stories.

This form of cultural production produced a rich collection of texts for Asian Americans to view, largely within a specific context—the Asian American film festival. Asian American film festivals have a symbiotic relationship with Asian American film, as both rely upon one another for their continued existence. Film festivals focusing specifically on Asian American content are held yearly in at least a dozen cities across the United States. The oldest and largest Asian American film festivals are connected to Asian American media arts centers—Asian CineVision in New York, Visual Communications in Los Angeles, and the National Asian American Telecommunications Association (now the Center for Asian American Media) in San Francisco. Such centers support Asian American filmmaking and media creation in a number of different ways. They provide instruction and equipment for making movies, preserve archival images, screen films to the community, and generally support

Asian American filmmaking. But their annual festivals are the center-piece of each organization, providing an opportunity to bring together large crowds and showcase the year's best Asian American films.

Like many other kinds of film festivals, such events serve to bring film into their local communities. But this seemingly simple undertaking actually has profound implications for minority audiences who otherwise would not have the opportunity to see themselves represented in the multiplex, or to see these particular films. For all minority film festivals—including those about African Americans, LGBTQ communities, people with disabilities, Latinos, and women—such community gatherings provide physical spaces for the building of cultural citizenship (Gamson 1996; Broyles 1983). Through the act of watching films together, communities who are traditionally excluded from mainstream media can feel accepted and even celebrated. Not only do people from these underrepresented identities have the opportunity to experience cultural productions made for and by people like them, but they can mingle and converse with like-minded filmgoers. Thus, film festivals allow communities to do more than merely view films; they allow them to come together and validate the work of their own artists and that of others who share their marginalized identities. Over the festival's duration there are multiple opportunities for discourse surrounding image production and consumption. The Q&A following screenings provides one clear forum for discussion. In addition, panel discussions and workshops provide other occasions for dialogue. By these means, Asian American filmmakers are most assuredly participating in changing the way Asian Americans are represented in the world of cinema.

This portrait of the way relationships between media production and distribution serve to create, develop, and sustain Asian American communities can help us understand what it means when these relationships are remediated through digital and online media. Many Asian Americans have taken advantage of the low barriers to participation in online video creation and distribution. While traditional filmmaking depends upon expensive film equipment, editing software, and training before even submitting a film to a film festival, digital tools have changed this equation. Using nothing more than a webcam and a broadband connection, individuals can create videos with the flip of a switch and instantly broadcast them to the public. Although this scenario describes the way many YouTubers started out, an entire generation of Asian Americans born digital has matured into a sophisticated collective of videographers in its own right, deploying the tools of digital media to make new interventions into the world of media production and consumption. In this move toward digital media creation, we might worry about the decline of spaces like Asian American film festivals that have proven vital in creating communities of practice around Asian American media.

Yet I argue that this is not the case—rather than subvert the potential for Asian American communities to organize around media, online media has produced new opportunities for the formation of meaningful networks and communities, both online and offline. In this chapter I investigate the different ways Asian Americans are using YouTube as a platform for distributing their media creations and developing communities. In particular, I look at the way increased visibility on sites like YouTube contributes to a new kind of Asian American celebrity in the digital sphere—a small group of individuals who have become hypervisible and influential due to their presence online. I argue that the connections these individual celebrities make reveal the development of transmedia branding across Asian American popular culture—a project that serves to create hubs of Asian American participatory culture that can be mobilized for different kinds of action. These actions are not always political or related to media activism, but the development of such networks nevertheless provides the potential for using popular culture to foster participation and helps shape our understanding of the term "Asian America" toward political ends.

Online media provides a new arena for Asian Americans to voice their opinions, organize themselves and their allies, initiate conversations, create their own media, and increase the impact of their messages—tactics which act in concert with or contribute to the efforts of other Asian American media activists. Konrad Ng has examined various sites of online activism among Asian Americans, contending that new media communication "is about the flow of content across media platforms and the formation of independent cultural industries and mission-driven digital networks that encourage community participation in shaping and amplifying the representation of the Asian American experience" (Ng 2012, 257). Here I focus on the way a new generation of Asian American celebrities is using digital media practices to create cultural formations around Asian American popular culture, including video, music, and dance. These interconnected networks of popular culture allow Asian American celebrities to express their understanding of cultural citizenship as the freedom for self-representation and creative control over their own images and stories. In this sense, cultural citizenship cannot be realized as long as hegemonic media industries are monopolizing the narrative about the Asian American experience.

This chapter begins with an examination of the discourse surrounding five of the most popular Asian American YouTubers—Michelle Phan, KevJumba, Nigahiga, Wong Fu Productions, and Clara C.[1]—in order to gain insight into how their work has been positioned. I argue that we need to understand them as celebrities, but I question the instrumentality of this kind of celebrity, focusing in particular on the way that their work intersects with the efforts of Asian American media activists. In examining the star texts of these celebrities I also question what kind of media work counts as activist or merely political, arguing that there is still much work to be done in connecting YouTube stardom to the deliberate project of working toward social change. I then examine the ways that these celebrities partner with organizations like You Offend Me You Offend My Family and ISAtv to create bridges between mainstream media and independent media. In doing so, they increase the value of each individual's celebrity status while also strengthening Asian America as a site for cultural identity and affiliation. My examination of these specific uses of online media and its affordances shows how their creation of cultural citizenship is strengthened through digital networks—it begins by having access to the means of media production but becomes more powerful when these networks are used to engage a broader Asian American public through online participatory cultures.

Asian American Uses of YouTube

As one of the most popular websites on the internet, YouTube has been heralded for its ability to allow anyone to upload and share videos. Since the site premiered in 2005, it has given amateur and professional videographers alike the opportunity to garner audiences of all kinds—from a handful of close friends to millions of strangers clicking through from across the globe. In 2006, YouTube was acquired by Google for $1.65 billion. Although YouTube continues to operate independently, the site is now supported by advertisements. Sites like YouTube contribute to a more participatory culture in which the ease of accessibility supports the creation and dissemination of creative work and allows users to freely seek out content and develop social connections (Jenkins et al. 2006). Asian Americans have been particularly prolific in doing so, creating thousands of their own original videos and sharing them with an international audience that continues to grow at an astounding rate. They have amassed millions of subscribers to channels within a diverse set of genres—including comedy (KevJumba, NigaHiga), music (David Choi, Clara C), makeup expertise (Michelle Phan), narrative storytelling (Wong Fu Productions), special effects (Freddie Wong), and fitness (Blogilates). Although their rankings wax and wane over time, many Asian Americans have maintained popular channels whose subscriber numbers have frequently eclipsed even mainstream stars like Rhianna, Lady Gaga, and Justin Bieber—an artist who himself was discovered and brought to fame on YouTube. This trend has not gone unnoticed by the mainstream news media or by scholars. A *New York Times* article in July 2011 reported that "on the democratized platform of YouTube . . . a young generation of Asian-Americans has found a voice (and millions of eager fans)" (Considine 2011). Josh Kun also noted in an article about the success of the Filipino American singing group Legaci that YouTube had become "a crucial launching pad for Asian-American artists seeking the kind of exposure rarely afforded them by the mainstream recording industry" (Kun 2010).

TABLE 4.1.

YouTube Channel	Subscribers on March 12, 2012
Nigahiga	5,128,429
KevJumba	2,286,724
Michelle Phan	1,851,349
Lady Gaga	1,473,348
Justin Bieber	1,321,646

In 2012, Asian American YouTubers dominated the charts in terms of number of subscribers—outpacing even mainstream celebrities such as Lady Gaga and Justin Bieber.

The participation of Asian Americans on YouTube is often believed to provide an alternative to the traditional gatekeepers in mainstream media, as it offers a seemingly democratized platform for minority media producers. For instance, Eun-Young Jung's study of three Korean American musicians finds that YouTube and other forms of online social media have allowed Asian American musicians to circumvent the institutional racism that previously limited their careers (Jung 2014). Yet this celebratory tone is tempered by the reality that the work of Asian American YouTubers is often ineffective in combating racism, for a number of reasons. Part of this failure must be attributed to the unfortunate reality that YouTube, like many online spaces, is an openly hostile and racist environment.[2] Asian Americans on YouTube are thus subject to racist feedback online, even as identities of privilege such as masculinity and heterosexuality serve to insulate popular personalities like Ryan Higa and Kevin Wu from other forms of discrimination (Saul 2010; Wotanis and McMillan 2014). Yet the videos of popular YouTubers show the additional problem that Asian Americans themselves do not always seek to counter stereotypes in their self-presentations. In their study of Higa and Wu's vernacular discourse on YouTube, Lei Guo and Lorin Lee (2013) argue that the revolutionary potential of their videos is undercut by their failure to undermine racist stereotypes. Although the discourse of the two Asian Americans is critical of dominant ideologies, their videos, which portray Asian Americans as diligent and obedient, nerdy, emasculated, or simply uncool, often end up reifying stereotypes. Elaine Chun echoes these problematic findings in her study of Wu's style of humor, which often goes beyond stereotypes of Asian Americans by upholding and mimicking stereotypes of black masculinity (Chun 2013).

Although these explorations of the perpetuation of stereotypes on YouTube are useful, an overreliance on the discourse of stereotypes from the perspective of antiracism can unnecessarily limit conversations about the way audiences engage with the media. As discussed in chapter 1 in relation to the Media Action Network for Asian Americans, it is important that we move beyond simply viewing content and critiquing the presence or absence of stereotypes. Here I consider the role of Asian American YouTube users more broadly, asking how successful YouTube celebrities frame their own participation in the media landscape via the construction of their star text, and what they seek to do with their performances. In their capacity as celebrities who interact with the public, they do more than simply star in popular media content—their own lives become part of their stories. Therefore we need to include the study of paratextual materials in order to make sense of their meaning. Celebrity scholars have noted that a star's image is a construction continually created through competing and contradictory forces, including authorized sources such as promotional materials and the star's website, and unauthorized sources such as fan forums and gossip blogs. Because of these multiple sources of information what we know about a film star is the result of much more than his or her filmic oeuvre; the person's star text is composed of the intersection between multiple forms of paratext—interviews, photographs, reviews, gossip columns, tweets, news stories, and other media that work together to create meaning (Gray 2010). As Richard Dyer argues, "star images are always extensive, multimedia, intertextual" (Dyer 1985, 3). So to make sense of what a star means we must take a close look at these different pieces of evidence.

If we translate this understanding of the more traditional movie star to the Asian American YouTube star, it makes sense to look beyond the content on the star's own channels. To assess the star text more broadly and its relation to media activism, I first look at interviews published online with Michelle Phan, KevJumba, Nigahiga, Wong Fu Productions, and Clara C. Interviews and "behind the scenes" discussions with these YouTubers gives us insight into how their work has been positioned— both the way media outlets have framed it, and the ways in which they have asserted their own perspective through their responses to questions. This allows us to see how their celebrity contributes to the kinds of cultural citizenship espoused by the long tradition of Asian American independent filmmaking, as well as the ways in which it departs from this tradition.

Who Are YouTube's Stars?

Ryan Higa (NigaHiga) has been one of the most consistently successful users in all of YouTube. With over 15 million subscribers in 2015, his channel is ranked in the top ten most subscribed of all time, and he has frequently been the top-ranked channel owned by an individual on You-Tube. Higa started making his own comedic videos with a friend in 2006 when he was in high school, and has continued to create his signature humorous sketches, lip-synch performances to popular songs, rants, and spoofs. The videos do not always call attention to his Asian American identity, but his background as a Hawaiian-raised Japanese American is mentioned in many interviews. Kevin Wu (KevJumba) is also a comedian and rose to prominence at the same time as Higa. Wu's channel became popular in 2008 when a video called "I experience stereotypes" was featured on YouTube's homepage. His channel has featured humorous exchanges with his first-generation Chinese American father, his friendship with basketball star Jeremy Lin, and self-deprecating rants about a number of light-hearted topics. Both Higa and Wu have participated in a number of transmedia endeavors beyond their work on YouTube, including Asian American independent feature films, live concerts, music videos, charity programs, and many collaborative projects with other YouTubers.

Michelle Phan is a makeup artist who started posting tutorials on YouTube in 2007. Her facial creations range from tips on how to look pretty in the upcoming season to dramatic re-creations of the makeup from movies or music videos. In interviews, she frequently discusses her parents as immigrants from Vietnam and shares stories about her financial struggles when she was a child, leading to her career as an artist. Michelle Phan is one of the few Asian American women to become successful on YouTube, as nearly all the other top Asian American performers on YouTube are men. Musician and singer-songwriter Clara Chung (Clara C) was added to the group of people being studied, but she has far fewer subscribers than the others. Chung's participation reflects the experiences of many Asian American musicians whose entire career is based on a YouTube persona, and she is frequently called upon to discuss her online celebrity. Based in Los Angeles, Chung rose to popularity after performing and winning at the 2010 Kollaboration Los Angeles—an Asian American competitive showcase of young and upcoming talent that often features YouTubers.

The channel Wong Fu Productions is run by Wesley Chan, Ted Fu, and Philip Wang. The three Chinese American filmmakers started making short films in 2003 when they were in college together at the University of California, San Diego. After graduating, they established a media company to manage the production of their music videos and short films, which range from darkly dramatic to comedic satire and farces. The filmmakers and their videos are extremely popular with Asian American youth, as evidenced by their subscriber base of over 2 million, invitations to over a hundred events on college campuses around the country, and the existence of multiple fan-created websites. Together with the pop music group Far*East Movement, they started the concert series International Secret Agents (ISA) in 2008. The tour, which traveled to LA, San Francisco, and New York, featured Asian American artists and musicians in sold-out performances.

Interviews with these YouTubers generally fall into the categories of teaching others how to do what they do—giving advice about making videos, the creative process, how to grow an audience—and learning more about who they really are—how they got started, their goals for the future, and details about their daily lives, personal preferences, and quirks. Yet these are the kinds of inquiries one might make of any celebrity. While this interest in their private lives and professional expertise is an important indicator of their cultural capital as celebrities, there is more analytical work to be done in unpacking the meaning of these interviews and their connections to media activism.

Traditional or Online Celebrity?

The YouTubers discussed here are more than just the creators of one-time viral hits—the people who run these popular channels create lasting relationships with their viewers by consistently producing new content. Their popularity in terms of the number of subscribers, coupled with the devotion of their fans, contributes to our understanding of them as a new kind of Asian American online celebrity. They are particularly well-known in Asian American youth communities, and are often invited to speak on panels at community festivals, appear at fund-raisers, serve as MCs, or give live performances. Alongside the jokes about the "countless dating and marriage proposals" (Chong 2012) they receive as a result of their fame, they are always careful to express their gratitude and affection for their fans. Such statements remind us of the affective relationship they have built with their followers. They are clearly beloved by their fans, but the existence of a vaunted few is noteworthy because it contradicts much of the discourse positioning YouTube as a democratic space for the reign of the amateur (Keen 2008). The ease with which users can participate in creating and sharing media is often assumed to mean that the distinction between the first-time participant and the media professional has been erased. In fact, the reality is that not all YouTube users are equally visible, and only a small percentage of videos get most of the hits. The algorithms that run the site are designed to boost the popularity of this marginal percentage of users through the most popular videos being highlighted on the main site and elevated to the top of the suggested set of links that run beside every video. Moreover, despite much discussion of the individual users who have risen to popularity, large corporations and industry-owned channels vastly outperform those of amateurs and individuals (Burgess and Green 2009). Thus the success of the few individuals who have gained a significant following despite these structural barriers is worthy of investigation.

But we must also interrogate how the success and social function of these YouTubers aligns with more traditional conceptions of the "celebrity." Although I argue that we should call these YouTubers celebrities, they are not celebrities in any traditional sense of the word. In fact, "celebrity" might seem like an odd term to use for people who are conspicuously absent from the mainstream media or among non-Asian viewers, and who struggle to monetize their popularity and fame. Burgess and Green argue that what distinguishes celebrity on YouTube from celebrity in the mainstream media world is the ways in which YouTube celebrity status remains connected to and measured by the standards of mainstream media celebrity. To their way of thinking, the marker of success for YouTube participants is their ability to "pass through the gate-keeping mechanisms of old media—the recording contract, the film festival, the television pilot, the advertising deal" (Burgess and Green 2009, 23–24). Using this model, there are only a small number of Asian Americans who have achieved such crossover success. One example might be Kevin Wu when he was a contestant on Season 7 on the CBS program *The Amazing Race* along with his first-generation Chinese father. Michelle Phan has undoubtedly made the most of her crossover efforts, becoming the official video makeup artist with Lancome and launching her own beauty line EM with L'Oreal, as well as starring in television commercials for Dr. Pepper.

But even so, in its first ten years YouTube cannot be said to have served as a dependable means for people to transition to a career in the mainstream media. Rather, it would be more accurate to describe the Asian Americans participating on YouTube as creating a counterpublic that makes no effort to appeal to a mainstream audience. Although few of the conversations happening on YouTube are explicitly political or even related to Asian American identities, these channels nonetheless serve as a space where Asian Americans can communicate with one another. All five of the YouTubers examined here frequently discuss the pleasure of participating in building their own community by making and sharing videos. When asked how she manages to accumulate so many hits, Michelle Phan explained:

> You just really have to have a two way conversation with people who are watching your stuff. Because traditional media, it was just a one way street. With new media, when you're watching the content, you start seeing all these comments from other viewers. And that in itself creates a new content too. Sometimes they're debating, sometimes they're adding value, sometimes they're just adding just funny comments. (Wall Street Journal 2012)

This interactive, participatory aspect of YouTube reminds us that the site is not simply pushing content onto its audience; it is creating a space for having a conversation about the videos where viewers can express their own opinions alongside Phan's. Internet communities like those circulating around these Asian American stars on YouTube enable participants to discuss and develop their identities away from the public eye. As theorists like Nancy Fraser (1990) and Catherine Palczewski (2001) have argued, subaltern counterpublics play an important role in creating identities for disenfranchised groups, serving to "enable marginal groups to overcome the discursive barriers to participation because, by definition, they expand discursive space and provide discursive systems counter to those that exist" (Palczewski 2001, 169). Although the potential for emancipation can be limited by barriers to access—and the internet is certainly not accessible to all Asian Americans—the existence of these participatory cultures provides opportunities for conversation, skills training, and identity development precisely because they are not connected to the mainstream media. In this arena, Asian Americans are able to articulate their own perspectives and participate in the formation of new interpretive frames, regardless of whether or not this kind of content appeals to a broader audience.

We must also consider the possibility that not all artists, producers, and media personalities are seeking to make the transition to mainstream media. Asian American YouTubers often discuss the fact that online media offer something different and desirable—an untapped community, the potential to disseminate media for free, and a space to build long-term connections with their viewers. The creators of Wong Fu discussed their relationship to mainstream media in one interview:

> For a while we were in the online world and we were trying to figure out how to get to the mainstream world. But now you see everyone's trying to come this way . . . [now] we're figuring out how to balance both. We are working in the mainstream world but at the same time YouTube online is where it's really headed and we know we have to keep our footing and presence there. (Triton Television 2014)

Thus they have come to seek a balance between different projects rather than abandoning the online modes of creation and dissemination that brought them success. They are also looking to build a sustained career—not simply the widespread fame of a single "viral video," but the stability that comes from having connected to the same community for years, as all these YouTubers have done.

Beyond the opportunities that online media offer, it must also be noted that the mainstream media is a historically racist, sexist, homophobic industry that has long ostracized and mistreated Asian Americans. Given the many difficulties that Asian American actors and producers face, these Asian American YouTubers are excited to participate in a media subculture that offers them more autonomy and less public glare, and that speaks more directly to their community. Although racism is certainly prevalent online, YouTubers often speak fondly of the strength of support from their communities and the lack of racism they have encountered. In fact, they rarely speak about racism, instead choosing to focus on the positive aspects of their participation in online spaces. Chung stated in an interview, "As far as music goes, I haven't felt any stigma, put downs, or obstacles for being Korean or Asian. . . . I feel really accepted." Similarly, while an early video by Wu did allude to the fact that he received a lot of racist comments on his videos, this was done in a humorous way without suggesting that racism had held him back in the online arena.

This lack of discussion of meaningful experiences of racism is even more interesting in light of the honest, confessional tone so character-istically deployed on YouTube. Unlike the more glamorous world of mainstream celebrities where professional studios and flashy produc-tion values create symbolic barriers between viewers and stars, amateur productions on YouTube emphasize a DIY aesthetic marked by both sincerity and accessibility. Many stars who have become famous on You-Tube make videos about their own lives, rather than playing characters or taking on fictional roles. Their pointed lack of monetary reward or mainstream success allows them to remain someone "just like you and me" rather than a distant, inaccessible star. As Kevin Wu stated in an interview:

> The goal is . . . to keep sharing my life with my audience. I think that's why people watch my videos, it's because I'm very honest and I'm very personal with them. It's scary for a lot of entertainers, like Hollywood celebrities, to make a video and share so much about them, they like to close people off. But I love YouTube because I use it to bring people in, to get for people to know me and me to get to know people. (Asians on Film 2012)

Like Wu, Higa also capitalizes on his ability to pull back the curtain, so to speak—in 2011, he created a second channel called "HigaTV" that provides a space for posting behind-the-scenes videos and humorous outtakes. Kelli Burns argues that much of the appeal of user-generated videos on YouTube can be connected to a frustration with scripted tele-vision, even so-called reality television, which leads viewers to seek something that seems "more organic, more natural, more real" (Burns 2009, 63). While I would not want to imply that YouTube celebri-ties are in fact more "authentic" than actors or even reality television stars—particularly given that their highly edited video creations are performances, offering merely one construction of themselves—the majority of Asian American YouTubers do seem to want to portray themselves from their personal perspective and much of their content is based around experiences that they purport to have actually had. Even when Asian American YouTubers participate in fictionalized or scripted stories, as in the case of Wong Fu Productions, they always accompany these videos with explanations in which they speak directly into the camera in a way that seems designed to represent their own experiences. This focus on the true, personal stories of Asian American YouTubers, coupled with the absence of any sort of media industry infrastructure that might distance the creators from their fans (such as handlers, agents, PR professionals, or even technical assistants and crew) serves to highlight the control that each individual YouTuber wields over the images that he or she shares.

The Politics of Participating in YouTube

Yet the failure of popular YouTubers to call attention to racism brings us back to a discussion of the political project of participating in You-Tube. In many ways, the site's ability to allow Asian Americans to share their own stories is a remediation of the work of the Asian American independent filmmakers and community media centers described in this chapter's introduction. Like independent filmmakers, Asian American YouTubers are working to create and disseminate representations of Asian Americans and increase the control they have over their own images. Within the online world, these particular Asian Americans have become highly visible and they now have the opportunity to articulate their own perspectives and realities. This cultural work is arguably political because it renders Asian American identities legible and disseminates Asian American narratives and voices.

Although these outcomes are aligned with those desired by Asian American media activists, it is not clear that these Asian American You-Tube celebrities themselves are activists. In fact, the impact of their participation is often explicitly unintentional, as evidenced in interviews in which they state that their participation in YouTube is motivated by a desire for personal success or entertainment rather than social justice. This intention is regularly reiterated, as Asian American YouTube celebrities are most commonly framed as entrepreneurs rather than activists. Authors and interviewers praise them for their success in terms of page views and fan adulation, while the YouTubers themselves consistently avoid discussions of political intentions or connections to activism. This apolitical orientation is particularly visible in an interview about one of Wong Fu's videos called *Yellow Fever*, which addresses the issue of interracial relationships. When asked about the politics of the film, founder Phil Wang responded:

> I think it's really funny because when we went to make it, we just thought it would be something fun to show, something funny that people talk and laugh about. We didn't think of it as "tackling" the subject and stereotypes, and we certainly didn't have a political stance. We never really thought it would make that much social impact. We just hope people don't read too much into it because we didn't make it with that intention. But we do know that there are a lot of Asian American studies programs out there that use it as course material. I just think that's hilarious! (Chie 2008)

In his response Wang deliberately positions himself in opposition to any sort of political stance, firmly identifying as an artist instead of an activist. Given that my definition of activism requires intentionality, statements like these affirm their desire to be seen as entrepreneurs, not activists. Their project has been to identify a unique need and fill it; in creating Asian American content they have been able to entertain Asian American audiences and disseminate Asian American content, but they did not seek to contribute to social reform or to right a social wrong. Although in later interviews members of Wong Fu Productions do note that they have taken up the responsibility of contributing to representing Asian Americans because they recognize that the mainstream media does not adequately do so, this political orientation is always described as something that was forced onto them by their fans and was never their original intention. In contrast, they consistently profess their discomfort with this responsibility and often turn the conversation to how they could never represent all Asian Americans and only seek to tell the stories that interest them.

Mobilizing Fans for Social Change

Despite a stated orientation toward nonactivism, in many ways YouTube celebrities are still striving for cultural citizenship by uniting and mobilizing communities of Asian Americans—moving beyond their own self-commodification to causes larger than their individual fame. We have already noted that their work in creating images of Asian Americans is productively aligned with the goals of media activists and the long history of Asian American cinema. But we can also consider their ability to mobilize their base as a way of activating the collective citizenry of Asian America. If we can call these YouTubers famous, this fame is the result of their being able to draw responses from millions of followers without any assistance from well-established promotional industries. There were no expensive advertising campaigns plastering their faces on billboards, no scheduled interviews with talk shows or entertainment tabloids, no arena tours or corporate tie-ins. Rather, it is simply the talent and personality of the performers that compels their fans to subscribe to their channel, buy tickets to see them in person, and respond with their support. In this sense, each of these celebrities is an adept mobilizer who participates in creating and shaping an Asian American collective that can be called upon to take action. Although in many cases this ability to mobilize their fans is simply used to increase hits to their own websites, sometimes it has also been seen to connect with social issues.

One example of the way Asian American YouTube celebrities deploy their social influence is to collect money for charitable causes. In 2009, Wu created a second channel called JumbaFund. Since YouTube pays channels with large subscriber bases, Wu could post his signature humorous videos on the second channel and collect money for charities such as earthquake relief in Haiti or habitat conservation for animals. In 2013, he raised $50,000 through this site and some additional fundraising, and was able to construct and operate a secondary school in Nairobi named KevJumba High School (Wu 2013). Others have undertaken similar charitable endeavors—Phan has a second channel called "RiceBunny" that directs its profits toward charities, and Wong Fu Productions holds regular charity events such as basketball tournaments, dance contests, and charity auctions. Chung frequently mentions her passion for fighting autism and human trafficking in her interviews.

We see from these examples that some Asian American YouTube stars are contributing toward a good cause, which demonstrates a creative use of their ability to mobilize their fans for reasons other than stoking their own fame. In doing so, Asian American YouTubers are following in the footsteps of the many mainstream celebrities who also deploy their celebrity toward charitable causes. In fact, as long as there have been celebrities they have engaged in philanthropic and charitable work. Alison Trope (Trope 2012) notes that stars "are reminded of the symbolic, and in turn, commercial value of giving and encouraged to pursue public displays of charity and altruism" (158). In her analysis of Angelina Jolie as a Hollywood star who publicly participates in both charitable and activist efforts, she argues that we should be careful not to naively celebrate these acts. Although a star's efforts toward philanthropy or charity can be understood as altruistic, these efforts can often be criticized for falling into quick fix, overly simplistic approaches or for highjacking a cause with a one-sided perspective. Nevertheless, as Trope argues, the participation of celebrities in charity work does indeed have the potential to change the public perception of those causes and is reflective of a long history of the complicated interplay between celebrities and philanthropy.

For Asian American celebrities, supporting a charity or nonprofit demonstrates one way to mobilize their fans into civic action—by turning their participation (their viewership) into monetary donations for a charity or by encouraging their viewers to donate directly. This mobilization is a commendable use of their social power, but we must also note that charity is not the same as activism. Charity has often been critiqued for focusing on emergency relief or local causes, in contrast to activist work toward reform at the broader cultural level or concrete policy changes (Poppendieck 1998; King 2004). While charity assists the victims of social injustice, activism attacks the root cause of the injustice. Moreover, causes for activism can often be risky and unpopular— activists call attention to systemic inequalities and the ugly consequences of oppression, and urge people toward societal change rather than a one-time fix. Indeed, discussions of race in the United States are often seen

as polarizing and taboo, making antiracist activism a much more challenging undertaking than charity.

It is clear from these examples that Asian American online celebrities
are being careful not to alienate any of their core fan base by taking on a
cause that is even remotely controversial or risky. Yet the consequence of
this choice to focus on charity rather than activism is that conversations
about racism become sublimated and there is no intentional engagement with the politics of representation for Asian Americans. Instead,
they disavow an activist identity and focus their social contributions towards charitable causes that veer from the world of media activism or
any number of issues rooted in systemic racism—such as Asian American poverty, drug use, homophobia, mental illness, or gang violence.
Of course there is no reason to insist that all Asian Americans take up
any of these issues, or that they must necessarily become activists. But
I seek to more clearly differentiate between the work of participating in
Asian American media projects and participating in Asian American
media activism. Rather than uncritically lumping every form of media
participation together as activism, it is important to pay attention to the
specific work undertaken by these YouTubers with a view to its contribution to systemic change in the media industries. Here, I argue that it
is not their contributions to charity that mark them as activists but their
creation of a base of participants who can be called upon to take action
as a collective.

In facilitating the identification of an Asian American subaltern
counterpublic through their media making, these Asian American You-
Tube celebrities do contribute to some of the goals of media activists.
What this examination of YouTube celebrities helps to illuminate is the
fact that not all celebrities who gain fame through the media are interested in the politics of visibility or the specific goals of media activism.
Rather, through the work of Asian American YouTube celebrities we can
see that the broader project of representational change for Asian Americans in the media needs to be understood as a complicated undertaking
in which both activists and nonactivists play a part. Only by clarifying
these distinctions and more accurately assessing how activists seek to
contribute to social change can we more productively, and collectively,
work toward those goals.

YouTube as a Bridge between Independent and Mainstream Media

While YouTube celebrities are already working in a collective mode through their mobilization for larger social causes, they are building connections between different communities in other important ways. Indeed, the celebrities on YouTube are just one node in an interconnected network of multiple forms of media that includes Asian American independent cinema and more mainstream film and television. Although Asian Americans on YouTube may struggle to use their videos to make their way into mainstream media, their images do not exist in complete isolation from other forms of media. YouTube celebrities work in many ways to create bridges between differently mediated communities of practice—specifically, between mainstream media, independent media, and online media. They are active in a wide number of transmedia endeavors beyond their own YouTube channels that together form part of a larger political project. As YouTube celebrities team up and take on collaborative transmedia projects, they create bridges between established and emerging forms of media. These bridges do more than create pathways for media creators to traverse; they also provide opportunities to more meaningfully engage with Asian American audiences. This act of identifying and uniting a collective Asian American audience further contributes to their ability to mobilize individuals, but also importantly connects to the work of Asian American advertising agencies described in the previous chapter to develop Asian American consumer-citizens. When Asian American audiences are collectively interpellated, they can take action together to support Asian American media projects.

One organization that demonstrates the way these bridges are built and utilized is the blogging community at You Offend Me You Offend My Family (YOMYOMF). YOMYOMF is a pop culture group blog started in the summer of 2009 by filmmaker Justin Lin and some of his friends and colleagues from the entertainment industry. The contributors include filmmakers, actors, writers, festival programmers, producers, and writers. Together they represent a wide range of industry affiliations, although they blog using only their first names and generally discuss humorous topics rather than industry information. Lin plays a somewhat controversial role in the world of Asian American film, given the course of his career. His first feature film *Better Luck Tomorrow* embodied the spirit of Asian American independent filmmaking—Lin funded the project on a shoestring budget and cast previously unknown Asian American talent. When the film was acquired by MTV Films and debuted to rave reviews at the Sundance Film Festival, Lin's career began to take a different trajectory. His next two films—*Annapolis* and *The Fast and the Furious: Tokyo Drift*—were decidedly mainstream fare, and his reputation as a sought-after Hollywood director continued to grow. Although he received some flak from the Asian American community for his failure to introduce more Asian American actors and content into his blockbusters, he continued to carefully balance his projects between big pictures and small independent Asian American fare. *Finishing the Game*, a low-budget mockumentary, comically explores a producer's hunt for a replacement for Bruce Lee. The phrase "You offend me, you offend my family" is used to audition each actor for the role, and is used to great comic effect in the film as each actor must give his or her own rendering of the line.

The use of this phrase as the title for the YOMYOMF website is a nod to Lin's efforts to embrace the Asian American community even as it fails to support him—with a budget of $500,000 *Finishing the Game* only made around $50,000 at the box office. This box office failure prompted Lin to write the blog post on YOMYOMF titled, "Am I 'retarded' for making Asian American films?" that I discussed in chapter 3. The blunt provocation headlining Lin's blog entry marks yet another important aspect of the YOMYOMF website—it creates a space for Asian American industry insiders to tell their own stories about their struggles, to debate the challenges of Asian American representation, and to initiate wider conversations about the work they are doing. In this way, YOMYOMF offers an interactive space for its fans and readers to learn about and participate in conversations about media representation. Bloggers, or "Offenders," as they like to call themselves, often participate in lengthy debates with their readers through the comments section, particularly with regard to serious media issues.

The YOMYOMF community intersected with YouTube in 2012 when YouTube launched its Original Channel Initiative—a $100 million dollar program funded by Google to launch a hundred new video channels.

The initiative was part of Google's plans to create more content to rival television. Among those Google approached to launch a funded channel were three Asian American YouTube celebrities—Ryan Higa, Kevin Wu, and Chester See. Instead of starting their own channel, they partnered with YOMYOMF to start a channel called "The YOMYOMF Network." On June 4, 2012, the channel was launched with a humorous video called "It Has Begun: the Bananapocalypse." The video ostensibly served to introduce the channel and its origins, featuring many members of the YOMYOMF community alongside the YouTube celebrities mentioned above. KevJumba takes viewers along a stroll through the YOMYOMF backlot, introducing the dozens of people working on the new channel. Yet its featured participants include much more than internet stars—it also features cameos from mainstream media, including Jessica Alba, Wayne Brady, Parvesh Cheena, Jamie Chung, Tyrese Gibson, Gillian Jacobs, Masi Oka, Harry Shum Jr., and others.

The use of such a wide, diverse cast of celebrities who hail from film, television, and YouTube begins to blur the boundaries between the different kinds of celebrities. They appear to seamlessly work together in the fictional space of the YOMYOMF backlot. Although these media professionals have never actually worked together, the illusion this video creates is that they all have something in common—that they are all part of the YOMYOMF network. Anderson Le, one of the founders of YOMYOMF, explains that their commitment to blending mainstream and online media goes much deeper:

> In traditional spaces there has been a paradigm shift when it comes to content. A lot of established writers and directors and actors within the Hollywood system are interested in engaging with an audience by thinking outside the traditional box. We want to provide an opportunity for people who are already established in the system to work with people who work in the online space. It's about breaking the barriers between the traditional Hollywood system and the DIY spirit of the online space. (Le 2014)

Le's comments show that their common interest in utilizing digital media provides a bridge between the Hollywood system and YouTubers. As a result, the YOMYOMF network provides professionals from the

The first video posted to the YouTube channel YOMYOMF was called "It Has Begun: The Bananapocalypse" and featured an array of YouTube stars like KevJumba and mainstream media professionals like Justin Lin working together on a single backlot.

more traditional Hollywood system an opportunity to work alongside well-established YouTubers—many of whom had never before been paid for their videos. These relationships are of course facilitated by the funding from Google, who hoped to turn a profit from investing in the talent and ready-made fan base of popular YouTubers. From this we can begin to see that the possibilities for change lie at the intersection of mainstream and online media. YOMYOMF provides financial and artistic support for the creation and development of Asian American content. This content finds a home in either the online or the mainstream realm, but through its association with the YOMYOMF brand it already begins to break down the barriers between these different institutional realms.

The community at YOMYOMF has been dedicated to building these bridges in several other ways as well. In 2010, YOMYOMF launched an initiative called Interpretations. It began with a contest in which aspiring filmmakers were given the same brief script from which to create their own original short film. A panel of judges reviewed the works and featured a select number of films on their website. Five finalists received a cash prize for their next project, a subscription to the *Writers Guild of America Magazine,* and the promise of mentorship within the industry to help them network and improve their craft. By featuring these films YOMYOMF helps Asian American filmmakers reach a broader audience. YOMYOMF also adopted this model of mentorship and project development at the 2013 Hawaii International Film Festival. The festival's New Media Academy invited six young, Hawaii-based filmmakers to produce videos in a forty-eight-hour window. The videos were featured in a special presentation and the participants were mentored by filmmakers working in traditional media and by YouTube content producers. The best videos were posted to the YOMYOMF YouTube channel and the film festival's Vimeo channel. Importantly, these initiatives bridge not only mainstream and online media, but the film festival world as well—both programs launched from the site of Asian American film festivals, where filmmakers and audiences were already gathered together in order to talk about where Asian American media was heading. These kinds of initiatives illustrate even more clearly the connections being created between Asian American independent media, digital media, and mainstream media.

This examination of YOMYOMF points to the different ways that media convergence has impacted the centrality of mainstream media industries. Under the logic of convergence culture (Jenkins 2006a), we must recognize the multiple media platforms audiences are using to access content—in particular, the growth of web TV, streaming media, and online content. Given the difficulties Asian Americans face in finding steady work in the mainstream media industries, organizations like YOMYOMF have begun to innovate and take advantage of these alternative sites for media production and consumption. The initiatives described here help develop Asian American talent in the media arts while creating new opportunities for Asian American content to gain visibility and connect with audiences. While we may have formerly assumed that only a job in mainstream film and television could play this role, websites like YouTube and Vimeo, Asian American film festivals, and blogs are now being used in a number of different ways. But we must also recognize the central role of Asian American celebrities in creating these new spaces for content and engagement. Only by coming together as a community in synergistic moments such as "The Bananapocalypse" or in the deployment of director Justin Lin's celebrity to back Asian American media initiatives can these bridges be developed.

Wong Fu Productions and the Value of Interactivity

Beyond the work of YOMYOMF, the YouTubers described earlier are also creating bridges between different media worlds by relying on the affordances of YouTube as an interactive platform. In 2008, Wong Fu Productions started collaborating with the pop music group Far*East Movement—the first Asian American group to break into the Billboard Top 10 Chart with their song "Like a G6." Together they created a concert series called ISA (International Secret Agents) that traveled to LA, San Francisco, and New York and featured Asian American artists, musicians, and YouTube celebrities. This gave the viewers of Wong Fu Productions a chance to move from the online world to a live performance starring their favorite Asian American celebrities. The blend of online and offline interactions is characteristic of each of the YouTube celebrities discussed thus far; all those who gained fame through their digital performance have also parlayed their career into a series of college campus visits, panel discussions, serving as MCs at special occasions, or simply showing up at events to engage with fans.

These offline engagements then connect back to the development of new online ventures. In 2011, the International Secret Agents' live tour became a YouTube channel called ISAtv. Although it predates the YOMYOMF network by a little, it has not had the same kind of funding from Google and has thus developed at a much slower pace. Nevertheless, the networks formed through these different avenues of Asian American cultural production come together to form a common language using the online space provided by YouTube. As with YOMYOMF, the success of ISA has relied on the deployment of Asian American celebrities and the creation of bridges between the realms of mainstream, online, and independent media. Yet the story of ISA and its work also reveals the potential for utilizing Asian American popular culture more broadly to call upon Asian American audiences to play a role in asserting their own cultural citizenship.

One of the aspects of ISA's live performances that contributes to creating this kind of cultural citizenship is its focus on Asian American dance crews. Asian American hip hop crews first became visible on the MTV program *Randy Jackson Presents: America's Best Dance Crew*. The dance competition show invited amateur hip hop dance groups to compete for the title of "America's Best Dance Crew" through weekly choreography and performance challenges. But it quickly became clear that there was a common element to the most successful crews—year after year, it was the predominantly Asian American crews who finished on top. As one blogger wrote, "Nearly every crew on America's Dance Crew has had at least one API member. It's interesting that American's Best Dance Crew is full of Asian Americans. So really should the show be called Asian America's Best Dance Crew?" (Nguyen 2009). From the Jabbawockees to Kaba Modern to Super Cr3w, Quest Crew, and Poreotics, Asian American crews were consistently the most popular with voting audiences and the judges. While this trend is due in part to the talent and charm of Asian American crews, it also reflects the participation of Asian Americans in voting for and supporting the crews. As with many competition reality shows, voting audiences play a role in determining the outcome of the competition, and the strong fan base of Asian American dance crews and their eager participation in voting clearly played a role in the continuation of this racialized trend.

The highlighting of Asian bodies in mediated representations of dance stands in stark contrast to the standard racialization of dance in the United States, which has largely been viewed through the lens of a black/white binary. Like all cultural forms that have been shaped through the institutional and cultural processes of racism, dance has been viewed as a centrally white cultural form. As Brenda Dixon Gottschild argues, white forms of dance are the norm, but the increasing presence of "black" forms of dance such as African dance, hip hop, and jazz have indelibly impacted the way we view dance. As she states, "the black dancing body (a fiction based on reality, a fact based on illusion) has infiltrated and informed the shapes and changes of the American dancing body" (Gottschild 2003, 14). These racialized distinctions are often posited between the realms of the merely black and white. The rise of Latin forms of dance, particularly within the realm of ballroom, have begun to disrupt this black/white binary. But in the absence of a traditionally "Asian" form of dance[3] that could be inserted into the mainstream, what Gottschild might call "the Asian dancing body" has remained invisible and unimaginable, until recently.

The show *Randy Jackson Presents: America's Best Dance Crew* initiated the process of raising awareness of one of many Asian dance

The Asian American hip hop crew Quest Crew won the first season of Randy Jackson's *America's Best Dance Crew*, with many other Asian American crews following its lead.

subcultures—Asian American hip hop. Documentaries like *Planet B-Boy* (2007), which investigates global b-boy culture, and *Among B-Boys* (2011), which focuses on Hmong hip hop culture, demonstrate the existence of a vibrant and thriving culture of hip hop among Asians in the United States and across the globe. The dominance of Asian American crews vying for America's Best Dance Crew has helped to move this conversation into more mainstream venues, where Asian Americans can more visibly acknowledge their participation in this beloved cultural form and claim it as their own. In fact, in 2010 an online rumor began to circulate that Randy Jackson was banning all-Asian crews from the show. As Phil Yu from Angry Asian Man reported, the email being passed around quoted Jackson as saying:

> The crews from the past four seasons have been dominated by prominently Asian members, leading to their win, with exception to the Season 4 winners, We Are Heroes. Although we are happy for the Jabbawockeez,

Super Cr3w, and Quest Crew, we think it's only right to give other races a
fighting chance within the show. (Yu 2010)

In the post, Yu told his readers that he was "100 percent sure that this
ridiculous rumor is completely false," and there was no evidence of the
rumor's claims. Yet the widespread sharing of such a rumor is nevertheless indicative of the enthusiasm evoked by the success of Asian
American dance and its place in the spotlight. Asian Americans who
were part of dance crews—just like those who had become popular on
YouTube—gained visibility and a minor brand of celebrity status from
fans of the show.

The growing popularity of Asian American dance performers provided the perfect opportunity for the ISA tour, which merged the fans
of Wong Fu Production's YouTube channel, Far East Movement's music,
and *America's Best Dance Crew* on MTV. But in a transmediated environment, this fervent participation by Asian American fans and audiences
could be deployed in a number of different ways beyond simply eliciting
votes. In particular, Wong Fu Productions created a number of video
projects that connected the development of Asian American audiences
through these celebrities' fans to the interactivity of participatory cultures created online. Just as Asian American YouTubers are periodically
invited to participate in charitable endeavors, Asian American participants online were invited to play a more creative role. In May 2012 Wong
Fu Productions produced a video series called "Away We Happened"
that exemplified many of these strategies for taking advantage of shifting
media practices—the combination of Asian American stars from different kinds of media, the interactivity of YouTube, and the instrumentality
of nascent fandoms. First, the video starred two nonactors—Jen Chae of
frmheadtotoe, a popular YouTube beauty channel, and Victor Wong of
Quest Crew, a winning team from *America's Best Dance Crew*. The first
video of the series tells the story of how the two characters accidentally
switch bags before heading their separate ways, and end up learning
about each other in the process of getting their bags back. At the end
of the first episode, viewers see the character Jean writing a letter and
they are presented with two questions: "How should Jean respond?" and
"Who is the letter for?" Viewers are then directed to go to the show's
website and submit their responses to these questions. Each subsequent

episode responds to the ideas that viewers submitted. Wong Fu Productions described the process:

> We've looked through a lot of the comments and have begun writing and preparing for the next episode! Some suggestions make a lot of sense and will help continue the story in a realistic and emotional way . . . and some are just hilariously impossible! But either way, we love the feedback, and this just shows that our fans are super creative and fun! (Wong Fu Productions 2012)

As this comment shows, Wong Fu Productions actively makes use of viewers' comments in the crafting of new episodes, relying on its fans to submit suggestions that are realistic and workable alongside their more humorous or impractical feedback. As described above with *America's Best Dance Crew*, reality television often relies on viewer participation for competition shows like *American Idol* or *So You Think You Can Dance*, where viewers can vote for their favorite contestants (Enli and Ihlebaeck 2011). Yet the quick production time for a YouTube web series makes interactivity possible in order to shape the basic narrative, as viewers can be consulted for input on the direction of the plot. This interactive strategy produces a number of favorable outcomes. First, as with all participatory cultures (Jenkins et al. 2006), viewers are recognized as meaningful participants in the process of content creation, wherein their contributions really matter and are taken seriously. But this strategy also produces deeper engagement with the video within a condensed timeframe—viewers are rewarded for watching the videos right away while their contributions are still being accepted, rather than waiting for the series to be completed. This contributes to a sense of collaboration and engagement that helps to create a more meaningful role for Asian American viewers or users.

The same strategies were put to use in another video series called "When It Counts," which was produced by Wong Fu Productions in November 2012. Underscoring the success of its previous strategy, this video also relies on a cast of Asian American dance celebrities—this time, Yuri Tag and Mike Song from *America's Best Dance Crew*'s Kaba Modern, and choreographers Aimee Lee Lucas and Anthony Lee. The story revolves around the world of dance, exploring the relationships between four friends on a college hip hop team. It is also noteworthy that both "When It Counts" and "Away We Happened" are scored by Asian American YouTube musicians, Paul Dateh and Kina Grannis. This strategy of uniting multiplatform performers and calling upon viewer participation is part of a larger movement to develop Asian American audiences—which, as explored in the previous chapter, contributes to the goal of media activists who are reframing Asian Americans as powerful consumers. By recognizing fans of specific YouTube artists or dance crews and enlisting them to play an active role in the creative process, these transmedia activities are working to shape Asian America as a brand. Those who participate in these activities feel part of a vibrant, thriving collective, united in their goal of supporting the media arts, contributing in a way that matters, and making their voices heard—all under the unifying umbrella of Asian America.

Uses of Intertextuality to Develop Asian American Audiences

This focus on fostering the development of interconnected performers and communities stands in contrast to the singularity of the celebrity. It is certainly the case that all the people I call Asian American YouTube celebrities have become personally successful through the skillful development of self-brands (other than Wong Fu Productions, which achieved celebrity as a trio). Each YouTube celebrity excels in his or her own genre, which includes comedy, dance, music, makeup, and video production. In this way, each Asian American YouTube celebrity clearly stands alone—each channel is definitively his or her own, often with no oversight or input from so much as an additional camera operator. But if we are interested in how these individuals connect to the larger project of Asian American media activism and a collective form of cultural citizenship, I argue that it is through the deliberate manner in which they connect to one another, as described thus far. This includes everything from bringing fellow stars onto their own channel's programming to participation in the kinds of collaborative projects mentioned here—live shows, musical performances, game shows, dances, movies, talk shows, and more. Together, these partnerships serve as a form of transmedia branding that helps to create and grow Asian American audiences. The celebrity of each individual grows stronger as he or she interacts with and creates new media with other YouTube celebrities. Fans of one celebrity can tune in to see one of their favorite personalities, and in the process be introduced to other celebrities worth following.

The collaborative YouTube channels YOMYOMF and ISAtv both provide ample opportunities for this kind of transmedia branding, as the channels themselves rely on the synergy of multiple celebrities coming together to sustain their own popularity. Both channels resist focusing on any one celebrity in favor of creating opportunities for cross-genre celebrities to interact. The show "ISA! Variety Game Show" on ISAtv provides a strong example of this. Starring an incredibly diverse cast of YouTube personalities from every genre,[4] the show is based on wacky Japanese game shows. As the host Ted Wang explains, these are the kinds of media "we grew up watching, or our parents watched." The use of this genre itself is a move toward creating a common Asian American culture, as we see in Wang's statement. Japanese game shows are popular with wide swathes of American audiences, as evidenced by the game shows *I Survived a Japanese Game Show* and *Wipeout!*, which was based on Japanese shows such as *Takeshi's Castle, Most Extreme Elimination Challenge*, and *Ninja Warrior*.[5] But in Ted's introduction to ISA! Variety Game Show we see that Asian American viewers are familiar with this genre of programming from having watched them in their original form, rather than the American dubbed versions. His explanation clearly assumes the presence of a pan-ethnic Asian American audience through the idea of a shared culture.

The genre of the game show provides a level playing ground, so to speak, for each of the individual celebrities. Yet as the game unfolds, the host makes a nod to each celebrity's individual talents. For instance, when hostess Amy Okuda heads down the line to introduce each contestant, she stops by Jen and says, "You're so pretty." This line makes more sense to viewers who already know that Jen is a makeup guru who regularly parades her perfectly groomed visage on YouTube. Similarly, one of the challenges asks participants to list which dance craze is most popular. When professional dancer and choreographer Mike Song guesses Gangnam Style and the Macarena, the host coos, "We just want to watch you dance," and invites him to perform each of the dances for the viewers.

While the show is funny on its own merits, viewers who are familiar with each of the celebrities will be rewarded with extra knowing glances

The ISA! Variety Game Show brings together a diverse assortment of Asian American YouTube personalities and uses intertextuality to create a kind of transmedia branding that benefits all the performers.

due to its intertextuality. The assumption that viewers are aware of this intertextuality is further emphasized through a game that requires audience participation via a Google Plus Hangout. Although some of the questions asked of audience members could be answered by anyone (as in "Who is your favorite Pokemon character?"), one of the questions is, "Who do you think has the highest SAT score?" This question is premised on the assumption that the viewers know something about the YouTube celebrity players. Indeed, the most common answer is Freddie Wong, whose YouTube oeuvre belies an incredibly technical set of skills. Wong's videos typically utilize complicated special effects, green screen technology, and digital manipulation, while many of the other celebrities simply talk into the camera or deploy skills in less technical arenas such as makeup or singing.

Beyond the assumption that viewers are already familiar with the individual performers, the decision to create programming that features the thirteen stars together reaffirms the statement by the YOMYOMF "Bananapocalypse" video—these Asian American celebrities share one thing in common, namely, their identity as Asian Americans. Clearly genre is unimportant in the world of YouTube Asian American celebrities, as makeup artists and guitar players and comedians all belong to one larger collective—the YouTube celebrity collective. If there is anyone with whom the audience is unfamiliar, the video directs them to click on the person's YouTube or Twitter sites and thus be introduced to his or her work. Given that all YouTube celebrities are not, in fact, equal— some have multimillion dollar contracts on account of their popularity while others are just starting out with small fan bases—this kind of transmedia branding raises the profile of the less successful celebrities through association. Viewers can begin to think of little-known actor Ally Maki in the same league as comedian KevJumba, whose fame has permitted him to successfully partner with mainstream media entities like NBC for his role in *The Amazing Race*.

This synergistic impact of bringing lesser-known performers into the spotlight alongside more famous performers can also work in reverse with Asian Americans who are in mainstream media. Many celebrities who have become famous on YouTube partner with Asian Americans who work in mainstream film, such as Justin Chon and Jamie Chung. Chon played Eric Yorkie in the *Twilight* saga and was one of the stars of the hit teen comedy *21 and Over*, which was written by the same writers as *The Hangover*. Actress Jamie Chung, who has been in movies such as *Sucker Punch, The Hangover Part II, Grown Ups*, and the NBC show *Once Upon a Time*, also participates in occasional YouTube projects with this same cohort of YouTube celebrities. Importantly, these intersections between mainstream media and YouTube are facilitated by the celebrities themselves rather than by any larger media corporation hoping to promote YouTube talent into mainstream productions. On the contrary, it is the mainstream stars who gain cultural capital with Asian American audiences through these collaborations.

The power of Asian American YouTube celebrities' cultural capital is also clearly highlighted by Jeremy Lin. Professional basketball player Jeremy Lin rocketed to fame in the summer of 2012 when he led the New York Knicks to an unexpected winning streak. The combination of the scarcity of Asian American talent in the NBA with his astonishing rise to prominence culminated in what was colloquially known as "Linsanity"—a worldwide burst of interest in the Taiwanese American Harvard graduate (Ng 2013). Although Jeremy Lin clearly has developed his own fan base from his performance on the court, he has also worked to carefully cultivate his own brand identity. For example, in interviews he frequently discusses his Christian upbringing, his education, and the racism he has faced as an Asian American—three issues that have served as framing devices for understanding Lin's story. Given that these topics are atypical for an NBA player, it is clear that Lin is working to manage his brand rather than sticking to the standard script.

Yet before Linsanity erupted, when Lin was still playing for the Golden State Warriors, he was already working to establish his brand amongst Asian American youth. In August 2011, he started his own YouTube channel under the handle "JLin7." According to Kevin Wu of KevJumba, Lin approached him and asked if they could make videos together. They made a handful for KevJumba's own YouTube channel before Lin started up his own channel. Lin has posted videos ranging from humorous sketches to more serious documentary work, but the first one is very telling—in the two-minute long video called "Youtubing with KevJumba," Lin gets tips from KevJumba on how to connect with an audience using YouTube videos. As KevJumba counsels, "The camera's over here, so what you want to do is be as comfortable in front of the camera as possible. Just talk to it, engage with it. Add some energy, if you're not energized the audience isn't gonna care." Lin fumbles, eventually trying to explain the economic crisis as he awkwardly addresses the camera. The video is humorous in tone and Lin plays the role of complete newbie, making it clear that KevJumba is the expert in shaping a YouTube persona and garnering a YouTube fan base—even to a professional athlete who later single-handedly caused the stock of the New York Knicks to rise 6.2 percent and sold thousands of jerseys bearing his name (Tuttle 2012). The deliberate forging of a connection between Lin and Wu demonstrates an important tactic for individual Asian American stars to create value and audience recognition beyond the limits of their individual brands.

Modeling Political YouTube: The Fung Brothers

The work of these YouTube celebrities clearly illustrates a number of cultural effects. First, we see the development of public figures who can communicate different ideas about what it means to be Asian American. The concept of visibility is of vital importance because if we cannot see a

NBA star Jeremy Lin plays to Asian American youth audiences by partnering with You-Tube star Kevin Wu (KevJumba) in a number of comic videos. In this video, Wu is jealous of Lin's relationship with Wu's Dad, "Papa Jumba."

minority population or hear from them about their lives and experiences in their own words, then their inclusion and participation as cultural citizens of our imagined nation becomes difficult or even impossible. By providing a venue for more Asian Americans to become hypervisible, even if only within their own community, YouTube creates more opportunities for them to better articulate their own perspectives and realities. Asian American narratives about falling in love or making new friends, and performances of Asian American hip hop dance, comedic game shows, and the wide diversity of content represented on You-Tube present different perspectives on what it means to grow up Asian American. The work of Asian American YouTubers is also connected to media activism through their claiming of artistic control. As with Asian American filmmakers and those who screen their work in Asian American film festivals, YouTubers share a commitment to claiming their identities, stories, and voices as their own—free from the influences of mainstream media's gatekeepers and institutional structures.

Although it is often difficult to find explicit political action in the cohort of Asian American YouTube celebrities described thus far, this is not to say that such work does not exist anywhere on YouTube. The Fung Brothers provide an interesting example, blending entertainment and comedy with explicitly political intentions. The comedy duo first became popular in May 2012 with their rap video singing the praises of the "626," the area code of the San Gabriel Valley. As the video describes it, the San Gabriel Valley is a neighborhood fifteen minutes east of Los Angeles dominated by Asian immigrants and known for its thriving food culture. Follow-up songs such as "Bobalife," describing the late-night culture of milk tea popular with Asian American teens, further illustrated their ability to tap into Asian American cultural norms. Their channel "Fung Brothers Comedy" began with significantly fewer fans than those of the YouTube celebrities described earlier; while in 2014 KevJumba and NigaHiga had upward of 5 million subscribers, the Fung Brothers were nearing 200,000. In an interview with *Tofu Magazine*, they spoke about how they view their own online popularity:

> YouTube has given us a voice and a vehicle to showcase our thoughts, music and personality. I would definitely say we are part of the "Asian YouTube community" although we are smaller (subscriber wise). Other artists know who we are, especially in SoCal. (Tung 2013)

They are remarkably similar to the genre of comedy deployed by users like KevJumba and NigaHiga—using fast cuts and dramatic inflection, they voice their opinions and tell stories for the clear purpose of entertainment. Part of their signature style includes saying their lines in unison, which adds to the comic effect.

Yet what sets the Fung Brothers apart is the fact that they address issues of identity and even politics in this same comic tone. For instance, in a video called "Internet Hates Lorde's Asian Boyfriend (Asian Response)," they state, "We don't usually make videos about celebrity gossip and stuff, most of the time it doesn't affect our lives. We don't care! But this particular piece of celebrity gossip does affect our lives—Lorde dates an Asian guy! A nerdy Asian guy!" They describe the way New Zealand pop singer Lorde's boyfriend, James Lowe, has been criticized as being "ugly" and making Lorde's fans uncomfortable. They identify this critique as squarely related to race, stating, "It was kind of some racist shit, no one wants to see Asian guys with popular girls!" Then they ask their viewers to comment on whether or not the race of Lorde's boyfriend matters, and what it means to them. Although many YouTube

The Fung Brothers create a humorous YouTube video that explicitly criticizes the racism that manifests in discussions of white pop star Lorde's Asian boyfriend as ugly and undesirable.

videos end with a request for response and interaction, this plea is a call for political discussion about racism and its manifestations. Such explicit description of racism against Asian Americans is indeed rare in the most popular Asian American YouTube channels—yet the Fung Brothers take a political stance without veering away from the genre of comedy. They are able to seamlessly integrate political and activist speech in their comic routine.

The Fung Brothers also ventured into the political realm when they teamed up with the Asian Pacific American Legal Center (APALC). As part of the "Your Vote Matters! 2012" campaign, they created a public service announcement called "Does Your Asian Mom Vote?!" In the video, the brothers are seen asking their mother if she votes. At first the mother says she doesn't vote because it doesn't matter and they should just take care of themselves. But then she starts to imagine a terrible world in which her sons can't get into good schools because funding disappears, or they can't find a wife because the job market is so bad, or what would happen if the San Gabriel Valley were to elect an old white man who didn't care about Asian interests. The video concludes with a message about how to register to vote and where to learn about issues, and offers multilingual voter hotlines in seven different Asian languages. This kind of partnership with an Asian American nonprofit was extremely rare in the early days of the rise of Asian Americans on YouTube, with most performers actively disavowing any sort of political message. Yet the Fung Brothers have been able to blend the struggle for cultural citizenship—through their humorous comedy that stakes a claim to their identities as everyday American youth—alongside the more explicitly political battle for rights such as funding for education, employment, and fair representation.

Conclusion: Gendering Asian American Cultural Citizenship

Although I have demonstrated that Asian American YouTubers are actively asserting multiple forms of cultural citizenship through their video creations and dissemination, I want to conclude by thinking about the intersection between race and gender. It is significant that nearly all the successful Asian Americans discussed in this chapter are men—from the dominant YouTube celebrities like KevJumba, NigaHiga and FreddieW, to the filmmaking trio at Wong Fu Productions, all four members of Far East Movement, the Fung Brothers, and nearly all the dance crews who found success on *America's Best Dance Crew*. In a November 2011 online article entitled "Top 10 Subscribed Asian American YouTube Channel" (Truong 2011), nine of the top ten people mentioned were men—including David So, duo Bart Kwan and Joe Jo, Mychonny, Peter Chao, Wong Fu Productions, Timothy Delaghetto, KevJumba, Freddie Wong, and NigaHiga. The only woman to crack this top ten list was Christine Gambito, or HappySlip, who rose to prominence in the early days of YouTube. The comedian's irreverent impersonations of family members and comic soap operas delighted viewers starting in 2008, but her channel started to fade into obscurity when she took a break from making videos in 2012 to focus on her family. In early 2015, she only had around 600,000 subscribers and was not even ranked in the top one thousand most subscribed videos.

These statistics are not benign; they begin to reveal some of the differential treatment that women receive in online spaces such as YouTube. Lindsey Wotanis and Laurie McMillan (2014) interrogate the underrepresentation of women on YouTube by connecting the gender imbalance to what they call a "hostile online environment" for women and other minorities. Their study focuses on the top male and female YouTube channels—Ryan Higa of NigaHiga and Jenna Mourey of Jenna Marbles. Both offer humorous social commentary and parody videos. When the comments for each channel are compared to one another, it becomes clear that female Mourey receives more hostile comments, which are also more likely to have a sexually aggressive tone. Yet these two top performers are not merely of different genders, but also of different races. While Mourey, who is a white woman, receives critical or hostile feedback in the form of inappropriate sexual comments, Japanese American Higa receives negative feedback that is racist. Higa has addressed this racist feedback in interviews, such as this profile of Higa's channel in *Pacific Citizen*:

> "There are a lot of racists ones," Higa said about the messages he receives. "In every racist comment there are three recurring themes: one mentions my eyes, another mentions 'Chinks.'" The third most common theme in the racist messages is a variation of "Asians don't belong on YouTube." . . . "It doesn't offend me or anything," Higa explained about the racist comments. "I get so many of them that's it not worth responding." (Ko 2009)

Although Wotanis and McMillan (2014) argue that gendered hostile comments are more common than racial ones, we should note that even the most successful Asian American men are subject to a particular form of marginalization and abuse. Again Higa chooses not to linger on the negative consequences of racism, but he cannot deny that racism abounds online.

It stands to reason, then, that Asian American women bear the brunt of this kind of intersectional oppression, suffering from YouTube's hostile climate in terms of both race and gender. This does not mean that Asian American women are never successful, as we can see in the case of Michelle Phan, but these multiple axes of oppression must be considered when looking at the gender divide between Asian American men and women on YouTube. In 2014, Phan was the most popular Asian American woman on YouTube, and her makeup tutorials and discussions of beauty have earned a significant following. Yet Phan has also attracted a loyal cadre of fandom's dark sister—antifans, who regularly post their hate-filled critiques on sites like Guru Gossip, Get Off My

The success of entrepreneur Michelle Phan's extremely popular makeup tutorials on YouTube led to the launching of her own makeup line.

Internets, and others whose name includes the phrase "Michelle Phail." Some might argue that Phan's much-lauded expertise in the realm of beauty invites critique due to its superficial nature. Moreover, we might brush off Phan's success as an Asian American woman because it relies so heavily on upholding the norms of gendered consumption and hegemonic beauty ideals that continue to oppress women of all races. Yet we must also connect her desire to showcase her skills and stories to all the kinds of labor mentioned thus far—including the work of advertising agencies in promoting Asian American consumer citizenship and consumer choice, and the work of Asian American media producers to tell their own stories and promote their own narratives. Phan's choices as an Asian American woman must be recognized as part of the same struggle for cultural citizenship, particularly when she and other minority women face increased hostility and opprobrium as a result of their participation.

The intersection between race and gender in different forms of media activism brings us back to the tension between establishing citizenship at the individual versus the collective level. As Anna Yeatman argues in her discussion of feminism, women have battled to be recognized as citizens. The historical positioning of citizenship as fundamentally linked to the ideal of self-government is itself a patrimonial conception, with women simply fighting for recognition as people capable of self-government. Yet this definition of citizenship was historically embraced by women who were privileged in terms of their race and class; namely, these assumptions may help women who are white and middle class to gain power, but it disregards the realities of those who are not in the same position of privilege. In moving beyond the assumption that self-government qualifies one for citizenship, Yeatman discusses the reconfiguration of citizenship as respect for group rights that include those of "diasporic, non-hegemonic, and fractured identities . . . [refusing] any closure that comes with notions of a singular, bounded and propertied identity of the patrimonial kind" (Yeatman 2001, 149). As the category of "women" encompasses an extremely diverse set of women, some of whom are relatively privileged while others are not, the battle for citizenship must be wide enough to include these different, disparate contingents. Ien Ang connects this reconfiguration of feminism and citizenship to what she calls a "politics of partiality":

> [that] accepts the principle that feminism can never be an encompassing political home for all women, not just because different groups of women have different and sometimes conflicting interests, but, more radically, because for many groups of "other" women other interests, other identifications are sometimes more important and politically pressing than, or even incompatible with, those related to their being women. (Ang 2003, 204)

As Yeatman and Ang show us, the fight for citizenship at the level of the collective is inherently messy, complicated, and contradictory, as no large group of people is completely uniform in its desires, practices, or identities.

Thus the category of Asian American too must be recognized as inherently fractured and diffuse, and the notion of Asian American cultural citizenship cannot be encompassed by any one ideal. We must be open to the possibility that Asian American women must fight for a different kind of citizenship than men, as evidenced by the differential treatment hinted at in this discussion of Asian Americans on You-Tube. An Asian American politics of partiality, as suggested by Ien Ang, might mean that specific identities such as one's gender identity, sexual orientation, ethnicity, or class background could become more salient in differently mediated spheres and communities. The participants in the world of YouTube and Asian American popular culture discussed in this chapter have been largely bounded by age—it is millennials who are currently being recognized by and drawn to the YouTube celebrities described here. Yet their specific form of activism, as demonstrated by their development of active communities of practice, nonetheless connects to the larger political project of reforming media institutions to create space for the broader community of Asian Americans. It is only by recognizing the specificities of these kinds of coalition politics that we can truly describe the landscape encompassed by the term "Asian American."

5

Utilizing Skills and Passion to Spread Online Activism

Although comedian Stephen Colbert is widely celebrated as a progressive political force, many Asian Americans refused to laugh at a line posted on his Twitter account in March 2014. Colbert had earlier made a joke on his show skewering Redskins owner Dan Snyder for his continued insensitivity to the demands of Native Americans that he change the name of his football team. Colbert stated that if the owner of the Redskins wanted to start an organization that continued to include the offensive term "redskins," then he would create an equally racist organization. As a later tweet from @ColbertReport echoed, "I am willing to show the #Asian community I care by introducing the Ching-Chong Ding-Dong Foundation for Sensitivity to Orientals or Whatever." Asian Americans took umbrage at this dismissive reference to Asians and tweeted en masse using the hashtag #CancelColbert. Media reports from the websites of *NPR, New Yorker, Huffington Post, Slate.com, Variety, Time, Wall Street Journal, New York Daily News*, and countless others jumped into the fray with discussions of the role of satire in politics and the efficacy of so-called "hashtag activism." The flurry of conversations surrounding #CancelColbert begins to reveal the complexities of using new media tools like Twitter as part of an activist strategy. In some ways this was an unusual moment that elevated Asian American media activism into the national spotlight, producing a rare conversation about Colbert and comedy. But soon the conversation about the power of Stephen Colbert as a media figure came to be about much more—ultimately it began to reveal who belongs in America, and who belongs in Asian America.

While the previous chapter examined the use of Asian American new media practices to cultivate a sense of cultural citizenship through Asian American popular culture, this chapter examines the use of digital media for explicitly activist, political aims. I look in particular at how the technological affordances of online tools intersect with the cultural and

On *The Colbert Report*, comedian Stephen Colbert criticized Dan Snyder's creation of an organization that continued to use the offensive term "redskins" by claiming that he was going to create an equally offensive organization for "Orientals or whatever."

political practices of real communities. That is, we cannot examine the role that certain technologies play in contributing to activism without a careful consideration of the cultural meaning already embedded in these technologies. For instance, when considering how the internet is used as a space for antiracist organizing, we must recognize the proclivity of online participants for engaging in hostile forms of racist, misogynistic, homophobic, and other kinds of personal attacks. In her work on race and the internet, Lisa Nakamura (2008) has found that racist user-created media abounds online in everything from interpersonal interactions to textual and visual manifestations. But the space provided by the internet does more than reflect racism and social inequalities—it also offers opportunities to reveal, rewrite, and respond to the wide range of complex and contradictory identities and communities participating in online spaces. Moments such as the one following Colbert's tweet reveal the possibilities for political resistance offered by social media. As Nakamura writes:

> The multilayered visual culture of the Internet is anything but a space of utopian post-humanism where differences between genders, races,

and nationalities are evened out; on the contrary, it is an intensely active, productive space of visual signification where these differences are intensified, modulated, reiterated, and challenged by former objects of interactivity. (Nakamura 2008, 34)

Along with the ease of access and participation comes the possibility for minority communities to organize and use these platforms as an agent of social change. As Miriyam Aouragh and Anne Alexander put it, "the Internet is both a product of imperialist and capitalist logics and something that is simultaneously used by millions in the struggle to resist those logics" (Aouragh and Alexander 2011). Thus it is important to examine both functions of the internet—the way it serves to affirm the social and political systems of oppression in the offline world, and the ways it might enable movements toward political subversion.

In order to do so, in this chapter I raise the question of what it is that new media facilitates—that is, not how new media provides a solution to the problem of Asian American media images, but rather what role cultural formations, political identities, and affective relationships play in the way new media technologies are adopted as part of an activist project such as Asian American media activism. I begin the chapter by focusing on a series of Twitter campaigns centering on images of Asian Americans in the media. By tracing the different conversations that took place around such hashtags as #HowIMetYourRacism, #NotYour-AsianSidekick, and #CancelColbert, we can more clearly see that media provides both a rallying point for activism and a means for shifting the conversation to what really matters—the place of Asian Americans in American society. I then go on to examine the activist community at Racebending.com, which organized around the casting controversy of *The Last Airbender*. The attention of the organization later centered on broader issues of equality in entertainment and casting, providing a rich case study for examining the ways that the skills developed as active online participants can translate into a new kind of Asian American media advocacy and activism. The efforts of both Twitter activists and groups like Racebending.com illustrate the possibilities for using the affective connections and skill development facilitated by new media to generate a form of politicized participatory culture for Asian Americans online.

The Revolution Might Be Tweeted

Alongside the development of digital technologies, scholars have undertaken countless studies to better understand the role that new media play in contributing to social change (Hands 2011). In recalling the evolution of such "new" media technologies as television, radio, or print, we are reminded that shifts in media practices have always been assumed to herald a social revolution (Hofheinz 2011). Interest in this topic reached a particular zenith in the 2000s when social uprisings in Iran, Libya, Tunisia, and Egypt resulting in political regime change seemed to be deeply intertwined with and even reliant on participation in Web 2.0. Scholars found that Twitter and Facebook had helped activists in logistical activities such as organizing demonstrations, in disseminating information and news, and connecting people around the world (Lotan et al. 2011). Although a diversity of users have access to online communication—including journalists, corporations, activists, nonprofits, and individuals—studies of informational flows during these moments of activism showed that communication could indeed be controlled from the bottom up, with activists and opinion leaders online flexing the power to shift dialogue rather than relying upon journalists and corporations to take the lead (Lindgren 2011).

This understanding of the role of digital technologies like Twitter in contributing to social change begins to intersect with racial politics when we look at the demographics of who uses sites like Twitter. The colloquial term "Black Twitter" is used to refer to the overrepresentation of African Americans using Twitter—what Sarah Florini describes as the "millions of Black users on Twitter networking, connecting, and engaging with others who have similar concerns, experiences, tastes, and cultural practices" (Florini 2014). While the success of Asian Americans on YouTube has caught the attention of media analysts, pop cultural enthusiasts, and academics alike, considerably less attention has been paid to the presence of Asian Americans on Twitter. Much of the interest in Black Twitter, both academic and otherwise, has stemmed from Pew Research Internet Project reports stating that African Americans use Twitter at higher levels than any other race (Smith 2014). Yet Pew, like other widely used research bodies such as Nielsen, does not measure data regarding Asian Americans as part of its standard demographic split. In an article explaining the decision to only aggregate data into the categories "Black," "White," and "Hispanic," a researcher from Pew explained that the number of Asian American respondents is statistically too small and language barriers limit the respondents to those who can complete the survey in English (Smith 2013). As discussed in my investigation of Asian American advertising agencies, this leaves a startling dearth of information about Asian American internet usage. Although "Asian American Twitter" has yet to be recognized or researched to the same degree as "Black Twitter," Asian Americans are indeed active participants in the endless stream of 140-character messages. In a report presented by Pew Internet to the OCA (Organization of Chinese Americans) in 2011, Lee Rainie estimated that 20 percent of Asian Americans used Twitter (Rainie 2011)—as compared to 9 percent of whites, 25 percent of African Americans, and 19 percent of Hispanics at that time.

Although much of the scholarly work on Twitter is sociological in nature and is thus interested in broad questions of how social movements are created and collective actions initiated, in this chapter I begin by looking at how Asian Americans are using Twitter to engage in media activism. While the social movements that erupted in Tunisia, Egypt, and on Wall Street sought to overthrow governments, rewrite social contracts, and challenge capitalistic structures, the media activists I examine here are seeking a much more specific goal—to bring about change within entertainment media. As seen in the past four chapters, this has included a broad range of desired outcomes: the representation of Asian American bodies and stories, the hiring practices and leadership bodies behind media institutions, the way Asian American audiences are understood and targeted, and the artistic control Asian Americans can wield through self-representation and the development of their own celebrities. But importantly, media activism is usually directed at media corporations who seek to make a profit rather than government officials, legislative bodies, or society at large. The kinds of targets chosen does not make media activism any less political; in fact, W. Lance Bennett argues that digital communication networks are increasingly important to resource-poor players whose targets are outside the realm of conventional national political processes (Bennett 2003). Yet I point to this distinction so that we can more carefully examine the relationship between activism and its intended goals—in this case, changes in media practices, the development of cultural citizenship, and the potential for new forms of Asian American participatory culture.

#HowIMetYourRacism

We can begin by considering some of the ways Twitter has been utilized to effectively contribute to Asian American media activism, such as the campaign against *How I Met Your Mother*. In January 2014, an episode during the sitcom's final season featured cast members in blatant yellow-face—in one scene in the episode, the characters portrayed by Colbie Smulders, Josh Radnor, and Alyson Hannigan each wore Chinese costumes and black wigs, and spoke in stereotypical Asian accents. Asian Americans took to Twitter to complain about the scene's racist use of stereotypical traits for comic effect. Here are two examples of tweets on the subject:

> Didn't we agree that Mickey Rooney's yellowface is an embarrassment that ruins Breakfast at Tiffany's? #HowIMetYourRacism
> Sister Farrah (@SisterFarrah) January 14, 2014

> Besides the gross orientalizing of the women, Ted wore a fuck-ing Fu Manchu stach! Who thought this was ok? @HIMYM_CBS #HowIMetYourRacism
> Juliet Shen (@Juliet_Shen) January 14, 2014

An activist named Suey Park initiated the use of the hashtag #HowIMetYourRacism, giving people who were upset about the use of yellowface and the mocking of Asians the ability to join together and call attention to the issue.

Hashtags serve as a way to tag a post on Twitter so that it can be linked to others on the same topic or theme. The top ten hashtags experiencing a dramatic increase in usage are listed as "Trends" on Twitter's homepage, which greatly increases the visibility of that topic. Hashtags must be understood first as simply an aggregating mechanism that anyone can create; it is then up to that person's followers to discuss, retweet, or otherwise amplify the hashtag. As with all participation on Twitter, hashtags tend to emerge in a largely organic and unpredictable fashion, evidencing the multiple ways that people use them, rather than providing a linear or organized form of discourse. Yet when activists deploy Twitter to call attention to an issue, they utilize the visibility of this function by trying to "trend" a specific hashtag. If thousands of users post the same hashtag, its reach goes beyond the range of their own followers to all Twitter users.

Trending #HowIMetYourRacism and its complaints about the show brought swift results. A day after the hashtag was introduced, one of the show's creators, Carter Bays, took to Twitter with an apologetic series of tweets:

> With Monday's episode, we set out to make a silly and unabashedly immature homage to Kung Fu movies, a genre we've always loved.
>
> But along the way we offended people. We're deeply sorry, and we're grateful to everyone who spoke up to make us aware of it.
>
> We try to make a show that's universal, that anyone can watch and enjoy. We fell short of that this week, and feel terrible about it.
>
> To everyone we offended, I hope we can regain your friendship, and end this series on a note of goodwill. Thanks.
> Carter Bays (@CarterBays) January 15, 2015

To receive an apology from an image's creators within twenty-four hours of calling attention to the problem is an unusual and noteworthy feat in the world of media activism. Indeed, Asian American activists using traditional methods of communication (even those that are instantaneous, such as phone calls and emails) are often stymied for months before media producers respond with any recognition of wrongdoing, let alone a sincere apology. The speed of online communication and the throng of negative publicity that an image can accrue in a short amount of time contribute to an environment in which media producers are pressured to respond immediately. Twitter also provides a medium for the individuals responsible for images to respond using that same medium to speak back to their audience, rather than needing to issue a press release or use the communication networks of the activists to convey a response. Indeed, Twitter is often celebrated for its ability to level the playing field between powerful celebrities or media executives and everyday media consumers who seek to contact them (Marwick and boyd 2011).

For all these reasons, it seems reasonable to argue that Asian American media activism can take place on Twitter using nothing but a hashtag. In response to *How I Met Your Mother*, we have a clear case of Asian Americans using Twitter to call attention to an offensive image, raise awareness about why it was problematic, and achieve the result of the image's creators apologizing and recognizing their mistake. They might then hope that such mistakes would not be repeated in the future, or that at the very least some education about that issue took place. Yet we should also note that this was not an act of deliberate organizing by Twitter users; although they were able to come together to create a collective outcry, they issued no organized set of demands or terms for success. If any organizing went on behind the scenes, that labor was largely made invisible by the fact that the hashtag seemed to emerge out of a collective sense of outrage that needed to be expressed rather than a carefully organized strategy designed to garner such an outcome.

#NotYourAsianSidekick

While the hashtag campaign against *How I Met Your Mother* provides an example of the way media activism can emerge from the participatory nature of Twitter, this example stands out due to the ease with which it was resolved. Although Twitter users did not call out for a public apology, when they received one it seemed to resolve the issue to everyone's satisfaction, and so the conversation died out. In other Asian American hashtag campaigns, there is often significantly less clarity about the intended goal or conclusive result. In many cases, the propagation of a Twitter hashtag seems simply to lead to a form of guided conversation rather than working toward achieving a desirable outcome from a media target. We can look at the conversation surrounding the hashtag #NotYourAsianSidekick as an example of this kind of conversation. This hashtag also helps us see that such Twitter campaigns are rooted in the fight for cultural citizenship at the level of the collective. In December 2013, Suey Park posted the following tweet:

> Be warned. Tomorrow morning we will be have a convo about Asian American Feminism with hashtag #NotYourAsianSidekick. Spread the word!!!!!!!
> Suey Park (@suey_park) December 14, 2013

Park, the same twenty-three-year-old activist and freelance writer who would later initiate the hashtag #HowIMetYourRacism, had cultivated a large audience of Twitter followers through her tweets about feminism and racial justice. Together with a small group of women of color feminists, Park began posting with the hashtag #NotYourAsianSidekick. Thousands of Twitter users contributed their own thoughts on the place of Asian Americans in American society, and within twenty-four hours over 45,000 tweets had been posted using the hashtag. Some messages focused on media-related outrage against stereotypes, invisibility, or the predominance of clearly subordinate "sidekick" roles.

> The last time Asian women where represented in film, in all their complexities: "The Joy Luck Club." 20 years ago. #NotYourAsianSidekick
> Jose Antonio Vargas (@joseiswriting) December 15, 2013

> Asian representation in the mass media needs to catch up to the mass audiences of Asian personalities on YouTube #NotYourAsianSideKick
> Mike Kwan (@mikekwan) December 15, 2013

From these tweets one might conclude that the theme of the "Asian Sidekick" related to these stereotypes, as if media representation itself was the central crux of the campaign. But other tweets moved beyond media issues to express frustration with a wide range of issues facing Asian Americans, including anti-immigrant sentiment, homophobia, colorism, patriarchy, and everyday experiences of prejudice and discrimination.

> White woman in ladies bathroom explaining I'm in wrong place. Thot I was Asian male foreigner, didn't speak English. #NotYourAsianSideKick
> Alice Y Hom (@JustFundQueers) December 15, 2013

> I'm #NotYourAsianSidekick because my immigrant parents sacrificed everything except self-respect.
> Hari Kondabolu (@harikondabolu) December 15, 2013

> Telling me I speak without an accent or that I'm "fair-skinned" isn't a compliment. Sorry. #NotYourAsianSidekick
> Josh Shahryar (@JShahryar) December 15, 2013

What emerges from these tweets and others that expand the meaning of the hashtag is a clearer picture of what it feels like to struggle for cultural citizenship. Although each tweet may operate on its own logic and represent only its individual author, the collective momentum developed through the accumulation of such messages moves beyond the individual. When a topic trends on Twitter, individual users click on that hashtag and are presented with an endlessly updating stream of comments that create meaning through the aggregation and accumulation of common themes. Again and again, tweets such as these make the point that the designation of "Asian sidekick" means being treated as a second-class citizen in American society—always being questioned, disrespected, and challenged, as if they do not really belong here. While media imagery plays a part in contributing to this loss of voice and identity as Americans, this broader idea of cultural citizenship more strongly characterizes the sentiment of the collective participating in using this hashtag.

We should note, however, that Park had initially called for a conversation about Asian American feminism, not simply a catch-all conversation about various forms of Asian American outrage. In interviews following the success of the trend, she reiterated that her goal was to create a conversation about feminism that was accessible to young girls, as she had personally felt frustrated with the tokenization of women of color in mainstream feminist communities. With hundreds of posts per day, Park was an active participant in the stream of messages surrounding this issue and many of her comments were directed at moving the conversation back toward her intended topic. In particular, she and other prominent participants criticized the use of the hashtag to uphold model minority discourses that contributed to antiblackness.

> #NotYourAsianSidekick was about NOT becoming sidekicks to white supremacy and suppressing other people of color. Not about our visibility.
> Suey Park (@suey_park) March 27, 2014

> Friendly reminder that while the popularity of #NotYourAsianSidekick is great, it originated as talk on Asian American FEMINISM. #dontderail
> Juliet Shen (@Juliet_Shen) December 15, 2013

These messages express some frustration with the diversity of messages using the hashtag, and in particular with the way Asian Americans might be inadvertently suppressing African Americans in their desire to be seen and heard. Although Park expressed her pleasure at the outpouring of participation engendered by the hashtag, her desire to use the hashtag to initiate discourse specifically about feminism and her frustration with the way the conversation had been "derailed" reminds us that Twitter conversations cannot be controlled by any one participant. As mentioned earlier, hashtags and other forms of communication on Twitter are marked by their fluid, unstructured, unpredictable nature. These factors, combined with the polyvocality of Twitter, make it an extremely unstable medium for communicating a targeted message. The stream of tweets on a subject cannot be policed or regulated, as individual participants can post any message they want.

Many corporations have learned this lesson the hard way when their attempts to initiate a hashtag in support of their company have inevitably been repurposed by individuals who use the hashtag to express their disapproval. For instance, when British Gas tweeted their followers to ask what they thought of the company, hundreds of users responded to the #askBG hashtag by criticizing the company's higher prices (Gard 2013). Celebrity chef Paula Deen has also been skewered on Twitter in the wake of her allegedly racist comments (Morrissey 2013). When a tweet from her account innocently asked for favorite potluck dishes, her Twitter followers were quick to respond with dishes like "poverty and potato salad," "Ku klux clams," and "colored greens." Such responses remind us that Twitter is largely a bottom-up form of mass communication wherein corporations and powerful individuals can participate and initiate dialogue, but that leaves them powerless to control the wave of individual messages that cluster together around a single hashtag or account.

This understanding of Twitter as a conversation that cannot be controlled by any one entity coincides with the use of Twitter in leaderless movements. Studies of the Twitter-fueled social movements in Egypt and Tunisia have found that these large-scale mobilizations were partly defined by their lack of a leader. As Manuel Castells (2012) notes, these movements are leaderless "not because of the lack of would-be leaders, but because of the deep, spontaneous distrust of most participants in the movement towards any form of power delegation" (224). Yet this inability to control the flow of communication on Twitter stands in stark contrast to much discussion surrounding #NotYourAsianSidekick, which positioned Suey Park as its leader. Many comments utilizing the hashtag praised Park for starting the conversation, while others described Park and her friends as "moderators" and "facilitators."

> Best wishes to @suey_park, who is moderating the #NotYourAsianSidekick discussion this morning. I guarantee you're going to want to read it.
> Kim Doel (@_kimmbot) December 15, 2013

> Hey #NotYourAsianSidekick followers, can you give some love and follows to @Juliet_Shen who helped @suey_park facilitate and is awesome?
> Julia Wong (@juliacarriew) December 16, 2013

> Important conversation about race and satire being facilitated by @suey_park and @clepsydras.
> Nia (@ArtActivistNia) March 28, 2014

The use of these terms to describe the propagation of a Twitter hashtag calls attention to the perception among participants that some individuals play a role in shaping the direction and flow of the conversation. To some extent this perception can simply be connected to the reality that certain Twitter users are more active in posting and have more followers than others, leading to a high number of replies and retweets. Sites like Klout, PeerIndex, and Kred have sprung up to systematically measure the social influence and reach of individuals on sites like Twitter. There are also occasions on Twitter when a user will announce that he or she is planning to tweet about a certain topic at a certain time, which is understood as facilitating a conversation on that topic. Yet even Park herself has called attention to the fact she is not the owner of the hashtag, and that no hashtag can trend without a community of supporters working to promote it.

> I want #NotYourAsianSidekick to be free from ownership. It is a shared space and anyone can participate in it however they choose to.
> Suey Park (@suey_park) February 13, 2014

In an article for XOJane.com about the success of the hashtag, she wrote:

"it actually takes a community to create a trending hashtag . . . people participate in social justice hashtags because of their invested interest in them and not because I simply tell people to join. The viral success of #NotYourAsianSidekick after I first tweeted the tag on December 15, 2013, wasn't about me, but all of us." (Park n.d.)

Her insistence on moving the conversation from her own specific role to the strength of the community that came together to voice its collective perspectives stands in contrast to the obsession of news articles and blog posts focusing exclusively on the young woman positioned at the center of the movement. Articles in outlets ranging from the *Washington Post* to *BBC* to *Al Jazeera* insisted on profiling the young woman and detailing her personal life, as if there could be no other explanation for the sudden burst of activity surrounding Asian American issues on Twitter. Although Park clearly played a role in initiating this conversation, the fixation on one individual demeans the participation of thousands of individual Asian Americans who came together to create this moment of mediated visibility. The widespread dissemination of #NotYourAsianSidekick is reflective of both the fluency of many Asian Americans in carrying on digital conversations and the insistent need for recognition of this particular topic—the invisibility, neglect, and mistreatment of Asian Americans in their everyday lives.

Trending #CancelColbert

The hashtag campaigns for #HowIMetYourRacism and #NotYourAsianSidekick set the context for the media flurry surrounding #CancelColbert. On March 14, 2014 the official Twitter account for *The Colbert Report* (@ColbertReport) published a tweet containing Colbert's joke about "the Ching-Chong Ding-Dong Foundation for Sensitivity to Orientals or Whatever" without context. As it stood, it seemed to propagate the very racism it ostensibly served to condemn. Just as in the previously discussed hashtag campaigns, Suey Park tweeted her response:

"The Ching-Chong Ding-Dong Foundation for Sensitivity to Orientals has decided to call for #CancelColbert. Trend it."
Suey Park (@suey_park) March 14, 2014

The #CancelColbert hashtag indeed caught like wildfire, spurring thousands of comments about how his satire contributed to the devaluing of Asian Americans. Media reports again fixated on Park's role in propagating the message of outrage and shaping the conversation surrounding it. Although she had earlier attempted to distance herself from being framed as a leader, with #CancelColbert Park stood firmly at the center. She wrote an article for *TIME* titled "We Want to #CancelColbert," and gave numerous interviews to media outlets about her reasoning behind the hashtag and her hopes for the kinds of conversation it would initiate. Such visibility came at a high cost to Park, as she was subject to an onslaught of online vitriol in the form of "racist and misogynistic slurs, rape threats, death threats and every other conceivable kind of invective" (Wong 2014)—a response which has unfortunately come to be expected for any woman or person of color who asserts his or her opinion online (Consalvo 2012; Shaw 2014; Marwick 2013).

But the ire directed at Park points to the fierce emotional chord that this campaign struck. Accusations of racism are always inflammatory, but Park's appearance on *Huffington Post Live* with Josh Zepps reveals the depth of the affective responses this issue provoked. In the segment, Zepps and Park began with a discussion of satire, with Park stating that it was unacceptable to use Orientalism in a critique of Native American mascots. Zepps responded by saying, "Part of the whole gag here is the use of the term Orientalism, which is such a weird, old, loaded (laughs) like, it's a stupid, stupid word, but to get upset about the use of that word when it's in a satirical context strikes me as misguided." This comment shows that Zepps has already slipped from his professional demeanor, calling the entire concept of Orientalism a "stupid stupid word" and denying that Orientalism might still be relevant in today's society. But the conversation continues to deteriorate after Park insists that because Zepps is a white man, he can't understand why people of color are responding to Colbert in this way.

PARK: . . . white men definitely feel entitled to talk over me, they definitely feel entitled to kind of minimalize [sic] my experiences, and they definitely feel like they are somehow exempt and so logical compared to women who are painted as emotional, right?

ZEPPS: No. No one's minimalizing your experiences. No one's minimalizing your right to have an opinion. It's just a stupid opinion.

At this point in the conversation both participants have begun to fail to use reason to support their arguments. Instead, they rely upon ad hominem attacks—Park invokes Zepps's race and gender in order to dismiss his points, while Zepps resorts to emotional name-calling to discredit Parks. This argument and the way it plays out reminds us that the affective stakes of this debate make it difficult for the parties to have the productive conversation needed to move forward toward change. Of course, the affective dimensions of this conversation are not specific to race alone—nearly all controversial political topics can be derailed when emotions get in the way of rational discourse. Yet this specific example reminds us of the confusion surrounding #CancelColbert and its goals.

Beyond the way that the stakes of the debate were often obscured, part of the problem was that the target of this campaign was an assumed ally in political comedian Stephen Colbert. The segment under question was ostensibly being used to condemn racism through satire, as did many of the jokes on *The Colbert Report*. As a result, much discourse surrounding the hashtag focused on alleviating confusion surrounding even the most basic inquiries—Did anyone really want to cancel *The Colbert Report*? Had Colbert really done anything wrong? While many Asian Americans and feminists of color echoed Parks's criticisms of Colbert, dissent flourished as well—Asian American journalists, celebrities, bloggers, community organizers, academics, and Twitter users spoke out against the entire campaign. Their criticisms ranged from an insistence that Colbert's satire was rooted in antiracism, to discomfort with the hostility of the campaign's tone, to frustration that the lack of clarity in the campaign had led to a decentering of Native issues. As with the conversation surrounding #NotYourAsianSidekick, Asian Americans who criticized #CancelColbert were accused of trying to:

uphold the model minority vision of Asian America as a monolithic and 'liberal' political group rather than addressing its multivocality, its potential radical political edges that align with other politicized WOC groups and feminists, its ability to create multigenerational and multiethnic politicized coalitions. (Kim 2014)

To some, the decision of individual Asian Americans to criticize or fail to support #CancelColbert was symptomatic of their desire to reify a monolithic, "mainstream" Asian America. These debates about the different Asian American responses to the campaign challenged what the category of "Asian American" really meant—in particular, whether or not Asian Americans fighting against racism needed to point to the specificities of their own oppression, or whether they should engage in acts of solidarity with other people of color.

This example demonstrates that despite the potential for Twitter to create a forum for conversation, the process is often fraught with complications because of the limitations of the medium. One clear limitation of Twitter is that 140 characters do not provide much room for sophisticated dialogue; in fact, whether Twitter even provides a platform for conversation or dialogue is questionable. In an analysis of "Twitter as Cultural Communication," Andre Brock (2012) argues that hashtags in Black Twitter contribute to a form of "call and response" where a user can request an affirmative response from his or her followers by initiating a hashtag. But in Brock's view, "Twitter's publication mechanism makes it difficult to keep track of conversations," and trending topics merely "highlight the conversational nature of the service" (541). Brock's research points to the fact that while Twitter is clearly a space for communication and interaction, its user interface and communicative practices do not easily allow for sustained, direct communication. This is particularly unfortunate when the topic at hand is emotionally provocative, complex, or nuanced, as is certainly the case with the conversation surrounding #CancelColbert. Statements on Twitter are also different from what we might characterize as "a conversation" in that every message is broadcast to one's entire network of followers, often with no expectation of direct response—what Marwick and boyd call a combination of broadcast media and face-to-face communication that entails conceiving of one's Twitter stream as many-to-many communication

(Marwick and boyd 2011). This does not mean that conversation does not happen on Twitter; indeed, through connected threads of replies, Twitter users regularly engage in what we would call conversations with their followers. Yet the limitations of message length, the ephemerality of each individual tweet, and the size of each individual's audience hinder Twitter from being a particularly strong medium for sustained or careful dialogue.

Don't Cancel Colbert, Just Grant Cultural Citizenship

These difficulties contributed to the failure of #CancelColbert as media activism. As with #HowIMetYourRacism, the #CancelColbert hashtag and its target centered directly on a problem in the media. Asian Americans were being used as the target of mockery and Twitter users were incensed by the message conveyed by this joke. Thus it would seem at first glance that the hashtag should be understood as yet another example of Asian American media activism. As defined in the introductory chapter, media activism occurs through the identification of a social problem in the media and the intentional action taken to remedy this mediated problem. Yet I argue that #CancelColbert was not about remedying the problem of Colbert's joke or the tweet that captured it. Indeed, even Park quickly backed away from a demand for the show's cancelation, stating in numerous interviews that she was deploying hyperbole as a means of gaining attention and that her hashtag was not meant to be taken literally. Moreover, in an interview with Salon.com she told interviewer Prachi Gupta that she had never watched the segment containing the joke, and that as a fan of the show she did not think *The Colbert Report* was oppressive. If #CancelColbert is not about media activism, then, what it more clearly reveals is the way media is connected to cultural citizenship—in this case, so much so that media activism can be bypassed in the fight to simply be seen, recognized, and heard. Media certainly plays a central role in the #CancelColbert campaign, as Colbert is seen to be in the wrong on this one joke. As Park said, "It's Colbert that doesn't realize how he's using racism as a vehicle to end racism, which is really just circular logic and doesn't lead to an end destination of liberation" (Gupta 2014). But the directive contained in the widely propagated hashtag did not seem to center around media change—rather, it simply provided the context for speaking out about the failure to grant Asian Americans cultural citizenship. While the messy, polyvocal, unpredictable nature of Twitter may stymy its facilitation of direct activist action, these attributes make it particularly well suited for a conversation about cultural citizenship and the multiple ways it has been defined and fought for throughout this book.

Although messages about #CancelColbert focused on the broader goal of inciting discourse and creating a space for developing community, we must be careful to distinguish its achievements from those of a traditional social movement. One of the aspects of #CancelColbert that weakened its ability to be understood as part of a social movement was the absence of any on-the-ground base building or organizing. Although the creation of political discourse alone can be seen as an activist project, researchers have found that the efficacy of using online networks for transitioning into a social movement lies in their ability to connect to real-life communities. As Aouragh and Alexander write:

> The value of Facebook as an organizer is lower where one can meet face-to-face, but it is perhaps more important to state that those physical meetings are also better for political planning and organizing and building trust and conscripting sacrifice, what is generally referred to as "strong ties"—even if Internet communication is faster and allows for (relative) anonymity. (Aouragh and Alexander 2011, 1350)

While we may want to be careful not to overstate the benefits of face-to-face organizing as being unilaterally superior to online organizing, the existence of offline participation is nevertheless conspicuously absent here. Manuel Castells argues that a characteristic of successful social movements in the internet age is the use of multimodal networks that include "social networks online and offline, as well as pre-existing social networks, and networks formed during the actions of the movement" (Castells 2012, 221). Social movement organizing takes place both in the space of the internet and in the public space of urban centers. While Castells is describing social movements that move far beyond the scope of media activism, there was an observable sense of deliberate resistance to any form of organization in #CancelColbert. While the propagation of the hashtag itself relied on various communities of practice which spread the conversation on this one topic, there did not seem to be any utilization of offline networks and certainly there was no attempt to turn this campaign into a movement. This is particularly noteworthy given that Park herself indicated her desire to do so with the #NotYourAsianSidekick hashtag:

> This is not a trend, this is a movement. Everybody calm down and buckle down for the long haul, please.
> Suey Park (@suey_park) December 16, 2013

While we can certainly see that the use of Twitter for building Asian American cultural citizenship has become a long-term project that connects across different responses to media imagery, it is difficult to argue that this conversation alone is part of a new or existing social movement. Nevertheless, it is important to understand the kind of activism embodied by these hashtag campaigns as being about much more than media activism; rather, they provide a moment of clarity which reveals the connection between media representations and the broader goal of fighting for cultural citizenship.

The uproar surrounding #CancelColbert thus illustrates the way that conversations about the media stand in for cultural citizenship to such a strong degree that the media activism itself becomes nearly irrelevant. There seems to be little actual desire for Colbert, *The Colbert Report*, Comedy Central, or other media entities to take action or respond. Rather, this campaign is centered on the fact that Asian Americans want to be taken seriously—they want to voice their pain and frustration with the continuation of harmful rhetoric, and they want to be recognized and heard when they do so. They are tired of being belittled as merely the butt of the joke, and they demand that the public respond with empathy and justice as they deem necessary. As the *New Yorker* blogger Jay Caspian King stated, "that a hashtag conversation on Twitter could have such resonance speaks to just how desperate Asian-Americans have been to talk about identity without deferring to the familiar binaries that shape most discussions of race in this country" (King 2014). Although in earlier chapters I argued that cultural citizenship meant different things to different Asian American media activists—including a desire to assimilate and be seen as "just like everyone else," to bring about systemic changes in the media industries, to be recognized as powerful consumers, and to control their own voice and representation—in these various Twitter hashtags there is no single unified message. Each individual Twitter user is free to contribute his or her own response to the images and provocations contained in the hashtag, and their range and breadth reflects the broad base of individuals who have done so.

Fan-Activists and the *Last Airbender* Controversy

While these different Twitter hashtags have provided an opportunity for Asian Americans to come together and demand cultural citizenship, Twitter is not the only new media tool being used to do so. Asian Americans are active in a number of different kinds of participatory cultures online, and their engagement with media and popular culture opens the door to many different kinds of political interventions. If we are interested in the way these politics play out in a case that does center specifically on media activism—an intentional fight to impact media practices for social change—we can turn to the activism surrounding *The Last Airbender*. In this example, Asian American activists yet again stirred up an emotional, politically complex battle surrounding the representation of Asian Americans in the media. Yet what this case reveals is the way that media activists can effectively tap into existing online cultures, and specifically media fandoms, in order to effectively express their demands.

In December 2008, producers of the film adaptation of the Nickelodeon cartoon *Avatar: The Last Airbender* set off a firestorm of criticism when they announced their casting decisions. Despite the fact that the television show seemed to have appropriated cultural practices, architecture, religious iconography, costumes, calligraphy, and other aesthetic elements from East Asian and Inuit cultures, four white actors had been cast in the lead roles. Many fans became irate, demanding that the roles go to Asian actors because they had always imagined that the characters were racially Asian. When one of the lead actors dropped out of the project he was replaced by Dev Patel, who is of Indian descent, as is the film's director, M. Night Shyamalan.[1] But fans insisted that the nation his character belonged to were the villains of the series, so now the problem was that the three white stars were heroes and the nonwhite actor and

The Nickelodeon cartoon *Avatar: The Last Airbender* created a fantasy world that was based on a variety of Asian cultural practices and aesthetics.

his people were villains. These conversations continued in heated online debates and culminated in a number of protest activities, ranging from the creation and spread of counter-media to a boycott of the upcoming film.

One of the reasons the protesters were able to so effectively embrace this kind of digital activism was because of their reliance on fans as their organizational base. Fan communities have long been active in online arenas, using digital tools to connect with like-minded individuals, share ideas and creative content, and create large communities of practice. In this case, fans were poised to use their skills to become politically engaged and align themselves with media activism movements. Usually when we talk about "fan activism" we are more accurately simply describing active fans—passionate viewers of a particular text who unite with like-minded individuals for a singular goal. Such fans participate in activities such as interacting in online forums, creating works of fan art and fan fiction, or consuming collectibles. Yet their goals are often confined to the world of the text itself, in "nonpolitical claims . . . culturally-oriented and consumer-based claims" (Earl and Kimport 2009, 220). Fans have used their collective power to demand that a certain romantic relationship blossom within the show's narrative (Scodari and Felder 2000; Tabron 2004), that a show stay on the air despite low ratings (Scardaville 2005), or as is sometimes the case with anime, that a show be imported to the United States (Levi 2006). Work that looks at this type of fan activity has been necessary in order to counteract the stereotype that viewers are passive, easily duped, or simply foolish. Yet fan activism can encompass a broader range of activities, some of which are distinctly political and may contribute to an increased level of civic engagement. Academics are now beginning to recognize the ways fans engage with issues that extend beyond the world of their fan text—in this case, by allying themselves with established nonprofit groups and seeking to expand their knowledge of political discourse and the real-world implications of their fandom. In this case the fans of *The Last Airbender* were able to transition from being everyday fans to political activists—but more significantly, this transition was facilitated by the language and culture of participatory culture and digital media literacy. Indeed, protests against *The Last Airbender* demonstrated the wide range of digital skills that can be used for media activism, and the points of intersection between these particular skills and the goals of traditional Asian American media activism.

One of the first responses to the news of the casting came from artists who had worked on the show. Under the handle "Aang Ain't White," they anonymously created a LiveJournal website and initiated a letter writing campaign. Although hundreds of fans and nonfans learned about the issue through the site and mailed letters, most were returned to the sender unopened. Soon thereafter, casting for the film was completed and production began with no changes to the cast. Although it is difficult to say why the traditional media activism tactic of letter writing failed in this instance, the participants did not lose hope and simply modified their strategies. Because of the earlier creation of the online forum to initiate the letter writing campaign, like-minded fans were able to meet each other in a virtual arena and establish a basis for future conversations. Two such individuals, known on the site as glockgal and jedifreac, decided to start a new forum. They created a site called Racebending.com, as well as a corresponding community on LiveJournal.

The name was a playful riff on the notion of "bending" that was an important part of the universe of *The Last Airbender*—each tribe is based on a natural element, and people known as "Benders" are capable of manipulating that element. The creation of this term can be read as an example of "textual poaching" (Jenkins 1992), or the act of fans repurposing ideas from their beloved texts to demonstrate resistance and agency. By referencing "bending" the activists acknowledged their fandom and attachment to the world of the franchise, even as they used the term to articulate their frustration with an industry in which roles are systemically taken from Asian Americans and filled by white actors. The filmmakers seemed to be saying that audiences would only support movies starring white actors, and as dedicated fans of a fantastical world populated by multiracial, multicultural peoples, they knew that this was not the case. Members of the community also noted that the casting call had used the phrase "Caucasian or any other ethnicity" when looking for these lead roles, which they found troubling and discriminatory, as it seemed to indicate that Paramount Pictures had specifically sought out white actors. In this sense, Paramount's definition of "racebending" was doing more than simply changing the race of a character. It had changed the race of characters of color to white for reasons of marketability.[2]

By the spring of 2009, the Racebending.com website was managed by six main contributors, three of whom were based in Los Angeles, one in British Columbia, one in New York, and one in Washington. Out of the six leaders of the movement, only one had been an active fan, participating in fan communities and engaging in fannish practices such as fan art and fan fiction. Four considered themselves general fans of the show but not at a serious level, and one had never seen an episode of the show and only joined the group to protest the casting. Nevertheless, the leaders of the group relied heavily on fan communities to provide the base to rally individuals to take action. In an informal poll of 1,200 Racebending.com supporters, the movement was found to be spread across fifty countries. Racially nearly half their supporters were white, with only a quarter of their participants identifying as Asian (Demographics of Racebending. com Supporters 2010).

This exploration of the desires of the fan community raises another important question—why was the Racebending.com movement so focused on fans? Interviews with the primary leaders of the movement made it clear that only one had been a serious fan of the show, as the others could not be said to have been part of the show's dedicated fan community. Thus, their continual reliance on fan communities for support of their cause was deliberate and strategic. This might seem counterintuitive at first, since passionate fans would seem to be the most difficult group to convince to boycott the film version of their beloved show. Yet this example shows us that the set of skills exercised and utilized by fan communities has the potential to translate effectively into skills for a new mode of activism that takes place largely online. Van Zoonen (2004) makes a strong case for the similarity between fan communities and political constituencies, arguing that the emotional investments of both are a result of performance, and that their activities are similarly concerned with things like knowledge, discussion, and participation. But the mobilization of fans around this particular issue takes us one step further—not only do the activities and affective realities of fans resemble those of political constituencies, but fan activities can be seen to facilitate the development of a set of skills particularly well suited to political activism in the era of Web 2.0.

Defining "Asian" in *The Last Airbender*

Although the Nickelodeon cartoon was created by two white Americans—Mike DiMartino and Bryan Konietzko—fans of the show had always been particularly attuned to its Asian aspects. They proudly noted that the visuals were remarkably accurate in their portrayal of Chinese, Japanese, Korean, and Inuit cultures, even though the story takes place in a somewhat mythical, alternate world. Despite the fact that the race of animated characters can be underdetermined, ambiguous, or deliberately obscured (Lu 2009), operating under the Japanese idea of *mukokuseki*, or "lacking any nationality" (Iwabuchi 2004), many fans actively searched for proof that these characters were actually Asian. To that end, there are countless video montages on their websites showing images from the show and comparing them to ethnographic photographs of Japanese clothing, Inuit housing, Chinese calligraphy, and other evidential images from those cultures. In making these comparisons they insist relentlessly that we can pinpoint what Asia and Asian culture[3] are by looking at these visual artifacts.

Yet we must consider how this discourse contributes to an essentialized or fixed notion of Asia. Not only do these images suggest that an escalating pile of artifacts can be used to ascertain what is really Asian and what is not, as if Asian identities cannot exist outside these artifacts, but we are expected to use this evidence to match a racialized body to this perfect image of Asianness. This becomes somewhat difficult given that the show seemingly appropriates and mixes cultural artifacts from a wide range of Asian cultures, none of which could be accurately represented by any single actor. Moreover, who and what constitutes "Asia" is also a debatable topic, given that the geographical, racial, and cultural boundaries surrounding what we might consider "Asia" are shifting and contextually constructed (Chuh 2003; Ono 1995). The demand that an Asian actor play the role of Aang also assumes that identity and representation can be collapsed within an actor's body, when representation is always a mediation and our identities can rarely be straightforwardly mapped out without any complexity or shading.

This fixing of Asian culture as a specific set of material practices and a particular physicality becomes even more problematic when accusations of Orientalism arise within the group. On the LiveJournal community site, one contributor posted the following message:

> I have a friend who says that the Last Airbender race fail does not bother him because he does not see it as whitewashing because he does not see the Avatar world as Asian in the first place. To him, the world and its cultures do not code as Asian, but as more in the vein of white Orientalism. It's characters putting on Asian costumes in an exotic Asian world, for white people. Essentially, to cast the characters as white is only fitting. (livejournal.com 2009)

In the discussion that followed this posting, the participants debated whether or not the show was at its core authentically Asian or superficially Asian, as well as who got to arbitrate such a debate given the diverse positionalities of those who were arguing each position. Given that over half the fans and most active Racebending.com participants were not Asian, they would likely not want to detract from their own ability to participate in the Asian fantasy of the show. One contributor added, "there's the undeniable fact that *Avatar: The Last Airbender* is a hybrid: . . . [it] is Asian American, and of course Asian Americans come in different flavors" (racebending.livejournal.com 2009). These debates, which began to spiral out of control rather than reaching any resolution, point to the slipperiness of authenticity and identity, and perhaps the weakness in the group because it was relying so heavily on these discourses.

Although arguments for authenticity proliferated on the websites, the leaders themselves rarely discussed the issue. Instead, they relied heavily on the more general concern that Asian Americans were being systemically excluded from "heroic roles." In a presentation at a college campus, Racebending.com leader Michael Le stated, "In an ideal world, John Cho could play George Bush and Keanu Reeves could play Martin Luther King Jr. But I think we can all agree that we are not there yet. People of color are still not being allowed to tell their own stories." These arguments are not connected to authenticity or accuracy, but to general casting practices in Hollywood and the overall invisibility of minorities.

We also see evidence of this position being upheld in the group's response to cosplay, or dressing up in costume to represent and perform characters from the show. When asked if they thought that only Asians could cosplay the characters from *The Last Airbender*, Racebending.com supporters strongly affirmed that people of all backgrounds could play the role of Aang and other "Asian" characters. This statement is confirmed in a video on Racebending.com of interviews conducted at Comic-Con. In the video, an African American woman playing the (arguably Inuit) Sokka and a white woman playing the (arguably East Asian man) Iroh are both given the chance to explain why they are against the casting decisions for the movie. The interviews show not only that Racebending.com supporters think that people of all backgrounds should be able to play the character of their choosing, but also that these "racebending/genderbending" individuals are part of the Racebending.com movement itself. It seems that in some instances, then, racebending is perfectly acceptable regardless of an individual's racial background or authentic connection to that culture, because these people and their decisions about what character they want to portray are not part of the larger discrimination against Asian Americans in the industry.

Using Participatory Culture for Action

The first move the activists made toward engaging with fans of the show was to create a website called Racebending.com and a community on LiveJournal. LiveJournal, a blogging website that has been a platform for fan communities since 2003 (Derecho 2006), was already a hub of fan activity surrounding *The Last Airbender*, so the community quickly grew in popularity. The Racebending.com leaders were able to tap into an already existing network of individuals who had a strong connection to the show. If they could make the argument that their beloved property was being mistreated, that passion could be redirected against the live action film. We can see that this move was extremely effective—the LiveJournal community continued to be the most active site for conversation surrounding the issue, with daily posts written by a large number of community members and an extremely active base of commenters turning each post into a rousing debate. It was not uncommon for a single post to have anywhere from forty to eighty comments following it.

The Racebending.com community on LiveJournal made use of the already existing online network of individuals, but also put them to work in sorting through and accumulating new information about the issue at hand. Fans have long been known as great collectors of information about their fan object; in an exploration of the wiki called *Lostpedia*, Mittell finds that the community website's "core function is as a shared archive of data, culling information from the show, its brand extensions, and its cultural references to make sense of the show's mysteries and narrative web" (Mittell 2009). The high level of fascination and attention to shows like *Lost* are multiplied when fan communities unite to pool their resources, making their data set incredibly comprehensive and detailed. Jenkins (2006b) further expands on this phenomenon, comparing the advantages of Pierre Levy's notion of collective intelligence to Peter Walsh's more traditional "expert paradigm." He argues that there are many pleasurable reasons for people to participate in the production of collective knowledge: the exercise of generally unacknowledged skills, the assumption that individuals have something worthwhile to contribute, and the generally democratic principles that lead to a dynamic process of acquiring knowledge. This notion of collective labor maps perfectly onto the case of Racebending.com, where it is not always the leaders who provide the latest news regarding the production and promotion of the film. Rather, it is a collective of motivated individuals who sporadically contribute, leaving no stone unturned in their search for new details and developments.

Beyond updates on the making of the film, the site also served as a place for a host of related discussions, including questions about racial politics, re-examinations of episodes of the show in the context of this new politicization, and attention drawn to similar issues in other media representations. In his examination of the cultural economy of fandom, Fiske (1992) finds that fans are "particularly productive," and that "all such productivity occurs at the interface between the industrially-produced cultural commodity . . . and the everyday life of the fan" (37). He specifically outlines three kinds of productivity, two of which we see in action here—enunciative productivity, or fan talk, and textual productivity, or fan art. With regard to enunciative productivity, we can see these regular conversations and debates on LiveJournal as evidence that fan talk is productive of deeper knowledge about the text itself, as well as the political implications of the way that the film has been cast. Through these discussions and debates, participants were able to sharpen their own arguments and solidify their stance on what is clearly a politically fraught issue.

With regard to textual productivity, we can look to the copious production of fan artwork and fan videos as additional components of knowledge creation. Coppa defines vidding as, among other things, "a visual essay that stages an argument" (2008), and indeed the videos made by Racebending.com participants articulate nuanced arguments through their humorous montages, sarcastic rants, and compelling collections of evidence. There was also a movement to create videos of individuals stating why they were participating in a boycott of the movie, which contributed to a show of strength in numbers. In addition to these videos on YouTube, many fan artists turned their visual arts skills toward the cause, creating original works of art that could be used as banners, T-shirts, buttons, icons, or personalized avatars. In this way, the artistic and creative skills that fans regularly employ in the creation of fan art and vids was used to propel the arguments of the Racebending.com cause.

Fan-activists created many works of art that reinforced their critique of the film's casting by communicating how they understood the visual world and racial identities embodied in *The Last Airbender*.

The group's collective use of "comment-bombing" can also be seen as related to Fiske's notion of "enunciative productivity." Any time that a news organization published information about the upcoming film, new behind-the-scenes information, interviews with actors and cast members, or promotional material for other whitewashed projects, Racebending.com participants directed members of the community to post comments. The community was very comfortable with the act of commenting since its members participated in regular online dialogues with others of their own community, and dozens complied with these requests, overwhelming the article with their viewpoint and offering counterpoints to any opposing arguments. In the era of online news-writing, comments can be seen as an important component of online discourse, and can even contribute to the creation of further legitimized conversation. For instance, the *Los Angeles Times* wrote an article based on an interview with director M. Night Shyamalan, and members of the Racebending.com community were encouraged to comment on the article. This action led to the writing of another article with the headline "The Last Airbender is causing a casting commotion," which was published in the *Los Angeles Times* blog. Although this blog often focuses on discussions that take place in the online comments, the fact that a respected newspaper like the *Los Angeles Times* would take note of online comments legitimates the commenting arena as important and worthy of concern.

Conversations around commenting are also important because they serve the purpose of policing the boundaries of acceptable fan behavior. This helped the group to retain its image as a respectable group of activists rather than flamers or trolls only interested in inciting anger or stymieing discourse. One LiveJournal post directing members to comment on a blog post included the warning, "Just remember to be polite and keep your cool. If you come off as angry (Season 1 Zuko!) they have yet another excuse to dismiss you. Make your points calmly and confidently." Since fan communities spend so much time engaging in online discourse, there are often strict rules about the kinds of participation that are allowed and the kinds that are discouraged. In her examination of soap opera communities, Baym finds:

> Politeness is a criterion of communicative competence. . . . If conflicts were to become personal (or degenerate into "flame wars"), people would be inhibited from contributing potentially controversial opinions, and the primary function of the group as an interpretive forum would be disrupted. (1997, 117)

If we apply this logic to the Racebending.com community, we see that the primary function of the group—propelling its cause into mainstream media and convincing viewers to boycott the film—could be inhibited by allowing a lack of respect and decorum.

The protest against *The Last Airbender* is also interesting within the realm of Asian American media activism because of the way the leaders of Racebending.com positioned their cause internationally, intentionally extending their work beyond the borders of the United States. In an informal survey of 1,200 of their participants, they found that 25 percent were not from the United States, with supporters hailing from over fifty countries around the world. Some of the largest contingents were in the United Kingdom, Australia, Singapore, and the Philippines. As a result of this data, they began to think about their cause as internationally relevant, and expanded some of their strategies to new locales. For instance, when the movie came out, they wrote to film critics in the United Kingdom, and articles about the casting began to appear in some of the largest and most influential British newspapers. Beyond the reach of their own base, they also took into consideration the fact that international sales contribute millions of dollars toward a film's bottom line. Blockbuster films like Shyamalan's are international media that have a much wider impact than in the domestic context of the United States and the film's financial success or failure would also be an indicator as to whether or not Paramount should produce a second or third installment of the film. In this sense, it was actually very important for the group to attempt to impact ticket sales beyond the United States.

The group's outreach to international news media resulted in news about the discriminatory casting extending to Canada, South Korea, Taiwan, and Japan. Marissa Lee, one of the founders of Racebending.com, explained another consequence of this extensive media coverage at a more personal level—when a Chinese-language newspaper in the United States covered the story, she was able to send the article to her Taiwanese American family in Irvine, California to finally show them what she had been working on all this time. These international efforts reflect the strength of online organizing, given the ease with which an activist in Los Angeles can find the resources to reach out to international press organizations. But this story also reminds us that the relationship between Asian Americans and Asia is sometimes as close as our own living room, where many Asian American families still prefer to learn about the world through in-language ethnic media and are highly attuned to stories from their country of origin. These transnational, cross-cultural connections provide an important base for conducting continued work in the politicization of Asian Americans through popular culture. This story also shows us yet another aspect of how cultural citizenship is embodied by media activists—they see their participation in media activism as an expression of their identities, and as Asian Americans they seek to demonstrate that they are part of a community that is doing valuable work. More broadly, we can see that one's identity is intimately connected to the activist communities in which one plays a part, and the struggle to improve the representation of Asian Americans becomes connected to a more personal desire to affirm one's identity within the context of their Asian American families and communities.

Moving the Movement

Beyond their work on *The Last Airbender*, activists at Racebending.com sought to sustain their momentum by taking on the more general cause of promoting equality in the casting of Asian Americans and other minorities. As Scardaville (2005) finds, many fan activist groups share a common origin story: "A single act or a pattern of offending acts mobilize individuals to unite. After the goal is either achieved or no longer attainable, the protesting group may, with time, evolve into a watchdog organization" (886). The Racebending.com movement seems to follow this typology, since the casting decision led to the mobilization of the group, but the ongoing issue of racism in representation is what continues to motivate their collective. The Racebending.com website lists as their mission: "We are a coalition and community dedicated to encouraging fair casting practices. As a far-reaching movement of consumers, students, parents, and professionals, we promote just and equal opportunities in the entertainment industry" (Racebending.com 2009). This statement clearly moves beyond the film itself to advocate for a change in casting practices in general.

One campaign that epitomized this expanded goal was against the whitewashing of a comic book called "The Weapon." The comic book starred an Asian American hero named Tommy Zhou, but when the story was set to be remade into a film, a white actor was cast to play him. Members of the Racebending.com communities were very supportive of efforts to protest this casting. The coordinators wrote a letter condemning the decision in the name of Racebending.com, and one coordinator actually had an extended phone conversation with the executive producer of the film to convey their message. The group's support for these actions revealed an interest in working on projects other than *The Last Airbender*. Overall, in the period between the movie's production and the premiere, the majority of new posts were about issues outside the world of *The Last Airbender*, and only infrequently contained updates on the progress of the film's promotion or the occasional tidbit of new information from the main contributors.

The case of Racebending.com and their work is important to consider in light of the work of the traditional media activists discussed in chapter 1. In some ways, the goals of MANAA and Racebending.com could be seen as overlapping—both groups took on the cause of protesting *The Last Airbender*, first attempting to call for a change in casting and then to impact ticket sales. Yet this close examination of the tactics of Racebending.com shows us that their goals are actually much more expansive—they also seek to educate themselves, to participate in an expanding dialogue about race and representation, to intervene into fannish discourse about authenticity and the fluidity of identity, and to disrupt mainstream conversations about the film. In this way, their fight comes to mirror some of the more direct struggles for cultural citizenship embodied by the hashtag campaigns on Twitter like #CancelColbert.

Like the online conversations initiated on Twitter, members of Racebending.com also struggled to transition between online and offline action, particularly early in the course of their organizing. For instance, a Racebending.com leader in New York organized a protest at the film's casting call for background actors in March 2009, but only a handful of people showed up. Together they held signs and tried to gain visibility, but with the lack of bodies their impact was minimal. Similarly, the Los Angeles "Street Team" organized a group of Racebending.com supporters at Comic-Con in San Diego in July 2009, but the two leaders ended up doing most of the work by themselves, "full-on yelling into the crowd, handing out flyers and buttons, getting signatures" (Livejournal.com 2009) with little support from their fellow Racebending.com members. Another missed opportunity for on-the-ground activism came when MANAA organized a protest at Paramount Studios against an offensive scene in its film *The Goods: Live Hard, Sell Hard*. MANAA approached Racebending.com to see if they wanted to use the protest to promote their cause, since Paramount was also the studio producing *The Last Airbender*, but only one member of the Los Angeles Street Team showed up at the protest. It was not until the premiere of the film on July 1, 2010 that members of Racebending.com were finally able to successfully organize their members for an in-person event. Partnering with MANAA, the National Korean American Service & Education Consortium, and the Korean Resource Center, over a hundred activists altogether gathered outside a movie theater in Los Angeles and attracted television news coverage from a variety of networks. Thus the seemingly boundless enthusiasm for the cause online did not always translate into offline action, making it difficult initially to get even the

Although fan-activists organizing through Racebending.com initially struggled to move their online activism onto the streets, they successfully partnered with other Los Angeles-based grassroots activist organizations for a physical protest around the film's premiere.

most vocal members of the group to put a name to their face and show up for a local event.

As we have seen in this discussion, the group effectively propagates its message by using online organizing and it has communicated its message to a broad audience of fans and nonfans. Further, it successfully moved its mission toward general casting and racial representation issues that are not even related to its original fan object—a trend that can only be seen as political, since it no longer relies on the affective ties of fandom—and through this shift it has become part of important conversations with industry executives.

Conclusion

This discussion of different online tools for communication—including Twitter, blogging platforms such as Livejournal, online forums, and websites—demonstrates some of the specific ways that cultures of participation impact the way that media activism takes place. For Asian Americans, the versatility of online social media can certainly lead to mobilization and the propagation of messages to a large audience. Yet exactly what that message is depends upon a number of different factors. We have seen that hashtag campaigns on Twitter can lead to an immediate response from media producers, but we have also seen that they can lead to the fracturing of Asian American communities and confusion about what kind of impact is truly desired. Reliance on fan communities can contribute to a wide range of creative production and the propagation of a multifaceted attack against racism in media practices, but online fandoms can reproduce Orientalism. Moreover, Asian American online activism often becomes a silo, with activists struggling to develop offline communities of practice that make use of their digital networks.

I have argued here that hashtags like #CancelColbert and #NotYour-AsianSidekick move past media activism to lay bare the dire need for Asian American cultural citizenship. For Twitter activists this seems to mean a desire to stand up for themselves in the face of insult and disrespect—whether this means being treated as a sidekick, as forever subordinate, or being used as the punching bag to demonstrate just how ugly racism can get. But at the confluence of all the different new media campaigns included in this chapter there is evidence of the many different ways that cultural citizenship has gained meaning for media activists. In fact, these different forms of digital activism illustrate all the definitions of cultural citizenship utilized throughout this book. As with the traditional media activists in MANAA, many tweets by Asian Americans reveal a desire to be treated "just like everyone else," to challenge stereotypes, and to be viewed as fully "American" rather than "Asian." Just as Asian Americans have attempted to systematically impact media industries through organizations like the APAMC, members of Racebending.com also fought to change representational practices at their root—through casting and the policies that govern casting. But the struggles surrounding *The Last Airbender* can also be understood as consumer activism, with activists organizing a boycott in order to show the strength of Asian American buying power, just like the work of Asian American advertising agencies. Thus although these different understandings of cultural citizenship may lead to different strategies of media activism, they are all deeply interconnected and reinforce one another despite their complexities and contradictions.

Conclusion

Producing Citizenship through Activism

Throughout this book I have made the argument that fighting to change representation in entertainment media and engaging with problematic images are political acts that work to produce cultural citizenship, and that there are many ways of doing so that have yet to be theorized as being part of the same battle. Whether it is by waving signs outside a movie theater, serving on an advisory board for a media ratings corporation, creating advertisements for life insurance to be placed within ethnic media, or making a silly YouTube video, these acts of calling attention to the inequalities and injustices facing the Asian American community are deeply interconnected. Together, each helps to redefine the nuances of an ever-changing Asian American identity, and insists upon recognizing and remedying the injustices that media industries and practices have long upheld.

This exploration of the connections between these activities helps to illuminate the different understandings of cultural citizenship that motivate these expressions of activism. For traditional Asian American media activism organizations, cultural citizenship is achieved by fighting for Asian Americans to be seen as "just like everyone else"—which they take to mean they are deserving of starring or heroic roles, love interests of their own race or romantic storylines at all, complex back stories, and all the other kinds of narrative entanglements that actors of other races are regularly given. Advocacy groups have also fought for citizenship through changes in more broad-reaching cultural policies, such as agreements with network television stations to give regular reports on the state of their minority hiring, or fighting to gain recognition in ratings from corporations like Nielsen. Recognition from large corporations has similarly played a central role in the strategies of Asian American advertising agencies, who gain respect and feelings of belonging from being seen as a powerful collective of consumers who vote with their dollars. Finally, we have also seen that Asian Americans have wielded digital tools to build communities online and develop strategies for a plethora of different activist interventions—from providing new venues for the distribution of Asian American images to bypassing traditional gatekeepers in media industries with their complaints when a problematic image arises.

In each of these examples, Asian Americans see cultural citizenship not as something that an individual media consumer or audience member can achieve alone but rather as something that requires working together with disparate allies and developing interlocking strategies that are often counterintuitive to our standard definitions of activism. For instance, the specific visions for cultural citizenship outlined in these chapters are what make a partnership between a grassroots activist organization and a corporation such as Comcast, McDonalds, or MTV viable as a strategy. But more importantly, these sometimes contradictory understandings of citizenship also help us understand what it means to identify as Asian American today. Although this identity encompasses a vastly diverse population whose members do not agree on a monolithic political strategy, their demands for recognition can only be met by working together. By participating in these kinds of media activism and discussions about representation, together Asian Americans are fighting for inclusion, belonging, recognition, and a voice within the national collective.

Although my investigation throughout has focused on strategies designed to impact mainstream entertainment media, my exploration of digital media in the later chapters of this book reminds us that media industries are shifting to accommodate the fact that we are all participating in creating media and developing the ability to tell our own stories. This investigation has examined how Asian Americans are working together, even if only by making strategic alliances for fleeting moments, because cultural citizenship is claimed through the collective body.

The need to work together becomes starkly apparent when we consider the risks of allowing individuals to stand alone without the support of their communities, as in the case of gay, lesbian, bisexual, or transgender people. Gay, lesbian, bisexual, or transgender people, including those who are undocumented, face real risks by making themselves visible by "coming out." This includes the threat of physical violence, ostracization from their communities, being kicked out of their homes, or in the case of the undocumented, being deported from the United States. Despite these threats, there is a growing movement for the creation and dissemination of "coming out" videos on YouTube by queer and/or undocumented youth.

In 2011, Suny Um posted a video on YouTube called "My Mini Story: Gay 2nd Generation Cambodian American." In the simply shot video set to a song by Bruno Mars, Suny uses hand-written placards to tell the story of his family immigrating to the United States from Cambodia as refugees. The placards then reveal that when he was sixteen, his father disowned him and kicked him out of the house for being gay. Suny became depressed and suicidal. But with a smile on his face, he writes, "I'm gay. So what? I'm still human; my heart still beats like yours. This is only a part of my story." The video is earnest and moving, demonstrating Suny's resilience while also providing a relatable story about the difficulties of growing up as a refugee, in poverty, with depression, or with a family who cannot accept who he is. Indeed, many of the comments on the video are from fellow Khmer youth who admit to having cried when watching the video, or who see themselves in his story. As one commented, "U r not Alone in this world and thanks for sharing his cuz even me, it makes me feel like im not the only one cambodian gay kid." Another wrote, "You're an inspiration to many gay Khmers out there. Like myself."

There are countless such videos on YouTube of young lesbian, gay, bisexual, and transgender people telling their coming out stories. YouTube and other video hosting sites clearly provide a way for these otherwise isolated or alienated individuals to find a supportive community online and connect with like-minded peers. Queer youth have found many different ways to connect using online social media and social software, from posting on YouTube to using online social networking sites, to sharing poetry and artwork or joining queer fandoms online (Gray 2009). But there are important differences between the act of posting a coming out video on YouTube and joining an LGBTQ networking community like TrevorSpace or Downelink.[1] In creating a video starring themselves and telling their own personal coming out stories, these individuals are broadcasting very public messages about their experiences and identities, and contributing to the broader collection of stories that comprise YouTube's vast database. Although I have earlier demonstrated that not everyone on YouTube is famous or popular, and certainly many videos fail to garner more than a handful of hits, there are countless videos of ordinary, everyday users that are passed around and begin accumulating audiences. Given the high risks for queer youth in revealing their sexuality in such a public, unrestricted way, it follows that there must be high rewards for doing so as well.

In connecting these stories to the fight for improving Asian American representations in entertainment media, it seems clear that one reason queer youth are interested in disseminating their own coming out stories on YouTube is because of the power and strength that come with media visibility. This is even more clearly demonstrated in the coming out videos of undocumented youth, given the real threat of deportation that the undocumented face in the United States. Arely Zimmerman has pointed to a shift in YouTube videos by undocumented youth—from carefully protecting their identities and obscuring any identifying information to boldly revealing their faces and names in the act of coming out as undocumented on YouTube (Zimmerman 2012). As Nancy Mesa, an immigrant rights activist in Los Angeles, put it, "Yes, it is dangerous, there are risks that we face in being so publicly active, but it is even more risky if they don't know we exist" (Zimmerman 2012). This statement clearly indicates the significance of making one's story public, no matter what the risk. These undocumented people refuse to hide and refuse to deny their right to exist in the United States, even if their paperwork says otherwise. In this sense, it seems more important for these undocumented youth to express their cultural citizenship—by creating online videos that tell stories of growing up, going to school, having hopes and dreams of living and working in the United States as an adult—than their legal citizenship, given their insistence on remaining active within this cultural sphere. But such expressions of cultural citizenship can lead to political mobilization, as many immigrant rights organizations use these kinds of YouTube videos as part of their campaigns to save people from deportation. Coming out videos and others are linked, emailed, and posted in order to mobilize their network of supporters to sign petitions, write news articles, and make phone calls to senators, members of the Department of Homeland Security, and U.S. Immigration and Customs Enforcement.

The narrative of journalist Jose Antonio Vargas also reinforces the importance of telling one's story in public, despite its risks. In June 2011, Vargas wrote a story called "My Life as an Undocumented Immigrant" in the *New York Times Magazine* in which he came out as gay and undocumented. The story details his inability to go to college and his attempts to secure his status and eligibility to remain in the United States. He was able to achieve an incredible level of success as a reporter, working for the *Huffington Post*, creating documentary films, and eventually writing for the *New York Times*, all while living in fear that the holes in his temporary paperwork would expose him and he would be deported. As he writes, "I'm done running. I'm exhausted. I don't want that life anymore." He first revealed his story to his editors and bosses, and then to the world with the publication of his article. Since then he has become an outspoken advocate on the issue, founding a nonprofit called Define American that facilitates dialogue about immigration issues and producing a documentary called *Documented: A Film by an Undocumented American* for CNN. Although it seems unlikely that Vargas will be deported, the high risk of his very public coming out story demonstrates the desperate need for these otherwise invisible members of society to be seen, heard, and recognized, no matter what the consequences.

Such stories of undocumented and queer communities rallying around online stories and videos reminds us of the overlap between visibility and cultural citizenship in entertainment and the political sphere. In the case of the media activists I have studied thus far, I argue that improving the representation of Asian Americans in entertainment media is connected to the issue of seeing Asian Americans as full members of society and thus reducing racially motivated discrimination and violence—consequences that will always be connected to the claiming of cultural citizenship. In connecting the visibility of Asian American actors or comedians to the stories of people like Suny Oum and Jose Antonio Vargas, we are reminded that visibility in all arenas is politically transformative, contributing to a wider belief that individuals from all backgrounds deserve fair treatment and inclusion. Those we can see and hear from are those we empathize with, stand beside, and understand. All the activists profiled in this book are working to change the way that Asian American lives are understood, and their fight engages with multiple sites—the marketplace, policy, the community, explicitly political realms, and above all, the media. For some, their targeted media extends primarily to other Asian Americans and creates a thriving counterpublic where Asian Americans can finally see and interact with people who share their identities and experiences. In these spaces there may be more potential for debate, exploration, and strategy building. For others, images of Asian Americans must be shared with the wider public to remedy the systematic silencing of a population who has historically been marginalized and mistreated. Their efforts target mainstream film and television industries in an effort to change the way audiences across the United States, and perhaps the world, are invited to view Asian America. Only through the recognition of what draws these sites together and produces different kinds of cultural citizenship can media activism continue to make an impact in the fight for justice and equality.

NOTES

INTRODUCTION

1 The practice of yellowface implies not only that an Asian actor is replaced by a white one, but also that the portrayal relies upon a combination of elements such as facial prosthetics that imitate Asian eye appearance and buck teeth, use wigs, glasses, costumes, and other props, and exaggerate accents and bodily gestures. Together these portrayals are designed to be humorous and mocking, ultimately serving to ridicule and demonize the Asian body (Fuller 2010).

2 Throughout the book I focus on the idea of "activism" rather than "advocacy," as I locate advocacy at the level of discursive impact—when a representative from a particular group is able to speak for the needs or concerns of that group. It is not always meaningful to distinguish between the act of advocacy and activism as described here, and indeed I do use the word advocacy to describe the work of some organizations. This reflects the extremely close relationship and frequent entwinement between these two concepts. But I take activism to be a more inclusive category as it involves individuals working to fight injustices that extend beyond the voicing of their concerns.

3 The way this book is written reflects the many roles that I assumed—that of activist, participant, academic, observer, historian, and cultural analyst. I use the names of activists and other participants when they are attached to public actions and documents, but I selectively remove identifying information from nonpublic comments made during interviews I conducted or that I heard during meetings. The decision as to when to anonymize and when to identify activists represents a delicate balance, since many of the people described here are public figures and want their actions to be documented as part of the important history of Asian American media activism. But I also want to be sensitive to the role that I play as an ethnographer in writing a story that allows me to make my own academic analysis while remaining true to the voices of the activists I describe here.

CHAPTER 1. THE LIMITS OF ASSIMILATIONISM WITHIN TRADITIONAL MEDIA ACTIVISM

1 Thanks to Karen Narasaki, former chair of the Asian Pacific American Media Coalition, for illuminating these five sites of action.

2 The history relayed in this section is based on items from the personal archives of Sumi Haru (1939–2014), an Asian American actress and activist whose collection is now available through the USC Digital Library.

3 Supporting organizations included the County of Los Angeles Human Rights Commission, Anti-Defamation League of B'nai Brith, the Equal Opportunity Commission, Council of Oriental Organizations, Japanese American Citizens League, NAACP (National Association for the Advancement of Colored People), TELACU (The East Los Angeles Civic Union), MAPA (Mexican American Political Alliance), CARISSIMA, Yellow Brotherhood, and Asian Hard Core.

4 There is much important scholarship in Asian American media studies documenting these common tropes (Ono and Pham 2008; Shah 2003; Kawai 2005; Dhingra and Rodriguez 2014; Wong 1978).

CHAPTER 2. LEVERAGING MEDIA POLICY FOR REPRESENTATIONAL CHANGE

1 This alliance mirrors a later collusion in the 1980s between Christian fundamentalists and anti-pornography feminists, both of whom sought to limit the influence of pornography, which they felt was degrading and harmful to women. For both groups, the effects of the media upon society are so deeply worrisome that even though they have radically different political views and constituents, they banded together in an attempt to control and limit the imagery in question.

2 Although the NAACP was originally a member of the Multi-Ethnic Media Coalition, it later separated from the Coalition in order to pursue its own strategies for African American media activism.

3 Asian American representatives to the group include members of MANAA, East West Players, the Asian American Justice Center, Visual Communications, SAG, the IW Group, and a number of Asian American actors and filmmakers.

4 The positions included in the statistics consist of: actors in regular and recurring roles, directors, writers, producers, entertainment creative executives, program development, and suppliers.

5 In the case of NBC, the meetings take place every quarter.

CHAPTER 3. SOCIAL CHANGE THROUGH THE ASIAN AMERICAN MARKET

1 In fact, the allocation of dollars for a company's Asian American budget is often (unfortunately) increased by decreasing the dollar allocation from its African American or Hispanic budget, given that many companies refuse to expand the overall amount of money allocated to minority markets. This effectively converts all minority marketers into competitors.

2 One executive in the Asian American advertising industry informed me that insiders do not actually use the term "Asian American market," and simply call it the "Asian market"—a title that would make sense if they are simply referring to race (such as black, or Hispanic), and not nationality (American). But since the marketing agencies explored in this chapter only work in the United States and do not do any advertising in Asia, I will continue to refer to the "Asian American market" to be as clear as possible.

CHAPTER 4. ASIAN AMERICAN YOUTUBE CELEBRITIES CREATING
POPULAR CULTURE NETWORKS

1 All the interviews were readily available online and the sample included articles
   from more traditional mainstream media organizations (Forbes.com, CBS, Glam-
   our.com, PBS Hawaii), posts on blogs and online magazines for Asian American
   online media organizations (Audrey Magazine, Asia Pacific Arts, The Other
   Asians), and video interviews with a variety of outlets (The Partners Project, Click
   Network TV, ISA TV).

2 Lisa Nakamura has discussed the proliferation of racism online in many of her
   books, including *Cybertypes: Race, Ethnicity, and Identity on the Internet* (2002)
   and *Digitizing Race: Visual Cultures of the Internet* (2008), as well as in an online
   article, "Glitch Racism: Networks as Actors within Vernacular Internet Theory."

3 Bollywood dance might be one form of "traditional Asian dance" that has begun
   to infiltrate mainstream America and represent the image of a dancing South
   Asian body. Yet for the most part, it seems clear that Asian dance forms are still
   largely neglected and marginalized.

4 Participants include Amy Okuda, KevJumba, Philip Wang, Ally Maki, Anthony
   Lee, Brandon Laatsch, Clara C, David Choi, Freddie Wong, Jen FrmHeadToToe,
   Mike Song, Ted Fu, and Wesley Chan.

5 Although the inspiration for Wipeout! is not explicitly acknowledged by the producers, I reference these three Japanese television shows because they were named
   in a 2008 lawsuit by the Tokyo Broadcasting System alleging copyright infringement because of their similarities. The parties settled privately (Belloni 2011).

CHAPTER 5. UTILIZING SKILLS AND PASSION TO SPREAD ONLINE
ACTIVISM

1 Patel was born to Gujarati parents who were from Kenya, and he was raised in
   England. Shyamalan was born in India but raised in Pennsylvania from the time
   he was six weeks old.

2 The group is identified throughout as members or participants of Racebending.
   com—an important distinction, since the group is actually "against racebending."

3 Although Racebending.com supporters also argue that Inuit culture is being represented in *Avatar: The Last Airbender* and thus should be represented in the film,
   the majority of their arguments focus on Asians and Asian Americans.

CONCLUSION

1 Both these websites are online LGBTQ communities which enable youth to chat
   and make friends with other LGBTQ-identified youth.

BIBLIOGRAPHY

About MANAA. n.d. Accessed June 20, 2011. http://www.manaa.org/about_us.html.

Alba, Richard, and Victor Nee. 2003. *Remaking the American Mainstream: Assimilation and Contemporary Immigration*. Cambridge, Mass.: Harvard University Press.

Ang, Ien. 1991. *Desperately Seeking the Audience*. London: Routledge.

———. 2003. "I'm a Feminist But . . . : 'Other' Women and Postnational Feminism." In *Feminist Postcolonial Theory: A Reader*, edited by Reina Lewis and Sara Mills, 161–189. New York: Routledge.

Aoki, Guy, interview by Author. 2009. November 1.

Aouragh, Miriyam, and Anne Alexander. 2011. "The Egyptian Experience: Sense and Nonsense of the Internet Revolution." *International Journal of Communication* (5): 1344–1358.

Appiah, Kwame Anthony. 2006. *Cosmopolitanism: Ethics in a World of Strangers*. New York: W. W. Norton.

Asian American Justice Center. 2011. "AAJC Welcomes Comcast/NBCU Joint Venture." January 19. Accessed June 20, 2011. http://www.napalc.org/en/rel/453/.

———. n.d. *Media Diversity*. Accessed June 20, 2011. http://asianamericancensus.org/tv_diversity/.

Asians on Film. 2012. *Kevin Wu aka KevJumba Interview: Rock Jocks & Hang Loose*. May 13. http://www.asiansonfilm.com/2012/05/kevin-wu-aka-kevjumba-interview-rock-jocks-hang-loose/.

AsianWeek. 2014. "MANAA Asks Fox to End 'White Only' Dating Policy on 'Mindy Project.'" March 25. http://www.asianweek.com/2014/03/25/manaa-asks-fox-to-end-white-only-dating-policy-on-mindy-project/.

Baez, Jillian. 2008. "Mexican (American) Women Talk Back: Audience Responses to Representations of Latinidad in U.S. Advertising." In *Latina/o Communication Studies Today*, edited by Angharad Valdivia, 257–281. New York: Peter Lang.

Bailey, Jason. 2014. "'I'm a Fucking Indian Woman Who Has Her Own Fucking Show': Mindy Kaling Fires Back at 'Insulting' Diversity Complaints." *Flavorwire*. March 10. http://flavorwire.com/444418/im-a-fucking-indian-woman-who-has-her-own-fucking-show-mindy-kaling-fires-back-at-insulting-diversity-complaints/.

Banet-Weiser, Sarah, and Roopali Mukherjee. 2012. *Commodity Activism: Cultural Resistance in Neoliberal Times*. New York: NYU Press.

Barlow, William. 1999. *Voice Over: The Making of Black Radio*. Philadelphia: Temple University Press.

Baxter, William. 1974. "Regulation and Diversity in Communications Media." *American Economic Review* 64 (2): 329–399.

Baym, Nancy K. 1997. "Interpreting Soap Operas and Creating Community: Inside an Electronic Fan Culture." In *Culture of the Internet*, edited by Sara Kiesler, 103–120. Mahwah, N.J.: Lawrence Erlbaum.

Belloni, Matthew. 2011. "ABC, Endemol Settle 'Wipeout' Copyright Lawsuit with Japanese Broadcaster." *Hollywood Reporter*. December 24. http://www.hollywoodreporter.com/thr-esq/wipeout-copyright-lawsuit-abc-endemol-276301.

Bennett, W. Lance. 2003. "New Media Power: The Internet and Global Activism." In *Contesting Media Power: Alternative Media in a Networked World*, edited by Nick Couldry and James Curran, 17–38. Lanham, Md.: Rowman and Littlefield.

Braxton, Greg. 2000. "Minorities Seeing Little TV Diversity; Television Coalition Issues More Poor Grades to Major Networks, Who Defend Their Efforts to Level the Playing Field." *Los Angeles Times*. November 15: F1.

———. 2001. "4 Networks Failing at Diversity, Group Says; TV: A Coalition Criticizes ABC, CBS, NBC and Fox, Saying Agreements Reached 16 Months Ago Haven't Been Honored." *Los Angeles Times*. May 25: C1.

Brock, Andre. 2012. "From the Blackhand Side: Twitter as Cultural Conversation." *Journal of Broadcasting & Electronic Media* 56 (4): 529–549.

Broyles, Yolanda Julia. 1983. "Chicano Film Festivals: An Examination." *Bilingual Review* 10 (2): 116–120.

Burgess, Jean, and Joshua Green. 2009. *YouTube: Online Video and Participatory Culture*. New York: Polity Press.

Burns, Kelli. 2009. *Celeb 2.0: How Social Media Foster Our Fascination with Popular Culture*. New York: Praeger.

Canclini, Nestor Garcia. 2001. *Consumers and Citizens: Globalization and Multicultural Conflicts*. Translated by George Yudice. Minneapolis: University of Minnesota Press.

Caramanica, Jon. 2006. "After the International Channel: AZN Narrows Its Audience and Widens Its Flaws." *New York Times*. July 30.

Castells, Manuel. 2012. *Networks of Outrage and Hope: Social Movements in the Internet Age*. Cambridge, U.K.: Polity Press.

Chambers, Jason. 2009. *Madison Avenue and the Color Line: African Americans in the Advertising Industry*. Philadelphia: University of Pennsylvania Press.

Chambers, Todd, and Herbert H. Howard. 2006. "The Economics of Media Consolidation." In *Handbook of Media Management and Economics*, edited by Alan B. Albarran, Sylvia M. Chan-Olmstead, and Michael O. Wirth, 363–386. Mahwah, N.J.: Lawrence Erlbaum.

Cheng, Anne. 2001. *The Melancholy of Race: Psychoanalysis, Assimilation, and Hidden Grief*. Oxford: Oxford University Press.

Chie, Ho. 2008. *From East to West with Wong Fu Productions*. November 14. http://taiwaneseamerican.org/ta/2008/11/14/from-east-to-west-with-wong-fu-productions/.

Chin, Elizabeth. 2001. *Purchasing Power: Black Kids and American Consumer Culture*. Minneapolis, Minn.: University of Minnesota Press.

Chin, Frank, and Jeffery Paul Chan. 1972. "Racist Love." In *Seeing through Shuck*, edited by Richard Kostelanetz. New York: Ballantine Books.

Cho, Margaret. 2001. *I'm the One That I Want*. New York: Random House.

Chong, Joelle. 2012. *YouTube Sensation Ryan Higa Has No Time for Love . . . Yet*. September 2. http://entertainment.xin.msn.com/en/celebrity/buzz/asia/youtube-sensation-ryan-higa-has-no-time-for-love%E2%80%A6yet.

Chuh, Kandice. 2003. *Imagine Otherwise: On Asian Americanist Critique*. Durham, N.C.: Duke University Press.

Chun, Elaine. 2013. "Ironic Blackness as Masculine Cool: Asian American Language and Authenticity on YouTube." *Applied Linguistics* 34 (5): 592–612.

Classen, Steven. 2004. *Watching Jim Crow: The Struggles over Mississippi TV, 1955–1969*. Durham, N.C.: Duke University Press.

Cohen, Lizabeth. 2008. *A Consumers' Republic: The Politics of Mass Consumption in Postwar America*. New York: Random House.

Communications Act of 1934. U.S. Code, Title 47, Chapter 5, Subchapter I, § 151.

Consalvo, Mia. 2012. "Confronting Toxic Gamer Culture: A Challenge for Feminist Game Studies Scholars." *Ada: A Journal of Gender, New Media, and Technology* 1. http://adanewmedia.org/2012/11/issue1-consalvo/.

Considine, Austin. 2011. "For Asian-American Stars, Many Web Fans." *New York Times*. July 29.

Coppa, Francesca. 2008. "Women, Star Trek, and the Early Development of Fannish Vidding." *Transformative Works and Cultures* 1.

Curtin, Michael. 1997. "Gatekeeping in the Neo-Network Era." In *Advocacy Groups and the Entertainment Industry*, edited by Michael Susman and Gabriel Rossman, 65–76. Westport, Conn.: Praeger.

Das Gupta, Monisha. 2006. *Unruly Immigrants: Rights, Activism, and Transnational South Asian Politics in the United States*. Durham, N.C.: Duke University Press.

Davila, Arlene. 2001. *Latinos, Inc.: The Marketing and Making of a People*. Berkeley: University of California Press.

"Demographics of Racebending.com Supporters." *Racebending.com*. April 30, 2010. http://www.racebending.com/v4/press/demographics-of-racebending-com-supporters/.

Derecho, Abigail. 2006. "Archontic Literature: A Definition, a History, and Several Theories of Fan Fiction." In *Fan Fiction and Fan Communities in the Age of the Internet: New Essays*, edited by Karen Hellekson and Kristina Busse, 61–78. Jefferson, N.C.: McFarland and Company.

Desai, Jigna. 2005. "Planet Bollywood: Indian Cinema Abroad." In *East Main Street: Asian American Popular Culture*, edited by Shilpa Dave, LeiLani Nishime, and Tasha G. Oren, 55–71. New York: NYU Press.

Dhingra, Pawan, and Robyn Magalit Rodriguez. 2014. *Asian America: Sociological and Interdisciplinary Perspectives*. Malden, Mass.: Polity Press.

Dyer, Richard. 1985. *Heavenly Bodies: Film Stars and Society*. New York: Routledge.

Earl, Jennifer, and Katrina Kimport. 2009. "Movement Societies and Digital Protest: Fan Activism and Other Nonpolitical Protest Online." *Sociological Theory* 27 (3): 220–243.

eMarketer. 2013. "Social Digital Video Drive Further Growth in Time Spent Online." *eMarketer*. May 8. Accessed September 7, 2013. http://www.emarketer.com/Article/Social-Digital-Video-Drive-Further-Growth-Time-Spent-Online/1009872.

Enli, Sara Gunn, and Karoline A. Ihlebaeck. 2011. "'Dancing with the Audience': Administrating Vote-Ins in Public and Commercial Broadcasting." *Media, Culture and Society* 33 (6): 953–962.

Erickson, Mary P. 2010. "'In the Interest of the Moral Life of Our City': The Beginning of Motion Picture Censorship in Portland, Oregon." *Film History* 22 (2): 148–169.

Espiritu, Yen Le. 1992. *Asian American Panethnicity: Bridging Institutions and Identities*. Philadelphia: Temple University Press.

Ewen, Stuart. 1976. *Captains of Consciousness: Advertising and the Social Roots of the Consumer Culture*. New York: McGraw-Hill Books.

Feng, Peter. 2000. "Recuperating Suzie Wong: A Fan's Nancy Kwan-Diary." In *Countervisions: Asian American Film Criticism*, edited by Darrell Hamamoto and Sandra Liu, 40–58. Philadelphia: Temple University Press.

Feng, Peter, ed. 2002. *Screening Asian Americans*. New Brunswick, N.J.: Rutgers University Press.

Filipino Americans Demand for Apology from ABC and Desperate Housewives. Accessed June 20, 2011. http://www.petitiononline.com/FilABC/petition.html.

Fiske, John. 1992. "The Cultural Economy of Fandom." In *The Adoring Audience: Fan Culture and Popular Media*, edited by Lisa Lewis, 9–29. London: Routledge.

Flores, William, and Rina Benmayor. 1998. *Latino Cultural Citizenship: Claiming Identity, Space, and Rights*. Boston: Beacon Press.

Florini, Sarah. 2014. "Tweets, Tweeps, and Signifyin': Communication and Cultural Performance on 'Black Twitter.'" *Television and New Media* 15 (3): 223–237.

Fraser, Nancy. 1990. "Rethinking the Public Sphere: A Contribution to the Critique of Actually Existing Democracy." *Social Text* 25/26: 56–80.

Freire, Paolo. 1970. *Pedagogy of the Oppressed*. New York: Continuum.

Fuller, Duncan. 1999. "Part of the Action, or 'Going Native'? Learning to Cope with the 'Politics of Integration.'" *Area* 31 (3): 221–227.

Fuller, Karla Rae. 2010. *Hollywood Goes Oriental: CaucAsian Performance in American Film*. Detroit: Wayne State University Press.

Gamson, Joshua. 1996. "The Organizational Shaping of Collective Identity: The Case of Lesbian and Gay Film Festivals in New York." *Sociological Forum* 11 (2): 231–261.

Gard, James. 2013. "#AskBG: British Gas Hikes Prices, Then Takes to Twitter." October 17. http://www.theguardian.com/business/2013/oct/17/askbg-british-gas-hikes-prices-then-takes-to-twitter.

Glickman, Lawrence. 2005. "'Make Lisle the Style': The Politics of Fashion in the Japanese Silk Boycott, 1937–1940." *Journal of Social History* 38 (3): 573–608.

Glickman, Lawrence B. 2009. *Buying Power: A History of Consumer Activism in America*. Chicago: University of Chicago Press.

Goldman, Robert. 1992. *Reading Ads Socially*. London: Routledge.

Gottschild, Brenda Dixon. 2003. *The Black Dancing Body: A Geography from Coon to Cool*. New York: Palgrave.

Gray, Herman. 1995. *Watching Race: Television and the Struggle for Blackness*. Minneapolis: University of Minnesota Press.

Gray, Jonathan. 2010. *Show Sold Separately: Promos, Spoilers, and Other Media Paratexts*. New York: NYU Press.

Gray, Mary. 2009. *Out in the Country: Youth, Media, and Queer Visibility in Rural America*. New York: NYU Press.

Grieveson, Lee. 2004. *Policing Cinema: Movies and Censorship in Early Twentieth-Century America*. Berkeley: University of California Press.

Griffith, Alison. 1998. "Insider/Outsider: Epistemological Privilege and Mothering Work." *Human Studies* 21 (4): 361–376.

Guo, Lei, and Lorin Lee. 2013. "The Critique of YouTube-Based Vernacular Discourse: A Case Study of YouTube's Asian Community." *Critical Studies in Media Communication* 30 (5): 391–406.

Gupta, Prachi. 2014. "#CancelColbert Activist Suey Park: 'This Is Not Reform, This Is Revolution.'" *Salon.com*. April 3. http://www.salon.com/2014/04/03/cancelcolbert_activist_suey_park_this_is_not_reform_this_is_revolution/.

Hamamoto, Darrell. 1994. *Monitored Peril: Asian Americans and the Politics of TV Representation*. Minneapolis: University of Minnesota Press.

Hands, Joss. 2011. *@ Is for Activism: Dissent, Resistance, and Rebellion in a Digital Culture*. London: Pluto Press.

Harmetz, Aljean. 1985. "Movie to Have Disclaimer." *New York Times*. August 30.

Harris, Albert W. 1954. "Movie Censorship and the Supreme Court: What Next?" *California Law Review* 42 (1): 122–138.

Hartley, John. 2012. *Digital Futures for Cultural and Media Studies*. Malden, Mass.: Wiley-Blackwell.

Hazlett, Thomas, and David Sosa. 1997. "Was the Fairness Doctrine a 'Chilling Effect'? Evidence from the Postderegulation Radio Market." *Journal of Legal Studies* 26 (1): 279–301.

Heinke, Rex, and Michelle Tremain. 2000. "Influencing Media Content through the Legal System: A Less than Perfect Solution for Advocacy Groups." In *Advocacy Groups and the Entertainment Industry*, edited by Michael Suman and Gabriel Rossman, 43–52. Los Angeles: UCLA Center for Communication Policy.

Hermes, Joke. 2005. *Re-Reading Popular Culture*. Malden, Mass.: Blackwell Publishing.

Hillenbrand, Margaret. 2008. "Of Myths and Men: Better Luck Tomorrow and the Mainstreaming of Asian American Cinema." *Cinema Journal* 47 (4): 50–75.

Hofheinz, Albrecht. 2011. "Nextopia? Beyond Revolution 2.0." *International Journal of Communication* 5: 1417–1434.

Horwitz, Robert Britt. 1989. *The Irony of Regulatory Reform*. New York: Oxford University Press.

Hu, Brian. 2010. "Korean TV Serials in the English-Language Diaspora: Translating Difference Online and Making It Racial." *Velvet Light Trap* 66: 36–49.

Imada, B. 2007. "Forget the Asian-American-Market Myths—But Remember These Truths." *Advertising Age* 11 (5): 14.

Imada, Bill, interview by Author. 2011. March 28.

Iwabuchi, Koichi. 2004. "How 'Japanese' Is Pokemon?" In *Pikachu's Global Adventure: The Rise and Fall of Pokemon*, edited by Joseph Tobin, 53–79. Durham, N.C.: Duke University Press.

Jenkins, Henry. 1992. *Textual Poachers: Television Fans and Participatory Culture*. New York: Routledge.

———. 2006a. *Convergence Culture: Where Old and New Media Collide*. New York: NYU Press.

———. 2006b. *Fans, Bloggers, and Gamers: Media Consumers in a Digital Age*. New York: NYU Press.

Jenkins, Henry, Katie Clinton, Ravi Purushotma, Alice Robison, and Margaret Weigel. 2006. *Confronting the Challenges of Participatory Culture: Media Education for the 21st Century*. MacArthur Foundation.

Jung, Eun-Young. 2014. "Transnational Migrations and YouTube Sensations: Korean Americans, Popular Music, and Social Media." *Ethnomusicology* 58 (1): 54–82.

Kang, Connie K. 1995. "'Girl' Undergoes Major Changes Amid Criticism." *Los Angeles Times*. March 11.

Kang, Samuel. 2010. "Greenlining Tells House Committee: Comcast/NBC Universal Merger Threatens Media Diversity." *Greenlining Institute*. July 7. Accessed June 20, 2011. http://www.greenlining.org/news/press-release/2010/greenlining-tells-house-committee-comcastnbc-universal-merger-threatens-media-diversity.

Kawai, Yuko. 2005. "Stereotyping Asian Americans: The Dialectic of the Model Minority and the Yellow Peril." *Howard Journal of Communications* 16 (2): 109–130.

Keen, Andrew. 2008. *The Cult of the Amateur: How Blogs, MySpace, YouTube, and the Rest of Today's User-Generated Media Are Destroying Our Economy, Our Culture, and Our Values*. New York: Doubleday.

Kellogg, Don. 2011. *Among Mobile Phone Users, Hispanics, Asians Are Most-Likely Smartphone Owners in the U.S.* February 1. Accessed March 1, 2011. http://blog.nielsen.com/nielsenwire/consumer/among-mobile-phone-users-hispanics-asians-are-most-likely-smartphone-owners-in-the-u-s/.

Kim, Dorothy. 2014. *#Twitterpanic: Feminist Killjoys, #TwitterPanic, and AAPI Feminist Digital Disruption*. June 30. http://modelviewculture.com/pieces/twitterpanic.

Kim, L. S. 2005. "AZN Television: The Network for Asian America." *FlowTV*.

Kim, Ted, interview by Author. 2009. *President and CEO, MNet*. June 9.

King, Jay Caspian. 2014. *The Campaign to "Cancel" Colbert*. March 30. http://www.newyorker.com/online/blogs/newsdesk/2014/03/twitter-campaign-to-cancel-colbert-report.html.

King, Samantha. 2004. "Pink Ribbons Inc.: Breast Cancer Activism and the Politics of Philanthropy." *International Journal of Qualitative Studies in Education* 17 (4): 473–492.

Ko, Nalea J. 2009. "Ryan Higa Snatches no. 1 Spot on YouTube." *Pacific Citizen*. September 16.

Kun, Josh. 2010. "Unexpected Harmony." *New York Times*. 18 June.

Labaree, Robert. 2002. "The Risk of 'Going Observationalist': Negotiating the Hidden Dilemmas of Being an Insider Participant Observer." *Qualitative Research* 2 (1): 97–122.

Lang, Robert. 1994. *The Birth of a Nation*. New Brunswick, N.J.: Rutgers University Press.

Le, Anderson, interview by Author. 2014. January 27.

Lee, Alice, interview by Author. 2011. *President of Research and Development, LA 18*. July 19.

Lee, Esther Kim. 2006. *A History of Asian American Theatre*. Cambridge: Cambridge University Press.

Lee, Rachel C. 2004. "'Where's My Parade?' Margaret Cho and the Asian American Body in Space." *Drama Review* 48 (2): 108–132.

Lee, Robert. 1999. *Orientals: Asian Americans in Popular Culture*. Philadelphia: Temple University Press.

Leong, Russell. 1991. *Moving the Image: Independent Asian Pacific American Media Arts*. Los Angeles: UCLA Asian American Studies Center.

Levi, Antonia. 2006. "The Americanization of Anime and Manga: Negotiating Popular Culture." In *Cinema Anime: Critical Engagements with Japanese Anime*, edited by Steven Brown, 43–64. New York: Palgrave Macmillan.

Lewis, Justin, and Toby Miller, eds. 2003. *Critical Cultural Policy Studies: A Reader*. Oxford: Blackwell Publishing.

Lim, Shirley Jennifer. 2006. *A Feeling of Belonging: Asian American Women's Public Culture, 1930–1960*. New York: NYU Press.

Lindgren, Simons. 2011. "The Potential and Limitations of Twitter Activism: Mapping the 2011 Libyan Uprising." *TripleC: Communication, Capitalism, and Critique* 11 (1): 207–220.

Lipsitz, George. 2008. "Breaking the Chains and Steering the Ship: How Activism Can Help Change Teaching and Scholarship." In *Engaging Contradictions: Theory, Politics, and the Methods of Activist Scholarship*, edited by Charles R. Hale and Craig Calhoun, 88–114. Berkeley: University of California Press.

livejournal.com. 2009. December 22. http://community.livejournal.com/ontd_political/4893219. 2009. *Livejournal.com*. July 27. http://community.livejournal.com/racebending/81024.html.

Lotan, Gilad, Erhardt Graeff, Mike Annany, Devin Gaffney, Ian Pearce, and Danah Boyd. 2011. "The Revolutions Were Tweeted: Information Flows during the 2011 Tunisian and Egyptian Revolutions." *International Journal of Communication* 5: 1375–1405.

Lotz, Amanda. 2007. *The Television Will Be Revolutionized*. New York: NYU Press.

Lowe, Lisa. 1996. *Immigrant Acts: On Asian American Cultural Politics*. Durham, N.C.: Duke University Press.

Lu, Amy Shirong. 2009. "What Race Do They Represent and Does Mine Have Anything to Do with It? Perceived Racial Categories of Anime Characters." *Animation* 4 (2): 169–190.

Lyons, Charles. 1996. "The Paradox of Protest: American Film, 1980–1992." In *Movie Censorship and American Culture*, edited by Francis G. Couvares, 277–318. Amherst, Mass.: University of Massachusetts Press.

———. 1997. *The New Censors: Movies and the Culture Wars*. Philadelphia: Temple University Press.

MacGregor, Ford H. 1926. "Official Censorship Legislation." *Annals of the American Academy of Political and Social Science* 128: 163–174.

Maeda, Daryl. 2009. *Chains of Babylon: The Rise of Asian America*. Minneapolis: University of Minnesota Press.

Maira, Sunaina. 2009. *Missing: Youth, Citizenship, and Empire after 9/11*. Durham, N.C.: Duke University Press.

Mako. 1970. "Chairman, Brotherhood of Artists." Los Angeles. June 8.

Malinowski, Bronislaw. 1922. *Argonauts of the Western Pacific*. New York: Holt, Rinehart, and Winston.

Marchetti, Gina. 1994. *Romancing the Yellow Peril: Race, Sex, and Discursive Strategies in Hollywood Fiction*. Berkeley: University of California Press.

Marwick, Alice. 2013. "Donglegate: Why the Tech Community Hates Feminists." *Wired*. March 29. http://www.wired.com/2013/03/richards-affair-and-misogyny-in-tech/.

Marwick, Alice, and danah boyd. 2011a. "I Tweet Honestly, I Tweet Passionately: Twitter Users, Context Collapse, and the Imagined Audience." *New Media and Society* 13 (1): 114–133.

———. 2011b. "To See and Be Seen: Celebrity Practice on Twitter." *Convergence* 17 (2): 139–158.

Mayer, Ruth. 2014. *Serial Fu Manchu: The Chinese Supervillain and the Spread of Yellow Peril Ideology*. Philadelphia: Temple University Press.

Mayer, Vicki. 2003. *Producing Dreams, Consuming Youth: Mexican Americans and Mass Media*. Piscataway, N.J.: Rutgers University Press.

Maynard, John. 2005. "TV Stations Worry 'People Meters' Miss Minorities." *Washington Post*. May 26.

McEwan, Paul. 2008. "Lawyers, Bibliographies, and the Klan: Griffith's Resources in the Censorship Battle over 'The Birth of a Nation' in Ohio." *Film History* 20 (3): 357–366.

McGuigan, Jim. 2003. "Cultural Policy Studies." In *Critical Cultural Policy Studies: A Reader*, edited by Justin Lewis and Toby Miller, 23–42. Oxford: Blackwell Publishers.

McMahon, Michael. 1994. "Rolling with the Punches: Margaret Cho Copes with Critics' Commentary." *USA Today*. September 19: 3D.

Miller, Toby. 1993. *The Well-Tempered Self: Citizenship, Culture and the Post-Modern Self*. Baltimore: Johns Hopkins University Press.

———. 2007. *Cultural Citizenship: Cosmopolitanism, Consumerism, and Television in a Neoliberal Age*. Philadelphia: Temple University Press.

Mimura, Glen. 2009. *Ghostlife of Third Cinema: Asian American Film and Video*. Minneapolis: University of Minnesota Press.

Mittell, Jason. 2009. "Sites of Participation: Wiki Fandom and the Case of Lostpedia." *Transformative Works and Cultures* 3.

Monkawa, David. 1974. "Jade: Magazine for Colonized Asians." *Gidra*. March: 9.

Montgomery, Katherine. 1989. *Target: Prime Time*. New York: Oxford University Press.

Morris, Meaghan. 1988. "Banality in Cultural Studies." In *What Is Cultural Studies? A Reader*, edited by John Storey, 147–167. New York: Arnold.

Morrissey, Tracle Egan. 2013. "Black People Troll Paula Deen on Twitter, Hilarity Ensues." *Jezebel*. July 12. http://jezebel.com/black-people-troll-paula-deen -on-twitter-hilarity-ensu-754919770.

Nakamura, Lisa. 2002. *Cybertypes: Race, Ethnicity, and Identity on the Internet*. New York: Routledge.

———. 2008. *Digitizing Race: Visual Cultures of the Internet*. Minneapolis: University of Minnesota Press.

———. 2013. "Glitch Racism: Networks as Actors within Vernacular Internet Theory." December 10. http://culturedigitally.org/2013/12/glitch-racism-networks-as-actors -within-vernacular-internet-theory/.

Narasaki, Karen, interview by Author. 2011. July 10.

National Asian Pacific American Legal Consortium. 2005. "Asian Pacific Americans in Prime Time: Lights, Camera and Little Action." Asian American Studies Department, University of California Los Angeles.

Nelson, Angela. 1998. "Black Situation Comedies and the Politics of Television Art." In *Cultural Diversity and the U.S. Media*, edited by Y. R. Kamalipour and Theresa Carilli, 79–87. New York: SUNY Press.

Nielsen Company. 2009. "Ethnic Trends in the Media 2009." http://www.nielsen.com/ content/dam/corporate/us/en/newswire/uploads/2009/03/ethnictrends_030309_fi- nal.pdf.

Ng, Konrad. 2010. "'You Offend Me You Offend My Family': Justin Lin and Asian American Cinema and Social Media in the Digital Age." *Flow TV* 11 (8).

———. 2012. "Asian American New Media Communities as Cultural Engagement: E-mail, Vlog/Blogs, Mobile Applications, Social Networks, and YouTube." In *New Media and Intercultural Communication: Identity, Community, and Politics*, edited by Pauline Cheong, Judith Martin, and Leah Macfayden, 255–273. New York: Peter Lang.

———. 2013. "#Linsanity." *Amerasia* 38 (3): 129–132.

Ngai, Mae. 2004. *Impossible Subjects: Illegal Aliens and the Making of Modern America*. Princeton, N.J.: Princeton University Press.

Nguyen, Mic. 2009. *Asian America's Best Dance Crew*. March 6. Accessed March 15, 2014. http://www.hyphenmagazine.com/blog/2009/03/asian-americas-best-dance- crew#sthash.iiqmdfdG.dpuf.

Nguyen, Viet Thanh. 2002. *Race and Resistance: Literature and Politics in Asian America*. New York: Oxford University Press.

Nishime, LeiLani. 2014. *Undercover Asian: Multiracial Asian Americans in Visual Culture*. Urbana Champaign: University of Illinois Press.

Noam, Eli. 2009. *Media Ownership and Concentration in America*. Oxford: Oxford University Press.

Nogales, Alex, interview by Author. 2011. July 19.

Ocampo, Keesa. 2011. "MYX TV Announces Partnership with Soompi." *PRWeb*. June 1. Accessed July 20, 2011. http://www.prweb.com/releases/MYX_TV/Soompi/prweb8517149.htm.

Okada, Jun. 2015. *Making Asian American Film and Video: History, Institutions, Movements*. New Brunswick, N.J.: Rutgers University Press.

Omatsu, Glenn. 2010. "The 'Four Prisons' and the Movements of Liberation: Asian American Activism from the 1960s to the 1990s." In *Asian American Studies Now: A Critical Reader*, by Jean Yu-Wen Shen Wu and Thomas C Chen, 298–332. New Brunswick: Rutgers University Press.

Ono, Kent. 1995. "Re/Signing 'Asian American': Rhetorical Problematics of Nation." *Amerasia Journal* 21 (1): 67–78.

Ono, Kent, and Vincent Pham. 2008. *Asian Americans and the Media*. Cambridge: Polity Press.

Onwuachi-Willig, Angela. 2007. "There's Just One Hitch, Will Smith: Examining Title VII, Race, and Casting Discrimination on the Fortieth Anniversary of Loving v. Virginia." *Wisconsin Law Review* 9 (29): 319–343.

Ouellette, Laurie. 2008. *Better Living through Reality TV: Television and Post-Welfare Citizenship*. Malden, Mass.: Wiley-Blackwell.

Palczewski, Catherine. 2001. "Cyber-Movements, New Social Movements, and Counterpublics." In *Counterpublics and the State*, edited by Robert Asen and Daniel Brouwer, 161–186. Albany: SUNY Press.

Pao, Angela. 2010. *No Safe Spaces*. Ann Arbor: University of Michigan Press.

Park, Lisa Sun-Hee. 2005. *Consuming Citizenship: Children of Asian Immigrant Entrepreneurs*. Palo Alto, Calif.: Stanford University Press.

Park, Suey. n.d. http://www.xojane.com/issues/suey-park-notyourasiansidekick.

Pew Research Center. 2012. *The Rise of Asian Americans*. Washington, D.C.: Pew Social & Demographic Trends.

Philip. 2009. "Hollywood and Asians: Why Protests Alone Won't Change Anything." You Offend Me You Offend My Family. August 31. http://youoffendmeyouoffendmyfamily.com/hollywood-and-asians-why-protests-alone-won%E2%80%99t-change-anything/.

Poppendieck, Janet. 1998. *Sweet Charity: Emergency Food and the End of Entitlement*. New York: Penguin Group.

Punathambekar, Aswin. 2009. "What Brown Cannot Do for You: MTV-Desi, Diasporic Youth Culture, and the Limits of Television." *FlowTV*.

Racebending.com. http://www.racebending.com. 2009. *racebending.livejournal.com*. December 23. http://community.livejournal.com/racebending/133219.html?thread=4072803#t4072803.

Rainie, Lee. 2011. http://www.pewinternet.org/files/old-media/Files/Presentations/2011/Jan/2011%20-%20pdf%20-%20Asian%20Americans%20-%20DC.pdf.

Ratto, Matt, and Megan Boler. 2014. *DIY Citizenship: Critical Making and Social Media*. Cambridge: MIT Press.

Roberts, Kathleen Glenister. 2011. "'Brand America': Media and the Framing of 'Cosmopolitan' Identities." *Critical Studies in Media Communication* 28 (1): 68–84.

Robinson, Russell. 2007. "Casting and Caste-ing: Reconciling Artistic Freedom and Antidiscrimination Norms." *California Law Review* 95 (1): 1–73.

Rosaldo, Renato. 2003. *Cultural Citizenship in Island Southeast Asia: Nation and Belonging in the Hinterlands*. Berkeley: University of California Press.

Rosenbloom, Nancy J. 1987. "Between Reform and Regulation: The Struggle over Film Censorship in Progressive America, 1909–1922." *Film History* 1 (4): 307–325.

———. 2004. "From Regulation to Censorship: Film and Political Culture in New York in the Early Twentieth Century." *Journal of the Gilded and Progressive Era* 3 (4): 369–406.

Said, Edward. 1979. *Orientalism*. New York: Random House.

Sang-Hun, Choe. 2012. "Bringing K-Pop to the West." *New York Times*. March 4.

Saul, Roger. 2010. "KevJumba and the Adolescence of YouTube." *Educational Studies: A Journal of the American Educational Studies Association* 46: 457–477.

Scardaville, Melissa. 2005. "Accidental Activists: Fan Activism in the Soap Opera Community." *American Behavioral Scientist* 48: 881–901.

Schilt, Kristen. 2003. "AM/FM Activism: Taking National Media Tools to a Local Level." *Journal of Gay and Lesbian Social Services* 16 (3): 181–192.

Scodari, Christine, and Jenna L Felder. 2000. "Creating a Pocket Universe: 'Shippers,' Fan Fiction, and the X-Files Online." *Communication Studies* 51 (3): 238–258.

Screen Actors Guild Affirmative Action and Diversity. 2010. "From Dollars and Sense to Screen: The API Market and the Entertainment Industry." http://www.sagaftra.org/files/sag/documents/SAG_API_Report_2010.pdf

Sender, Katherine. 2004. *Business, Not Politics: The Making of the Gay Market*. New York: Columbia University Press.

Shah, Hemant. 2003. "'Asian Culture' and Asian American Identities in the Television and Film Industries of the United States." *Studies in Media & Information Literacy Education* 3 (3): 1–10.

Shankar, Shalini. 2012. "Creating Model Consumers: Producing Ethnicity, Race, and Class in Asian American Advertising." *American Ethnologist* 39 (3): 578–591.

———. 2015. *Advertising Diversity: Ad Agencies and the Creation of Asian American Consumers*. Durham, N.C.: Duke University Press.

Shankman, Arnold. 1978. "Black Pride and Protest: The Amos 'N' Andy Crusade." *Journal of Popular Culture* 12 (2): 236–252.

Shaw, Adrienne. 2014. "The Internet Is Full of Jerks, Because the World Is Full of Jerks: What Feminist Theory Teaches Us about the Internet." *Communication and Critical/Cultural Studies* 1–5. doi:10.1080/14791420.2014.926245.

Shigekawa, Joan. 1974. "Through Jaded Eyes." *Bridge*. April: 31.

Shim, Doobo. 1998. "From Yellow Peril through Model Minority to Renewed Yellow Peril." *Journal of Communication Inquiry* 22 (4): 385–409.

Shimizu, Celine Parrenas. 2007. *The Hypersexuality of Race: Performing Asian/American Women on Screen and Scene*. Durham, N.C.: Duke University Press.

———. 2012. *Straitjacket Sexualities: Unbinding Asian American Manhoods in the Movies*. Palo Alto, Calif.: Stanford University Press.

Shohat, Ella, and Robert Stam. 1994. *Unthinking Eurocentrism: Multiculturalism and the Media*. New York: Routledge.

Sinha-Roy, Piya. 2010. "'Outsourced'—NBC's Latest Foray into Racist Xenophobia." *Neon Tommy*. September 24. Accessed June 20, 2011. http://www.neontommy.com/news/2010/09/outsourced-nbc-s-latest-foray-racist-xenophilia.

Slack, Jennifer Daryl, and Laurie Anne Whitt. 1992. "Ethics and Cultural Studies." In *Cultural Studies*, edited by Lawrence Grossberg, Cary Nelson, and Paula Treichler, 571–592. New York: Routledge.

Smith, Aaron. 2013. "Why Pew Internet Does Not Regularly Report Statistics for Asian-Americans and Their Technology Use." *Pew Internet*. March 29. http://www.pewinternet.org/2013/03/29/why-pew-internet-does-not-regularly-report-statistics-for-asian-americans-and-their-technology-use/.

———. 2014. "African Americans and Technology Use." *Pew Internet*. January 6. http://www.pewinternet.org/2014/01/06/african-americans-and-technology-use/.

Spivak, Gayatri Charkavorty. 1993. *Outside in the Teaching Machine*. New York: Routledge.

Squires, Catherine. 2014. *The Post-Racial Mystique: Media and Race in the Twenty-First Century*. New York: NYU Press.

Stokes, Melvin. 2007. *D. W. Griffith's "The Birth of a Nation": A History of the Most Controversial Motion Picture of All Time*. Oxford: Oxford University Press.

Story, Louise. 2007. "Anywhere the Eye Can See, It's Likely to See an Ad." *New York Times*. January 15. Accessed September 7, 2013. http://www.nytimes.com/2007/01/15/business/media/15everywhere.html?pagewanted=all&_r=0.

Tabron, Judith. 2004. "Girl on Girl Politics: Willow/Tara and New Approaches to Media Fandom." *Slayage: The Online International Journal of Buffy* 13.

Tokuda, Marilyn, interview by Author. 2011. July 11.

Triton Television. 2014. Wong Fu Productions. https://vimeo.com/82061298

Trope, Alison. 2012. "Mother Angelina: Hollywood Philanthropy Personified." In *Commodity Activism: Cultural Resistance in Neoliberal Times*, edited by Sarah Banet-Weiser and Roopali Mukherjee, 154–173. New York: NYU Press.

Truong, Ky. 2011. *Top 10 Subscribed Asian American YouTube Channels*. November 15. http://www.jackfroot.com/2011/11/top-10-subscribed-asian-american-youtube-channels/.

Tung, Susan. 2013. *Tofu Interview Series: YouTube's The Fung Brothers*. August 7. Accessed March 20, 2014. -http://www.tofumag.com/tofu-interview-series-youtubes-the-fung-brothers/.

Turner, S. Derek. 2006. *Out of the Picture: Minority and Female TV Station Ownership in the United States*. Free Press. http://www.freepress.net/sites/default/files/fp-legacy/otp2007.pdf

Tuttle, Brad. 2012. "The 'Linsanity' Effect: NY Knicks' Guard Jeremy Lin's Surprise Success Leads to Sold-Out Arenas, Jerseys." *TIME*. February 13. http://business.time.com/2012/02/13/the-linsanity-effect-ny-knicks-guard-jeremy-lins-surprise-success-leads-to-sold-out-arenas-jerseys/.

Van Zoonen, Liesbet. 2004. "Imagining the Fan Democracy." *European Journal of Communication* 19 (1): 39–52.

Vaughn, Stephen. 2005. "The Devil's Advocate: Will H. Hays and the Campaign to Make Movies Respectable." *Indiana Magazine of History* 101 (2): 125–152.

Volpp, Leti. 2001. "'Obnoxious to Their Very Nature': Asian Americans and Constitutional Citizenship." *Citizenship Studies* 5 (1): 57–71.

Vu, Kevin, interview by Author. 2011. June 29.

Wall Street Journal. 2012. *Internet Star Michelle Phan WSJ Exclusive Interview Full*. May 18. https://www.youtube.com/watch?v=6ZZfb1hp1dk.

Wallace, Michele. 1990. *Invisibility Blues: From Pop to Theory*. London: Verso.

Wallace, Michelle Faith. 2003. "The Good Lynching and 'The Birth of a Nation': Discourses and Aesthetics of Jim Crow." *Cinema Journal* 43 (1): 85–104.

Wang, Albert. 2008. "Another One Bites the Dust: Comcast Shuts Down AZN TV." *Hardboiled: APA Issues Newsmagazine of UC Berkeley*. March: 10.

Weems, Robert. 1998. *Desegregating the Dollar: African American Consumerism in the Twentieth Century*. New York: NYU Press.

Wong, Eugene Franklin. 1978. *On Visual Racism: Asians in the American Motion Pictures*. New York: Arno Press.

Wong, Julia Carrie. 2014. "Who's Afraid of Suey Park." *Nation*. March 31. http://www.thenation.com/blog/179084/whos-afraid-suey-park.

Wong, Sau-Ling. 1995. "Denationalization Reconsidered: Asian American Cultural Criticism at a Theoretical Crossroads." *Amerasia* 21 (1–2): 1–27.

Wong Fu Productions. 2012. *"Away We Happened"—New Series, Where YOU Help Us, Launches!* May 23. Accessed March 17, 2014. http://wongfuproductions.com/2012/05/away-we-happened/.

Wood, James Playsted. 1962. "Arthur C. Nielsen." *Journal of Marketing* 26 (3): 77–78.

Wotanis, Lindsey, and Laurie McMillan. 2014. "Performing Gender on YouTube: How Jenna Marbles Negotiates a Hostile Online Environment." *Feminist Media Studies*. doi:10.1080/14680777.2014.882373.

Wu, Ellen. 2014. *The Color of Success: Asian Americans and the Origins of the Model Minority*. Princeton, N.J.: Princeton University Press.

Wu, Kevin. 2013. *How I Built a School in Africa with YouTube Views*. August 26. http://www.huffingtonpost.com/kevin-wu/how-i-built-a-school-in-a_b_3658623.html.

Xie, Anna, interview by Author. 2011. June 16.

Yang, Jeff. 2005. *AZN, R.I.P.* December 8. Accessed June 20, 2011. http://www.sfgate.com/cgi-bin/article.cgi?f=/g/a/2005/12/08/apop.DTL&type=printable.

———. 2011. "Looking for a 'Hangover' Cure." *San Francisco Chronicle*. June 3.

———. 2013. http://blogs.wsj.com/speakeasy/2013/12/19/why-notyourasiansidekick-started-a-social-media-brushfire/.

Yeatman, Anna. 2001. "Feminism and Citizenship." In *Culture and Citizenship*, edited by Nick Stevenson, 138–152. London: Sage.

Yin, Kaitlyn [KaitlynYin]. 2014. "#FreshOffTheBoat normalizes the term. Whites will think it's acceptable to use w/o realizing historical origins [Tweet]." May 13.

Yu, Phil. 2010. *Is ABDC Banning All-Asian Crews? (NO)*. March 22. Accessed March 16, 2014. http://blog.angryasianman.com/2010/03/is-abdc-banning-all-asian-crews-no.html.

Zimmerman, Arely. 2012. *Dreaming Out Loud! Youth Activists Spoke about Their Fight for Education, Immigrant Rights and Justice through Media and Art*. January 9. Accessed March 7, 2012. http://henryjenkins.org/2012/01/dreaming_out_loud_youth_activi_2.html.

INDEX

ABOUT THE AUTHOR

Lori Kido Lopez is Assistant Professor of Media and Cultural Studies in the Communication Arts Department at the University of Wisconsin-Madison. She is also an affiliate of the Asian American Studies Program and the Gender and Women's Studies Department.

Made in the USA
Middletown, DE
02 April 2020

87608572R00156